Feast
of Laughter

An Appreciation of R. A. Lafferty

Fourth Edition - February, 2017

Ktistec Press

Feast of Laughter
An Appreciation of R. A. Lafferty
Volume 4, February 1, 2017
Published by The Ktistec Press

Front cover: "Facing the Storm" © 2016, Ward Shipman
Rear cover: "Thoughts on The Rod and the Ring" © 2017 Ward Shipman.
Cover layout: Anthony Ryan Rhodes

ISBN-13: 978-0998536408
ISBN-10: 0998536407

Contact:

Feast of Laughter
The Ktistec Press
10745 N. De Anza Blvd. Unit 313
Cupertino, CA 95014

www.feastoflaughter.org
editor@feastoflaughter.org

Table of Contents

My Grave, and I in It – Reprinted Essays

King-Maker – Reviews

At the Naked Sailor – Interviews with Lafferty

The Deformity of Things to Come –
Works Inspired by Lafferty

Nine Day King – The Master's Own Work

The Ultimate People – List of Contributors

"Rimrock the Ansel" © *2017 Bill Rogers*

Dedication

Dedicated to my father, John Cheek (1935 – 2016), who taught me to read everything, and to question everything I read.

This issue is also dedicated to Robert Bee and the staff of the Mercer County Library System in Lawrenceville, NJ, who so graciously hosted LaffCon 1, the first in what we hope will be a growing, living tradition of Lafferty Conventions. Thank you!

Illustration © 2017 Bill Rogers

Introduction - It Must Not End

R. A. Lafferty exhorted the SF writers attending the 1979 DeepSouthCon to create new worlds with the words "It must not end." He said the world we had known until very recently had vanished without notice or fanfare, and it was up to writers to bring new worlds into existence by the powers of their collective imaginations. This speech was published as the essay "The Day After the World Ended," and we are lucky to have reprinted it here—turn to the last few pages of this issue.

This issue of *Feast of Laughter* is loosely built around a theme of world building. We are trying to create and maintain the world of Lafferty studies and to preserve the worlds he so graciously gave us. The ingredients here are an eclectic mix of old names and new, well-known and unknown, of essays, artwork, poems, opinions, and stories. And one great first.

In this issue of *Feast of Laughter* we are publishing for the first time, Lafferty's story "The Rod and the Ring." Let me say this again: we are publishing for the first time a **new Lafferty story**!! This is the first unpublished Lafferty story to see the light of print in fourteen years, since Steve Pasechnick published "There'll Always be Another Me" in 2003. We owe a massive word of thanks to the Locus Foundation and the JABberwocky Literary Agency for making this literary coup possible. Read this apocalyptic, almost-the-end-of-the-world story for yourself and see how it complements the motif of world building. Darrell Schweitzer and Lawrence Person introduce and review "The Rod and the Ring" in this issue, and R. Ward Shipman created our magnificent back cover as a response and interpretation of the story.

There are other worlds, worldlets, and pocket universes packed into this issue. Gardner Dozois and Robert Silverberg introduce several of Lafferty's worlds. Gene Wolfe directly explores Lafferty's role as a builder of worlds in his seminal essay "Scribbling Giant." Michael Swanwick gives us a report on LaffCon. And we have another befuddlingly brilliant story from Howard Waldrop.

There are also literary cosmoses created by authors who are perhaps worthy of the same accolades and who I hope will soon be as well known. Experience the surreal worlds brought into existence by J Simon, Stephen R. Case, and Daniel Otto Jack Petersen. See a show in the almost-too-familiar world of Robert Jeshonek. Climb the mountains with Bill Rogers and dance with Logan Giannini. And many others—31 in all.

Some creative world maintenance issues must be attended to here as well: *Feast of Laughter* is moving to a longer publication cycle. The first three issues increased in quality, each above the previous. Realistically, it takes about a year to maintain the same standards in publication. After all this is volunteer work by a dedicated group of enthusiastic Lafferty fans who all have families and day jobs. Therefore, the Feast will now be prepared annually.

Deadlines for *Feast of Laughter 5*

- Expression of interest: August 31, 2017
- Content: October 31, 2017
- Tentative publication date, January 2018

Lafferty said we must write to build the new world, and we at *Feast of Laughter* are trying to do our part. We have lovingly crafted this small collection of worlds. The mice have labored and brought forth a mountain—perhaps a bit of terra firma on which to rest your literary legs. We strongly, vociferously, joyously encourage you to join the effort. The first four *Feasts of Laughter* have only begun to scratch the surface. There are Lafferty translations being written in many countries; there are thousands of great writers taking inspiration from him; there is a second LaffCon coming in June; there are great minds thinking and writing about his work the world over. It must not end!

Kevin Cheek
January 2017

"When they cleared out his office, most of Ray's books wound up in places where they served no function, mostly due to Ray's spines. Regardless of their intellectual contents (and their previous owner), school librarians would not keep them on the shelves and bookstores could not move them, not for more than a few coins."

"Pennies" © *2016 Anthony Ryan Rhodes*

Anthony Ryan Rhodes spent his formative years in Tulsa, Oklahoma. He went by his middle name (pronounced "Ron" in some parts of the state), only changing it in high school to his first after realizing how much more fun Anthony was to sign on paper. He showed a proclivity for art, math, and science and went to college for science. For decades he's worked with persons with developmental disabilities, or studied to do so, and only recently picked back up his artistic pursuits. In addition to making illustrations based on Ray Lafferty's work, he has created logos for small businesses and freelanced artwork for Google. He keeps an artists blog with sketches and insights into the illustration process at arr-illustrator.blogspot.com.

Graced Narratives: Themes of Gift and Will in R.A. Lafferty

by John Ellison

As in previous essays I wish to continue exploring concepts from Catholic theology that may cast light on key themes in Lafferty's writing. In looking at the relationship between grace and history I will examine aspects of the short stories, "Days of Grass, Days of Straw", "Among the Hairy Earthmen" and the novel *The Three Armageddons of Enniscorthy Sweeny*. I also hope to bring to the fore the role of gift and self-will within contemporary culture and the way these were interpreted through Lafferty's writings.

One paradox that confronts any critic of Lafferty is the sense in which his thought, so far removed from the ideology of individualism, is still concerned with how the individual acts and chooses. This is shown in a quite intense form in the short story, "Days of Grass, Days of Straw." Here we see how the struggle with the absolute occurs in individual contexts that involve sweat, blood, and the occasional headless torso.

The contrasts set up within this story are quite clear. We are given a description of the "straw world" that Christopher inhabits:

> Christopher Foxx was walking down a city street. Things were mighty even here, mighty neat. There was just a little bit of something wrong about their rightness.
>
> The world was rubbed, scrubbed and tubbed; it was shaved, paved and saved; it was neat, sweet and effete.

We are then given an account of the "grass world" in which Christopher is now Kit-Fox:

Strange Buffalo had a shoulder of dog and Kit-Fox had a rack of ribs. There was fried bread also and hominy and pumpkin. There was choc beer dipped with gourd dippers out of a big crock. Thousands of people were there. It was crowded and it was supposed to be...Now the strong smoke and savor could visit all the places, and the folks in every shop could see into every other shop.

There is an evocation of sensation and encounter in the descriptions of the "days out of count" which shows them as graced days. Yet this grace is shown as being won by individual contest, by the prophets who wrestle with God.

Before some more detailed theological considerations of this we may briefly mention the influence of agonistic and dramatic modes of thought in other discursive realms. Multidisciplinary thinkers such as Mircea Eliade and C.G. Jung have shown how the hero and shaman figure is closely linked to the type of the creative artist. Writers, painters and musicians through the ages have agreed that there is a disciplined ascent to some unspecified "place" from where the gift of a new creation is then returned, as it were, to earth. We can even catch hints of a transactional and contractual nature in descriptions of this as possible versions are somehow compared, chosen or discarded in some extra-temporal zone.

In developmental psychology it is recognized how the sportsman and even the businessman and politician can engage in a kind of inner drama. The gift of success is thereby struggled over rather than chosen by means of logic and mechanical selection.

But what "Days of Grass, Days of Straw" most obviously makes reference to are the insights of the Judeo-Christian tradition. The theological paradigm in this area is the account of when Jacob wrestles with an unknown person, receives a "wound and a blessing", and becomes aware of the transcendent nature of the being with whom he had struggled. (Genesis 32:22-32)

The following passage from the book *The Wound and the Blessing*, by Luigino Bruni can offer some ways of expanding these ideas further:

One of the great insights of...John Paul II is that we grow as humans only by giving ourselves in love to others, that the other is necessary for our authentic human development. ...Of course, few activities are more risky and scary than to give oneself to another with the possibility of it not being reciprocated; hence the Wound that is always a possibility as we share the blessing. This is a paradox best understood at the deepest level—theologically. Bruni describes how we have institutionalized protective belts such as markets and hierarchies to avoid the Wound...This comes from the "either/or" perspective of the Enlightenment. Yet as Catholic philosophy teaches us we are made as "both/and" creatures; we are material and spiritual, we do good and evil, we pursue our own interest and we are concerned for others... We seek the One and the Many knowing that they cannot be fully separated. As humans we will experience the wound and the blessing, as successfully avoiding the former will inevitably prevent the latter.[1]

Another quote from the mainstream Catholic tradition is worth giving here:

He who casts away the pleasant yoke and the light load of charity will have to bear unwillingly the unbearable burden of his own will.[2]

Out of all this style of thinking there emerges the concept of gift, which runs counter to the dominant cultural strands of post-modernity and atheistic secularism. In a wider cultural sense we are all trapped within a late capitalism in which there is indeed a "late-afternoon" feel to things. Most things seem robbed of promise and significance; there is a

---

[1] From p. 12 of the foreword by Charles M. A.Clark in, Luigino Bruni *The Wound and the Blessing: economics, relationships and happiness* (New York: New City Press, 2012)

[2] *On Loving God,* Bernard of Clairvaux, *On Loving God* (Kalamazoo: Cistercian publications, 1995), p. 145

presumption that the individual will conform to predictable patterns of behavior in which gift is squeezed out by self-enriching transaction. Lafferty, though, as I have suggested in previous writings, is a prophet of the morning and of the new things, which lay in wait to surprise and gratify.

This may be expressed in "Days of Grass, Days of Straw" by discourses of motion and abundance:

> ...I tell you it is not enough if only the regular days flow... There must be overflowing and special days apart from the regular days.

Another typical mode of expression, from the same story, centers on the sensations of taste and food:

> ...It's striking that the word for putting a condiment on should be the same word as a division of a year. Well, the seasons out of the count are all seasoned and spiced.

The dividing line between graced and fallen experience is explored in multiple ways in Lafferty's stories. In "Days of Grass, Days of Straw" there is a kind of rhetoric of compensation whereby the sweat and blood of the contest are justified by the gain of the "days out of the count." The emergence in recent times of an elaborated theology of gift can perhaps make sense of this perspective. Asceticism was once seen as something to be discarded forever along with other doctrines from the past in which the body was perceived as being punished. Yet, as mentioned before, it is evident that athletes and those, believers and non-believers, who have regular recourse to structured methods of contemplation, do indeed enter into a pact in which pain and endurance are the pre-conditions for gift. In this it is also clear that form and relationship help to give meaning to the context of gift.

In the novel *The Three Armageddons of Enniscorthy Sweeny* there are further nuanced meditations on themes connected to grace. Here the narrator seeks to capture the sense of unexpectedly being caught up in a Golden Age:

> ...In mythologies, gold stolen out of hoards used to turn overnight into acorns or twigs or stones or nutshells or klinkers or ordure or trash. In our time the process is reversed. All the minor and the common things in their collectivity are turning into gold. What? Have ten million items of crass materialism been transmuted into new and transcendent gold in our time! Is this the elevation of commonness with the improvement of everything opening up new aspects? For everything *is* better, hoes and hoecakes, shoes and saddles, baggage wagons and baseball bats...brass bands and bicycles...fads and fashions. [3]

The use here of the list as a kind of incantation is a familiar trope in Lafferty. We may describe this as a kind of ontology of the particular. The commodity and the artifact almost act as nets in which the transcendent is entangled. Something, no matter what it is, is always for Lafferty a victory over the blank abyss. Quotes from the "In the Days of Silent Radio" section of the novel expand on this insight of living in graced times.

> ...It is said that great art must always be the representation of evil and of agony, and that there will therefore not be any great art in our happy times. This may not be correct. Out of the catastrophes *that do not come* out of the sparkle and health we are able to say, "We Must Have Been Doing Something Right." Doing something right is great art. *We Must Have Been Doing Something Right* is the name of the comedy of our times, and it is full and fervent art. "Great Art" is just a term someone thought up. It isn't definitive. [4]

The comic mode of understanding history is interesting here in that it goes against the grain of the default world-view

---

[3] R.A. Lafferty, *Apocalypses* (Los Angeles: Pinnacle Books, 1977) p. 272

[4] ibid. p. 268

of detached-pessimism that pervades much academic research. We may recall that Lafferty is a writer who, in his short story, "Maybe Jones and the City", offered one of the more audacious responses to Voltaire's accusation of God as the willful creator of catastrophes. Characteristically, in this novel, there is a character who argues:

> "Even the most unkempt of things add to the holy totality."[5]

Other typical themes emerge in further passages from this section:

> We have had unearned luck...We are out of the slough and we are up on the good land. These are the green pastures and in us is scripture fulfilled...they are not quiescent green pastures. They are buzzing and clacking with life...There are plenty of moving parts in the pastures, ourselves.
>
> We break the monotony with all the lovely strength and roughness we can bring, and we heap it up with more of everything. We are Chinese for a while, and we pile up the seven sweets and seven sours. [6]

For readers unfamiliar with this novel it is relevant to stress here the wider, complex whole from which these excerpts are taken. The Armageddons of the novel's title refer to operas composed by the hero of the narrative. An alternative description is that the operas refer to the world wars and post-world war catastrophes which are actively instigated and brought into being by the anti-hero of the narrative. The tension between these simultaneous truths forms the core discourse of the novel.

---

[5] ibid. p. 274

[6] ibid, p. 274

Some passages from an article about the writer and theologian E.I. Watkin describing the dissolution of modern thought seem pertinent here:

> ...In Blake, man was deified not by grace but by a gnostic self-realization. German philosophy as represented by Hegel provided the rationale for the immanentist spirit of the age...Such a "pantheist indefinity" according to Watkin, was pseudotheism. The Dark Night of Wagner's *Tristan and Isolde*, a hymn to the indefinite, bears a delusive resemblance to the Dark Night of St. John of the Cross, a hymn to the infinite. [7]

Andrew Ferguson on his "Continued on Next Rock" site had cited Lafferty documents that showed that he was aware of Watkin's work. Certain of Watkin's theological ideas about color and the spectrum were used as a conceptual plan for a series of Lafferty's short stories. It may not be unreasonable, then, to see Watkin's comments on Wagner as also having some influence on the thematic construction of *The Three Armageddons of Enniscorthy Sweeny*.

In the "In the Days of Silent Radio" passages of the novel we are struck by the specificity and localism of the descriptions of life. No one thing serves as a dominant and totalizing narrative. Yet the combination of lots of little things and a variety of persons do provide the ingredients for a de-centered vision of Utopia, i.e. one that always admits Utopia is not quite arrived at, but senses that the "rehearsals" don't seem too bad.

Turning to the way the Sweeny operas function as surrogate forms of the Armageddons that afflict the world we may offer the following analysis. There are connecting features between the atonal music of Wagner, Stravinsky and Richard Strauss, the rise of surrealism and the avant-garde movement, and the waging of world wars. In each there is a reliance on the technique of shock. There is an impatience

---

[7] James Sullivan, 'E.I. Watkin: Herald of the New Spring', *Crisis* magazine, online article, May 1998

with conventional modes which have to function over extended periods of time and space. By contrast the single elements of fire or deafening noise presume to act in a "totalizing instant." Rather than preservation there is a kind of consummation of those caught within range of these elements. One of the music critics in the novel describes the operas of Enniscorthy Sweeny as effective. But the adjective is used in a guarded way: "effect" is revealed as shock, as a stunning of the senses by sound and spectacle.

As critical readers we may concur with a kind of skepticism about the cathartic role of alienation within modern art. Lafferty seems to suggest that when the norm of beauty is abandoned by artists this is a moment of danger. When Dada and the extreme avant-garde wanted to propagate shock and revulsion their audiences did seem to be used as a kind of cannon fodder. The new kinds of elites of the twentieth century, whether intellectual or military, were not overly touched by compassion or empathy with the masses.

There was no benign sub-narrative whereby the audience was meant to return to normal life purged and renewed. In this respect, then, we may see that Lafferty's insight was correct: *certain cultural and political forms of the twentieth century were effectively the same thing.*

The rise of modernism does see a war waged against tradition and memory. There is a break away from the contrapuntal culture of Christianity and the ideals of harmony and balance. A vacuum at all levels opens up in which assertion and dissonance are able to rush in and produce the kind of versions of Armageddon described in the novel.

The now discarded wisdom of the past included medieval philosophers such as Duns Scotus. He believed that we could blend elements of the intellectual and the charitable at an interior level before actually "creating" an act of will. He saw this process as analogous to musical technique by which separate notes and melodies are combined into a harmonious whole. (On-line lectures by the Catholic theologian Mary Beth Ingham are a rich resource for this topic.)

What seems still important in these old patterns of thinking is the way a sense of agency is preserved. The musical composer and the person willing a good act have a reliance on a social framework by which feedback is anticipated and communicated in traditional flesh and blood forms. The rise, though, of totalizing and abstract narratives erases the feeling of agency. Identity is then submerged by waves of disconnected signs and images.

What is important in the novel is the problematizing of our understanding of time and reality. What kind of truth can do justice to variant worlds that seem to exist alongside each other?

There is a tension shown between amnesiac and delusory modes of thought. The accounts of happy, local communities in the "Silent Radio" sections are almost a "sign of contradiction" in that the people do not act as if wars have taken place. Yet personal memory of parents and other deceased members of my own local community involved in the Second World War confirms how subtle and benign our understanding needs to be. The dread of war itself as something inhuman and threatening stayed with them. Yet these people, and the generations after them, all over the globe, do keep re-building the world from the ruins of history. So we may infer there had occurred a type of accommodation of memory in which past thoughts could be sifted in accordance to the needs of the present. This kind of "amnesia" when done in the context of family and community-building is obviously non-ideological. In this way agency can continue to exist within community.

In previous essays I have focused on the way addiction and other "enclosing" habits erode the sense of self and lead to the person being absorbed in their senses. This appears as a Lafferty theme again when a character describes features of the "peaceful" era of the third Armageddon:

> But we have not done away with sin, the great relaxer and friend of men, nor do we intend to. ..Sin and solace will we now turn to, and we will not have to turn to war ever again.[8]

---

[8] ibid. p. 360

Lafferty wants us to see that this perspective is a cause of the third Armageddon and that rather than ushering in an era of stable peace there is instead a kind of war being waged against the self. By way of explanation we might glance back to the earlier quote from St. Bernard while recognizing how the "unbearable burden of the self-will" is also portrayed in the writings of Dante in a critical-prophetic manner. The loss of gift occurs when the individual withdraws from the living continuum of charity. Dante and other Catholic thinkers don't in all this, I hope, come across as fulfilling the common stereotype of "Catholic guilt" and judgment. Dante knows that those who are alive have the potential to change for the better and that charity demands that we all build communities in which sinners are happier by turning from sin.

2.

Vigen Guroian in his article on Human Rights and Christian Ethics makes the following observation:

> I am not sure the liberal theory of human rights has much staying power outside of certain historical political societies in which a deeply embedded tradition of democratic constitutionalism and the rule of law already exists. And while in some places liberty and justice make gains, in other places the autochthonic powers of racism, sexism and tyranny arise and stalk humanity with new ferocity, easily overwhelming paper declarations of human rights.[9]

This image of powers stalking humanity is perhaps startling in the way it implies the quite palpable existence of malign forces within history. What is to the point, though, in this quote is that if we grant that there are such powers, then paper declarations and abstract defenses will be useless against them. This kind of discursive territory is in fact where Lafferty often pitches his tent. We hear the narrator's refrain at the end of the short story, "Among the Hairy Earthmen":

---

[9] Vigen Guroian, *Rallying the Really Human Things,* (Wilmington: ISI Books, no date), p. 225

We consider a new period—and it impinges on the Present—with aspects so different from anything that went before we can only gasp aghast and gasp with sick wonder:

"Is it *ourselves* who behave so?

"Is it beings of another sort, or have we become those beings?

"Are we ourselves? Are these our deeds?"

The story describes the incursion into Eretzi (Earth) history of seven "Children" who are entities able to act across the boundaries of body and space:

The children exploded into action. Like children of the less transcendent races running wild on an ocean beach for an afternoon, they ran wild over continents.

Reading copies of the original magazines that Lafferty's work appeared one is sometimes struck by the number of adverts for board games and war-gaming. It is perhaps appropriate to see this phenomenon refracted through Lafferty's own ironic vision:

He grabbed off gangling old forts and mountain-rooks and raised howling Eretzi armies to make war... One day the deposed Wenceslas came back, and he was possessed of a new power

...They clashed their two forces and broke down each other's bridges and towns and stole the high ladies from each other's strongholds. They wrestled like boys. But they wrestled with a continent... They smashed Germany and France and Italy like a clutch of eggs.

There is an interesting delineation of the contrasting types of the Children:

Of them all, Hobble had the least imagination. He didn't range wide like the others. He didn't outrage the Eretzi.

There are subtle ironic devices in the way the narrative voice conveys information in this middle section of the story. The "sick toys" of Hobble are the inventions which will benefit and advance human technology. By contrast the cruel and arbitrary nature of the other Children is shown in a detached and matter of fact manner. There is a kind of rhetorical ploy here in which the narrator has a shifting register, even ready to deliver things with a "monstrous" indifference, if the text requires it:

> There is an advantage in doing these little melodramas on Eretz. You can have as many characters you wish—they come free. You can have them as extravagantly as you desire—who is there to object to it?

The superiority of the Children in terms of their being able to manipulate persons and contexts does, of course, contrast with their moral deficiencies. There is a sense in which they are able to sample and taste emotions to their depths. What disturbs is the disordered lack of empathy they display in their actions. As we leap to interpret this as "just being like real children before they reach a certain stage of development" we also see glimpses in which the Children are in fact more like real-life and contemporary adult Eretzi.

> The children left off the game. They remembered (but conveniently, and after they had worn out the fun of it) that they were forbidden to play Warfare with live soldiers.

This convenient way of memory being over-ridden by will seems typical of a human sensibility that finds out, in the very spaciousness and extension of the moment, that vices can be enjoyable.

Many of the scenes in this story seem to have a lack of grounding in reality: the Children are just monsters, while the Eretzi are just puppets. Yet the text points to a certain historical events and patterns of historical happening which also somehow make the story true.

A brief theoretical detour may be relevant at this point. Strands of Post-modern philosophy assert that the concept of the simulacrum is an important way of grasping the break between the traditional relationship of model and image. In Christian spirituality there is the belief that we have been made in the image of God and that our life's activity should be a kind of creative mirroring of the transcendent realm. Post-modernity denies such connections and perceives the free play of images now on offer to the individual consciousness as a force for liberation. The surrealist aesthetic of the visual is often brought into these debates and we can see how an ideology of individualism may arise, in which, having cast to one side the "yoke of charity", there is a free rein to sample images and even persons, who may all be simulacrum anyway, with no moral restraint.

In the short-story "The Six Fingers of Time" the actions of Charles Vincent are described:

> Nor did he ever feel any shame for the tricks he played on unaccelerated humanity. For the people, when he was in the state, were as statues to him, hardly living, barely moving, unseeing, unhearing. And it is no shame to show disrespect to such comical statues.

I had always remembered Vincent as the hero of this classic Lafferty tale but, for all his holding out against the beings from the Pit, he too in this passage has his own lapses and moral lacunae.

And what about Enniscorthy Sweeny? He is revealed as an Everyman figure towards the end of the novel so maybe he is not all that innocent and does keep secretly writing new scripts for the Armageddon...

Casting around for a "clean" Lafferty hero figure we may best settle on the Pilgrim in "Among the Hairy Earthmen":

"I know you", maintained Pilgrim mountainously. "You are ignorant Children who have abused the Afternoon given you on Earth. You have marred and ruined and warped everything you have touched."

"No, no, "Ralpha protested,"... We have advanced you a thousand of your years in one of our afternoons. Consider the centuries we have saved you! It's as though we increased your life by that thousand years."

"We have all the time there is", said the Pilgrim solidly. "We were well and seriously along our road, and it was not so crooked as the one you have brought us over..."

This concluding excerpt sums up Lafferty themes nicely. The Faustian temptation to the accelerated state, the drive towards short-cuts and power do not offer the gifted life of grace. Instead when entities offer these bargains humanity is belittled and driven into contexts without love. The elemental figures of the Pilgrim and Adrian Mountain in "Days of Grass, Days of Straw", show instead how "in scare-shaking and laughter shaking" we are, humanly, rooted in the earth, and, divinely, moving ever-upwards, beyond the mountain, and beyond the sky.

John Ellison lives in England. At an early age, he selected Lafferty as a favorite author after discovering his short stories in SF magazines and anthologies in the late 1960s. John writes that at this time, Catholicism informs most of his choices in life—indeed he has shifted between the quite different milieu of Damon Runyon (he used to be a manager of betting shops) and Dorothy Day (he now works in the charity and voluntary sector). John is a frequent commenter on Andrew Ferguson's Tumblr, "Continued on Next Rock."

A Carny in Nebraska lifted his head and smelled the air.
"It's come back," he said. "I always knew we'd know. Any other Romanies here?"
R. A. Lafferty, "Land of Great Horses"

Illustration © 2016 Anthony Ryan Rhodes

Lafferty and Milford
by Andrew Ferguson

It's no exaggeration to say that the career of R.A. Lafferty would look very different without Milford, PA. Though most important as the location of Virginia Kidd and her Agency, Milford also served as a waypoint for almost every science fiction luminary who helped Lafferty on his way—and, moreover, shaped science fiction into something which could, however sporadically, make room for a writer like him.

The Milford group was an offshoot of the Futurians, a New York-based SF fan and writer's group that at one time or another boasted a membership including Isaac Asimov, Damon Knight, Donald A. Wollheim, Judith Merril, Fred Pohl, Cyril Kornbluth, Robert A.W. "Doc" Lowndes, and James and Virginia Kidd Blish. In the mid-Fifties, the Blishes moved from NYC to Milford, a smallish town tucked just on the Pennsylvania side of the Delaware river, a few miles from the New York border. Knight and Merril followed soon after, and that group would go on to found the Milford Science Fiction Writers' Conference, an annual workshop and retreat so central to in-genre networking that its participants were half-jokingly referred to as the "Milford Mafia." In addition to the above, a Milford con would often feature Robert Silverberg, Harlan Ellison, Terry Carr, Lester del Rey, Samuel R. Delany, and many others who would play some part in the coming SF New Wave—and, not so coincidentally, most of those who would buy stories from Ray Lafferty.

The Blishes divorced in 1963; eventually James Blish took the Milford workshop across the Atlantic, where it continues to be held yearly—albeit no longer at Milford-on-Sea. Virginia Kidd, of course, would remain in Milford for the rest of her life, building up and maintaining what, for a time, was the most important literary agency in the field. She held court at Arrowhead, the stately and somewhat ramshackle riverside house she and James purchased on their arrival in town, and which was almost immediately thereafter flooded in a hurricane; despite continued threats of flooding—and from the National Park Service, which purchased the land via eminent domain for the doomed Tocks Island Dam project—the Virginia Kidd Agency perseveres there still today.

Six decades on, a visit to Milford still showcases many of the charms that led writers to forsake, temporarily or otherwise, the allure of big city life. It's not really on the way from any one place to any other; approach from the south or east in particular takes you through thickly wooded US routes where most days you're likely to see as many deer as other cars. At ground level, the town seems a pleasant jumble of architectural styles, dominated by white-board Yankee dwellings, red-brick mid-century churches, and Late Victorian gables; only from higher ground—in particular, from The Knob, a promontory several hundred feet above town, reached by a short, strenuous hike through a historic graveyard and up the side of an escarpment—does the beauty of the place fully register.

I've visited Milford twice now in the course of Lafferty research. Although the University of Tulsa archive contains the bulk of the immeasurably important correspondence between Kidd and Lafferty, there are gaps in that record, a few of which I filled in through finds in the VKA files. Additionally, Tulsa is missing some original manuscripts, those of early stories in particular—possibly because he sent those copies onto the Agency, which is where I found them. The Kidd Agency also has one of three (as far as I can discern: the University of Iowa has the other publicly available one) complete manuscripts of the third Dana Coscuin novel, *Sardinian Summer*—for whatever reason, the Tulsa copy is missing the final couple of chapters. But the wealth of material there is not limited to drafts and correspondence between the two: Kidd kept tabs on her clients, and was sent clippings of reviews from many sources, including several of works not widely reviewed in genre press sources. Additionally, there is correspondence between Kidd and various SF editors relating to Lafferty, as she carried out the author's business dealings. It was in the Kidd Agency files that I found out about Harlan Ellison's proposal to adapt "Narrow Valley" for the TV show *Eerie, Indiana*; it was also there that I learned the fuller story of the royalties for "Six Fingers of Time" that would greatly snarl Lafferty's probate case.

Of course, when I say "files," I do not mean the sort that one would find in a university archive, such as at Tulsa or Iowa. What I found at the Agency was boxes, many of them. Some held correspondence, some copies and tear sheets of stories, some complete manuscripts of unpublished novels. The files have been preserved fastidiously—even heroically, as when another hurricane in 2004 flooded the basement, forcing agency staff to haul box after box of material up narrow rickety basement stairs ahead of the rising damp—but in only a semblance of order, so that my first task was undertake a full catalog of the holdings. (And even after two visits, this is not complete: in particular, I have yet to take stock of the foreign contract file, which will likely be the only way to get a full listing of Lafferty's works appearing in translation during his lifetime.)

Still, the unusual setting offers luxuries few university archives can match—in particular, working on the famous screened porch, where dozens of famous SF writers overnighted in sleeping bags, with a background of leaf rustle and river babble and a cool summer's breeze. As well, there was the hospitality of Kidd-trained agent Vaughne Hansen and assistant Christine Cohen, eager to show off not only the boxed treasures of the archive, but also the historical wealth of Milford more generally—through them, I got a special tour of the Pike County Historical Society Museum and its prized artifact, the flag that sopped up President Lincoln's blood after Booth's bullet; additionally, I saw Arisbe, the house of pragmatist philosopher Charles Sanders Peirce. Though Peirce's prose is not at all Laffertian, still I feel a strange kinship between them: at the same time that Ferdinand de Saussure was struggling with the linguistic gaps that would birth first structuralism, and then poststructuralism, Peirce approached the same problem from a wholly different angle, putting together a model of signification that remains too little explored or understood to this day—in part because of the idiosyncratic and somewhat goofy terminology Peirce developed, mostly to make sure nobody would appropriate those terms for other ends.

The days of Lafferty in Milford may be numbered. For one thing, the house itself is in legal limbo, technically owned by the Park Service but of no use to a dam project that will never now be carried out. The Agency continues to conduct business for its clients, but Lafferty is no longer among them; the estate now is represented by the JABberwocky Literary Agency, back in the City that Kidd once left. One hopes that the files kept in Milford will in time find their way to another archive, either to Tulsa, which would greatly ease travel burdens on future Lafferty researchers, or to another institution willing to preserve the material legacy of Kidd's agency. For my own part, I hope to return not only to finish the Lafferty dig, but to undertake more thorough research into Kidd herself, as preliminary to one day writing a biography and testament to the considerable debt science fiction and fantasy owe to that remarkable woman.

Lafferty only once met Kidd in person, and he would never make it to Milford. But it's appropriate that so much of his life is documented there: the pair's friendship, apart from the odd gap here or there, was one of the constants of his life for more than three decades. In their messages they bickered and flirted, traded critiques and advice, debated literature and social mores, and discussed everything from the present moment to eternity. Their final letters, often dispatched in rare bursts of health amid the ailments of old age, and as often finding the other in no condition to respond, are touching and terrifying in equal measure. That "old soul" Kidd, as Lafferty addresses her in one letter, was as close to his heart as anyone outside his immediate family; theirs was a match made in language, and no small amount of love.

This work © 2017 Andrew Ferguson.

Andrew Ferguson is the author of a critical biography of R. A. Lafferty forthcoming in the University of Illinois' Modern Masters of Science Fiction series. He is presently teaching English (and hopefully opening young minds to Lafferty) as a postdoctoral lecturer at the University of Virginia while seeking more permanent employment. His blog, "Continued on Next Rock," is at ralafferty.tumblr.com.

"There Are Three Ways to Open a Secret Door": R.A. Lafferty's *Bricolage* Aesthetic

by Gregorio Montejo

"There are three ways to open a secret door. One is to find the edge of it and pry it up. One is to say the words that will make it open. One is to have someone show you how."[1]

On more than one occasion R.A. Lafferty disclaimed any abilities as an artist: "I have tried several times to draw and paint, and I sure cannot make any mark with pencil or brush."[2] Nevertheless, despite his self-avowed lack of technical proficiency, Lafferty demonstrated a keen interest in the visual arts throughout his life. His writings are full of references to art and artists, his non-fiction often addresses questions of aesthetics, his visual descriptions of objects and events in various stories and novels often evince a discerning eye for color, form, texture, and shape, and on occasion he proffered decidedly critical opinions about many of the illustrations used in his published works. Perhaps Lafferty's most absorbing and protracted engagement with art was carried out in private and only emerged after his death, when his library and office, ornately festooned with hand-made collages, were briefly revealed (See Fig. 1).

---

[1] R.A. Lafferty, "Saturday You Die," in *The Early Lafferty* (Weston, Ontario: United Mythologies Press, 1988), pp. 24-29; at pp. 27-28.

[2] R.J. Whitaker, "Maybe They Needed Killing & The Importance of Happiness," in *Cranky Old Man from Tulsa: Interviews with R.A. Lafferty* (Weston, Ontario: United Mythologies Press, 1990), pp. 8-25; here at p. 14. This interview is also reprinted in the current issue of *Feast of Laughter*.

Figure 1. R.A. Lafferty's office after his death in 2002. Photo © 2016 Andrew Ferguson. Used per CC-BY-4.0 license.

When Lafferty's Tulsa home was renovated and subsequently sold, the elaborate decorations that covered much of the walls were destroyed, all except for the similarly adorned office door, which was also almost completely covered in collages, save for the keyhole and crystal knob. "Down the center were clippings of images of fine art, mostly women in portrait; a cacophony of cartoons and children's Valentines framed them. Ancient animals and obsolete farming tools were pasted in a corner together, destined to forever coexist"[3] Since this is the only surviving example of his decorative art, the door offers us a unique glimpse into Lafferty's visual imagination at work, yet the seemingly haphazard juxtaposition of imagery taken from reproductions of famous works of art, as well as advertisements, newspaper clippings, book illustrations, comic books, greeting cards, magazines, calendars, postage stamps, catalogues, and other ephemera resists easy interpretation (See Fig. 2).

---

[3] Natasha Ball, "Lafferty Lost and Found," *This Land*, Vol. 5, Issue 21 (November 1, 2014), pp. 6-7. Available online at http://thislandpress.com/2014/11/05/lafferty-lost-and-found/.

Figure 2. Lafferty's door. Photo © 2016 Andrew Ferguson.
Used per CC-BY-4.0 license.

Warren Brown, who salvaged the door, believes the obscure concatenation of visual elements somehow mirrors the rich profusion of colorful characters and complex concepts in Lafferty's mind, an idea echoed by Andrew Ferguson, a scholar who is writing an R.A. Lafferty biography: "I have to imagine it was an emblem of how his mind must have worked, this huge array of kaleidoscopic imagery, all shuffling in and demanding attention all at once... filling every available area. That's certainly what his stories do."[4] In order then to more fully appreciate the significance of the door, and further probe how its imagery may be linked to the written oeuvre, a broader Laffertarian aesthetic should be discerned and explicated. This essay will posit that Lafferty's visual art along with his speculative fiction can be subsumed under the category of *bricolage* aesthetic, and that all of his creative activities may best be explicated as the work of a *bricoleur*. In the course of establishing this aesthetic claim, I hope to "open" Lafferty's "secret door" in the three distinct ways that he advocates: first by "finding the edge" and thereby "pry open" the theoretical underpinnings of *bricolage*; by saying the "word" and thus elaborating how Lafferty's narrational method, particularly in one of his signature texts, is structured in a characteristically *bricoleur* manner; and finally by having Lafferty's images themselves "show" us "how" they evince the techniques of assemblage, discontinuous juxtapositions, and patterned relationships of elements in time and space which are the hallmarks of a *bricolage* aesthetic.

---

[4] Ibid.

I

The doors between different situations or worlds may be opened in peculiar ways such as this, but they may not be opened very wide or very often. And the knowledge of how they are opened cannot be left lying around. Even those who may sometimes have to use such means cannot be allowed to remember the trick of them.[5]

It would seem that mythological worlds have been built up only to be shattered again, and that new worlds were built from the fragments.[6]

A Portrait of the Artist as *Bricoleur*

In the first chapter of *La Pensée Sauvage*, the anthropologist Claude Lévi-Strauss introduces the concept of the *bricoleur*, a kind of jack-of-trades who is "adept at performing a large number of diverse tasks." In contrast to the engineer, he does not subordinate each of these tasks to the "acquisition of raw materials and tools conceived and procured for the project: his universe of tools is closed, and the rule of his game is to always make do with 'what's available;'" in other words, the *bricoleur*'s materials constitute "a set, finite at each instance, of tools and materials, heterogeneous to the extreme," since the components of the set are not necessarily related to the current project, or, indeed, to any particular project, but are rather "the contingent result of all the occasions that have occurred to renew or enrich the stock, or to maintain it with the remains

---

[5] R.A Lafferty, *Not To Mention Camels: A Science Fiction Fantasy* (Indianapolis, IN: The Bobbs-Merrill Company, 1976), p. 55.

[6] Anthropologist Franz Boas, in his Introduction to James Teit, *Traditions of the Thompson River Indians of British Columbia*, Memoirs of the American Folklore Society, VI (1898), p. 18; quoted by Claude Lévi-Strauss, "The Structural Study of Myth," *The Journal of American Folklore* 68: 270, Myth: A Symposium (1955), pp. 428-444, at p. 428.

of previous constructions or destructions."[7] For Lévi-Strauss, the *bricoleur* is an artist who constructs his work as a form of *bricolage*, or an assemblage of different pre-existent forms that result in a new whole, and a kind of poet who "derives his poetry from the fact that he does not confine himself to accomplishment and execution"—that is to say, he "'speaks' not only *with* things . . . but also through the medium of things: giving an account of his personality and life by the choices he makes between the limited possibilities" that his found materials provide.[8]

As a social anthropologist and ethnologist specializing in mythology and folklore, Lévi-Strauss was also particularly perceptive to the ways in which mythical thought appears to be an intellectual form of *bricolage*. As he explains in *La Pensée Sauvage*, the characteristic feature of mythical thought, as of *bricolage*, is that it "builds up structured sets, not directly with other structured sets but by using the remains and debris of events."[9] In other words, like the *bricoleur* who selects his tools and materials from an already existing stock that bear no necessary relation to his present purpose, the mythmaker considers the inventory of images at hand in his culture and recombines them through a series of transformations into a novel system of meanings. "Myths, like all things in constant use, break and are fixed again, become lost and are found, and the one who finds them and fixes them, the handyman who recycles them" is a kind of mythopoeic *bricoleur*, a recombinant shaman who takes some of the most enduring and recalcitrant elements of a culture—death, birth, war, sexuality, time—and attempts to fashion new meanings in order to resolve seemingly irresolvable paradoxes.[10]

---

[7] Claude Lévi-Strauss, *The Savage Mind* (Chicago: The University of Chicago Press and London: Weidenfeld and Nicolson Ltd., 1966), p. 17.

[8] Ibid, p. 21.

[9] Ibid, pp. 21-22.

[10] Wendy Doniger, "Foreword" to Claude Lévi-Strauss, *Myth and Meaning* (New York: Schocken Books, 1995), p. ix.

Moreover, according to Lévi-Strauss the mythopoeic imagination of the *bricoleur* stands in sharp contrast with the instrumentalized thought-processes of modern science and commercialized technocracy. Unlike the combinatorial methodology of the *bricoleur*, who works within the self-closed parameter of elements which are already to hand, and who incorporates the innate resistances to incorporation inherent in these elements into his work, the technocratic engineer attempts to transcends the particular constraints of the "natural and material world in order to achieve a total mastery of them;" it is a "predominantly conceptual mode of operation" that is constitutionally "indifferent to the contingent (substitutable) tools and materials that are constructed to achieve its ends."[11] The engineer works in conceptualizations that strive to be independent of cultural and material contexts, while the bricoleur works with a set of signs which are already embedded with symbolic meaning. And while symbols do not yet attain to abstractive conceptualization, since they do not "yet possess simultaneous and theoretically unlimited relations with other entities of the same kind," nonetheless they are "already *permutable*, that is, capable of standing in successive relations with other entities." But only, according to Lévi-Strauss, in a limited number of ways that follow identifiable rules, among which the most important may be the "condition that they always form a system in which an alteration which affects one element automatically affects all the others."[12] This indicates that beyond their methodological differences both modern science and the mythopoeic imagination follow similar cognitional exigencies to interpret and classify data, because they each follow the same unique human imperative to find meaning in things and events.

At its most expansive, the notion of *bricolage* denotes all the myriad ways in which the pre-scientific, oral (or "savage," to use Lévi-Strauss' preferred parlance, a term that by no

---

[11] Christopher Johnson, "*Bricoleur* and *Bricolage:* From Metaphor to Universal Concept," *Paragraph* 35:3 (2012), pp. 355-372; at p. 367.

[12] Lévi-Strauss, *Savage Mind*, p. 20.

means implies "primitive" so much as "wild" or unfettered by scientistic thought-patterns), mythopoeic mind encounters and responds to the world. This process "involves a 'science of the concrete' (as opposed to our 'civilized' science of the 'abstract') which," very far from being illogic or arbitrary, is actually a complex procedure that "carefully and precisely orders, classifies and arranges into structures the *minutiae* of the physical world in all their profusion by means of a 'logic' which is not our own."[13] The *bricolage* structures created in response posit reciprocal orderings between nature—in both its material and transcendent aspects—and the social world of the *bricoleur*. In effect, this mythopoeic logic is not only precisely structured, but also meticulously structuring, since the logical grammar whereby the mind finds order in the world is mirrored in the ordered cognitional grammar whereby the world is symbolized by the ordering mind:

> Myths signify the mind that evolves them by making use of the world of which it is itself a part. Thus there is simultaneous production of myths themselves, by the mind that generates them and, by the myths, of an image of the world which is already inherent in the structure of the mind.[14]

Hence the mythopoeic system of *bricolage* and the modes of representation it employs "serve to establish homologies between natural and social conditions or, more accurately, it makes it possible to equate significant contrasts found on different planes: the geographical, meteorological, zoological, botanical, technical, economic, social, ritual, religious and philosophical."[15] In this regard, both the scientific and the mythopoeic imagination are valid in their own terms—the

---

[13] Terence Hawkes, *Structuralism and Semiotics* (London: Routledge, 2003), p. 36.

[14] Claude Lévi-Strauss, *The Raw and the Cooked, Mythologiques* vol. 1, trans. J. and D. Weightman (Chicago: The University of Chicago Press, 1983), p. 341.

[15] Lévi-Strauss, *Savage Mind*, p. 93.

bricoleur "builds up structures by fitting together events, or rather the remains of events," while the scientific mind-set "creates its means and results in the form of events, thanks to the structures which it is constantly elaborating and which are its hypotheses and theories—and in Lévi-Strauss' estimation this locates art "half-way between scientific knowledge and mythical or magical thought," the artist being something of both the engineer and the *bricoleur*, since by "his craftsmanship he constructs a material object which is also an object of knowledge."[16]

Indeed, Lévi-Strauss' aesthetic theory finds close parallels between the mythographer and the creative artist, since the creative act that "gives rise to myths is in fact exactly the reverse of that which gives rise to works of art." In the case of artistic creation, the point of origin is usually a set of objects or events "which aesthetic creation unifies by revealing a common structure," while the mythopoeic endeavor "travel the same road but start from the other end." In other words, it utilizes a structure to produce what is itself an object consisting of a set of events, since all forms of mythology relate a narrative: "Art thus proceeds from a set (object + event) to the *discovery* of its structure. Myth starts from a structure by means of which it *constructs* a set (object + event)."[17] So while there are analogical relations between mythopoeic thought on the conceptual plane, and the praxis of *bricolage* on the practical level, for Lévi-Strauss only artistic creation can be located at the crucial mid-point between the scientism of the engineer and the forms of creative activity engaged in by the mythographer and *bricoleur*, and in this manner art bridges the divide between them. This privileged mediatory location also allows art to create a structure of knowledge-communicating signification that is in direct relation to the structure of the events or objects that it representationally signifies. The signifying structures of the creative artist can thus be likened to a symbolic microcosm, a small-scale assemblage or model (*modèle réduit*), of the

---

[16] Ibid, p. 22.

[17] Ibid, 25-26.

macrocosmic structures that it attempts to represent, which functions as an "immediate synthesis of the properties of the object (properties that science aims to isolate analytically) and the material givens of its apprehension (colors, smells, tastes, tones, perspectives, and so on)," and it is precisely this "integration of structure and event, this giving of the intelligible in the sensible, this offered whole" like a *compendium mundi* that results in the tell-tale aesthetic pleasure of a work of art, whether it be pictorial, literary, or musical.[18]

Lévi-Strauss' elucidation of the *bricoleur*'s characteristic technique of building up impromptu structures by appropriating pre-existing materials finds a close parallel in R.A. Lafferty's own acknowledged working techniques as a writer. Asked how he composed a story, Lafferty explicates an improvisatory process of recombining previous fragments in order to devise new forms very much like the combinatorial methods utilized *bricolage*:

> The only honest answer is that I prowl back through a bunch of busted or unfinished satires and salvage pieces out of several of them and put them together for a story that might go. It seems that time in discard is necessary for most of them, and the tension and juxtaposition that a story has to have can be made by a combination of old things. I usually make an outline of the new story then, though often only in my head and not written down. I usually do about two-thirds of the first draft writing. Then I start what I hope will be the final version and go right through without slowing down at the old stopping place. About half the time, this proves to be the final version, and I rewrite completely after letting it set aside for a month or so. In other cases, I will rewrite only two or three pages of it. Likewise after letting it set for a while.[19]

[18] Marcel Hénaff, *Claude Lévi-Strauss and the Making of Structural Anthropology*, trans. M. Baker (Minneapolis and London: University of Minnesota Press, 1998), p. 194.

[19] Whitaker, "Maybe They Needed Killing," p. 14.

In another interview Lafferty linked this method of composing with the older extemporaneous story-telling technique of the tall-tale as found in folk and pre-literate oral cultures:

> DS: How much of the traditional material turns up in your fiction, or do you simply borrow the method?
>
> RAL: More method, because the tall story has to be spontaneous. You just start raveling one out and pretty soon things start to happen in it.
>
> DS: Do you write your short stories the way you would tell a tall tale?
>
> RAL: I try to, yeah, but the handwriting gets in the way of it, if you want to put it that way. I think the oral tales are more authentic than the written ones that came later, and I think the oral ones are better.[20]

Lafferty also explicitly endorses the notion that the type of speculative fiction that he creates can be seen as a kind of mythopoeic activity. Even more interestingly, he echoes Lévi-Strauss' contention that despite their distinctive methodologies, myth and science both share a deeper common structure of analyzing the world and a mutual affinity to find order and meaning. "For that matter, science is a form of mythology. Myth isn't something false ordinarily. It's just a way of handling or coming on to a truth. When it can't be direct, there are lots of mythical things in science. They were in there quite a while before science was finally formulated."[21]

Most interesting, perhaps, is the way in which Lafferty's work manifests an inherent creative tension, a characteristic tension that Lévi-Strauss discusses at some length in his studies of myth, between the signifier and the signified; that is, between the representational aspects of a work of art that

---

[20] Darrell Schweitzer, "An Interview with R.A. Lafferty," in *Cranky Old Man from Tulsa: Interviews with R.A. Lafferty* (Weston, Ontario: United Mythologies Press, 1990), pp. 1-7; here at p. 4. This interview is also reprinted in the current issue of *Feast of Laughter*.

[21] Ibid, p. 3.

are ultimately based on the sensible attributes of the object or event being represented, and the signifying dimension of art, which designates the conceptual content of the representational image, and thereby institutes the represented object/event within a relational system of conceptual signs. According to Lévi-Strauss, the secondary qualities of anything that is creatively represented, whether it be its shape, color, texture, sound, movement, etc., are not mere descriptive signifiers, but are in fact also bearers of signification, so that any represented object/event, along with its attendant qualia, is also the "site of a series of formal operations, the locus of a mytho-poetical calculus."[22] In other words, these objects or events are constituted as signs in an operational semiotic structure that contain a meaningful content over and beyond their purely mimetic features, and in this manner the poetic and visual imagery of the creative artist can function analogously to the symbols analyzed by Lévi-Strauss in his anthropological work.[23] Moreover, this process of mythopoeic creation or *bricolage*, whereby secondary qualities are converted into a system of signification, is often mirrored in the very structure of the creative work itself, so that a structuralist analysis of such works—whether it be a myth or poem, a story or a painting—may upon closer scrutiny reveal the latent conceptual and functional paradigms undergirding the sign-system. Similarly, as a *bricoleur*, Lafferty's work often displays the inherent creative tensions between its constitutive mimetic elements and their significatory structural function, so that his artistry can be perceived not

---

[22] Boris Wiseman, *Lévi-Strauss, Anthropology and Aesthetics*, Ideas in Context 85 (Cambridge: Cambridge University Press, 2007), p. 88.

[23] As Lévi-Strauss explains, the mythopoeic and the creative act consists at once in the "extraction of constitutive units from sensible reality and their integration into a system 'which plays the part of a synthesizing operator between ideas and facts, thereby turning the latter into *signs*. The mind thus passes from empirical diversity to conceptual simplicity and then from conceptual simplicity to meaningful syntheses." *Savage Mind*, p. 131.

only as a representational system, but also simultaneously conceived as an illustrative exploration of the semiotic potentialities of that system.

II

There is a magnitude we missed,
Nor know we why it could not be
That comes to lesser folks than we.
Terribilis est locus iste!

In other days at other doors
May we be otherwise redressed,
And in the dimness put to rest
The ghosts of all our metaphors.

And you like some remembered dawn
Grow goldener when you are gone,
Who like the lithic wife of Lot
Was saltier when she was not.

The fog is fast about the trees,
And I will watch the midnight sea
And in the dark remember thee
With antipodal thoughts like these.[24]

Myths are not merely things that were made in times past: myths are among the things that maintain the present in being. I wish most strongly that the present should be maintained: I often live in it.[25]

---

[24] R.A. Lafferty, *Archipelago* (Lafayette, LA: Manuscript Press, 1979), pp. 32-33.

[25] R.A. Lafferty, "Boomer Flats," in *The Man Underneath*, The Collected Short Fiction, Vol. 3. Ed. J. Pelan (Lakewood, CO: Centipede Press, 2016), pp. 85-104; at p. 99.

Recurring Myth-Person Events[26]

Once, when asked to explain the genesis of one of his most celebrated tales, Lafferty gave a curious response:

> How did I write "Continued on Next Rock" then? Upside down and backwards, of course. I started with a simple, but I believe novel, idea that had to do with time. Then I involuted the idea of time (making all things contemporary or at least repeating), and I turned the system of values backwards, trying to make the repulsive things appear poetic ("the nobility of badgers, the serenity of toads") and trying to set anti-love up as comparable to love (the flattest thing you can imagine has to have at least two sides; it can have many more). I let the characters that had been generated by this action work out their own way then...[27]

This involution of the temporal order, which renders events in the narrative "contemporary or at least repeating," has been recognized as one the most characteristic features of this story, as well as a thematic leitmotif present in many of Lafferty's other fictions. As Sheryl Smith points out, a cyclical pattern of "endlessness and often of regeneration" frequently shapes Lafferty's most inherently mythopoeic compositions.[28] This observation is particularly true for "Continued On Next Rock," which traces a "recurring personal drama of unrequited love and destruction, in which three progressively-more-recent records in stone build to a present-time climax"

---

[26] Lafferty uses this term twice in "The Man Who Walked through Cracks," in *Chrysalis* 3, ed. R. Torgerson (New York: Zebra Books, 1978), pp. 223-245.

[27] R.A. Lafferty, "How I Wrote 'Continued On Next Rock,'" in *At the Sleepy Sailor: A Tribute to R.A. Lafferty* (1979), pp. 19-20; at p. 19.

[28] Sheryl Smith, "Lafferty's Short Stories: Some Mystagogic Goshwow," *Riverside Quarterly* 7:2 (1982), pp. 73-81, at 75.

but not, as Smith points out, "it seems, an end;" in fact the two "primordial-persons involved have little hope of achieving their mutually-exclusive aspirations except in death," adding to this "mythic comedy a near-tragic countertheme which is beautifully supported by the writing."[29]

In this brief yet penetrating descriptive analysis Smith isolates certain key constitutive elements in Lafferty's narrative, as pointed out by Lafferty in his own account of how he constructed this tale out of various disparate components, such as the seemingly irreconcilable binary opposition of the two protagonists which drive the narrative forward, or the curious temporal unfolding of the plot which simultaneously bends back upon itself in a seemingly atemporal manner, that find a striking functional correspondence with the structural building blocks of mythopoesis as described in Lévi-Strauss' anthropological work on *bricolage*. Like Lafferty, Lévi-Strauss recognizes the conflict of opposites (light/dark, young/old, fire/water, male/female, birth/death, earth/sky, day/night, etc.) as the basic engine of narrational movement and motivic development within all mythopoeic creations. This antipodal logic of paired contraries wherein certain functions are linked to a given subject, discloses its meaning not in isolated instances of binary opposition, but rather in bundles of such relations. Each of these bundles is an agglomeration of all the distinct iterations of one of these dyadic relations, "being simultaneously perceived, or sensed beneath and through whichever particular version is being used at any particular time."[30] Lévi-Strauss' groundbreaking insight is that myths always function simultaneously along two axes, much like a musical score does, which to be meaningful must be read both diachronically along one axis, "that is, page after page, and from left to right," but also "synchronically along the other axis, all the notes which are written vertically making up one gross constituent unit, i.e. one bundle of relations."[31]

---

[29] Ibid, p. 76.

[30] Hawkes, *Structuralism and Semiotics*, p. 30.

[31] Claude Lévi-Strauss, "Structural Study of Myth," p. 432.

Now, in point of fact, when we hear a tale being told, or read a narrative, we experience it largely as we would an orchestral score during a performance, that is, diachronically, and only perceive the synchronic aspects of the score as an overall pattern of harmonic resonances. Extending the metaphor, Lévi-Strauss posits that mythopoeic narrative are usually given as a sequence of disparate events that open up in a unilinear series, so that we are confronted with a sequence of the type: 1, 2, 4, 7, 8, 2, 3, 4, 6, 8, 1, 4, 5, 7, 8, 1, 2, 5, 7, 3, 4, 5, 6, 8 . . . The task of the anthropologist who wishes to uncover the way the various architectonic elements relate to each other within the overall mythopoeic structure is to re-arrange those components into rows of bundles, which Levi-Strauss will later call *mythemes*, according to their common thematic links:

1	2		4			7	8
	2	3	4		6		8
1			4	5		7	8
1	2			5		7	
		3	4	5	6		8

In this schema we are confronted with several vertical columns, "each of which includes several relations belonging to the same bundle. Were we to *tell* the myth, we would disregard the columns and read the rows from left to right and from top to bottom," however, if we want "to *understand* the myth, then we will have to disregard one half of the diachronic dimension (top to bottom) and read from left to right, column after column, each one being considered as a unit."[32] Lévi-Strauss' structural analysis thus attempts to read the myth along both axes: as *mythemes* or discrete units of recurrent thematic elements arranged in opposing yet static dyadic pairs, and as the unfolding of the inherent oppositional dynamic within those antipodal pairs across a temporal expanse. All the events and their respective constitutive elements are organized simultaneously in a median vertical plane, and also arranged in a continuous series across a

---

[32] Ibid, p. 433.

transverse axial plane. In conjunction, these two planes can account for all the cyclical variations upon the basic dyadic theme of a myth as it is progressively articulated in time.

According to Lévi-Strauss, the paradigmatic reduplication of images, events, and figures of speech in mythography, and to a more general extent in all forms of oral storytelling, can be attributed to the fact that such repetition has as its function to make the structure of the myth apparent. Lévi-Strauss' methodology makes this reticulated twofold synchro-diachronical structure manifest, thereby allowing us to map out the mythopoeic narrative in a diachronous sequence (across the transverse axis) that can also be read synchronously (down the vertical plane). Consequently, myths analyzed in this manner will exhibit a "slated" configuration that "seeps to the surface," or perhaps we should rather say, which emerges as layered three-dimensional strata by means of this "repetition process;"[33] a structured and structuring pattern of stratification that can be read "left to right," "top to bottom," and "front to back"[34] (See Fig. 3).

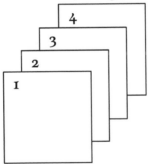

Figure 3. *Mythemes* organized in a three-dimensional ordering that can be read both diachronically and synchronously.

"Continued On Next Rock" may be unique among Lafferty's speculative fiction for the boldness with which it articulates its mythopoeic structure along both synchro-diachronical axes, and the manner in which the story itself

---

[33] Ibid, p. 436.

[34] Ibid, p. 443.

allows the strata of encoded significations to emerge to the surface of the narrative as it is read. In accordance with Lévi-Strauss' dictum that the process of signification emerges from a fundamental oppositional dynamic at the heart of any given myth, Lafferty's narrative proceeds from a fundamental binary conflict between love and "anti-love" as embodied in the two main protagonists, Magdalen and Anteros. In Greek mythology Anteros was an ambiguous figure, said to be the brother of Eros, the god of love, and whose function some ancient writers describe as an avenger of slighted eros or unrequited love. However, the prefix "ante-" means "equal of"—thus leading ancient writers like Plato to describe the essential concept of *anteros* as reciprocating love, the eros-in-return without which true love cannot flourish or grow.[35] Lafferty's Anteros Manypenny seems to personify both aspects of the myth, at once a figure that eternally seek to both give and receive a reciprocating love and ultimately an avenging angel of love spurned. The object of his affection is the antithetical figure of Magdalen Mobley, who exemplifies a counter-love or *anti-eros* to Manypenny's *anteros*.

This primordial antagonism establishes the mythopoeic mechanism whereby oppositional pairs will be projected into further levels of signification. In "Continued On Next Rock" the binary divergence at the core of the tale extends itself even to the landscape in which the outgrowth of the archetypal conflict is progressively disclosed. The symbolic and thematic focus of much of the tale centers upon a petrified "up-thrust, a chimney rock that is half fallen against a newer hill" that is "only a little older than mankind, only a little younger than grass. Its formation had been up-thrust and then eroded away again," a piece of the Earth were time was "heaped up, bulging out in casing and accumulation, and not in line sequence. . . striated and banded time, grown tall, and then shattered and

---

[35] Plato, *Phaedrus*, 255b: "And in the lover's presence, like him he ceases from his pain, and in his absence, like him he is filled with yearning such as he inspires, and love's image, requited love, dwells within him." Cf. Craig E. Stephenson, *Anteros: A Forgotten Myth* (New York: Routledge, 2012).

broken."[36] The complexly graded topology which Lafferty so richly describes mirrors the convoluted terrain of the character's inner landscape, an isomorphism that Lévi-Strauss acknowledged, and which allowed him to describe the various layered groupings of mythemes in terms of stratification.[37] Indeed, Lafferty has one of the characters explicate this morphic resonance between the signifying psyche and landscape, as both the material signifier and the conceptual signified, from within the narrative itself:

> "It bedevils me sometimes why I am the only one to notice the analogy between historical geology and depth psychology," Terrence Burdock mused as they grew lightly profound around the campfire. "The isostatic principle applies to the mind and the under-mind as well as it does to the surface and under-surface

---

[36] R.A. Lafferty, "Continued On Next Rock," in *Lafferty in Orbit* (Cambridge, MA: Broken Mirrors Press, 1991), pp. 73-89; at p. 73.

[37] In *Tristes Tropiques* (1959), an account of his first voyage into the Amazonian rain forest in order to collect aboriginal myth, a report that is itself structured according to bricolage aesthetics, Lévi-Strauss recalls an early experience of *topos*, a physical place located in space and time, as an analogue for the topology of the human psyche and the site of the mythopoeic process of signification: "And sometimes the miracle happens. On one side and the other of a hidden crevice we find two green plants of different species. Each has chosen the soil which suits it; and we realize that within the rock are two ammonites, one of which has involutions less complex than the other's. We glimpse, that is to say, a difference of many thousands of years; time and space suddenly [become one]; the living diversity of that moment juxtaposes one age and the other and perpetuates them. Thought and sensibility take on a new dimension, in which every drop of sweat, every movement of muscle, every quick-drawn breath becomes the symbol of a story; and, as my body reproduces the particular gait of that story, so does my mind embrace its meaning. I feel myself [immersed in a denser form of intelligibility, in which time and space answer one another and speak languages that have at last been reconciled]." Quoted in Wiseman, *Lévi-Strauss, Anthropology and Aesthetics*, p. 47.

of the earth. The mind has its erosions and weatherings going on along with its deposits and accumulations. It also has its upthrusts and its stresses. It floats on a similar magma. In extreme cases it has its volcanic eruptions and its mountain building. . . .The mind has its hard sandstone, sometimes transmuted to quartz, or half-transmuted into flint, from the drifting and floating sand of daily events. It has its shale from the old mud of daily ineptitudes and inertias. It has limestone out of its more vivid experiences, for lime is the remnant of what was once animate: and this limestone may be true marble if it is the deposit of rich enough emotion, or even travertine if it has bubbled sufficiently through agonized and evocative rivers of the under-mind. The mind has its sulphur and its gemstones—"[38]

To which the acerbically antipodal Magdalene responds "Say simply that we have rocks in our heads;" a superficially sarcastic comment that masks a deeper relevance, for as she goes on to point out "It isn't the same with us as it is with the earth. The world gets new rocks all the time. But it's the same people who keep turning up, and the same minds." That is, the same basic mythopoeic thought-structures are continuously recapitulated by a recurring ensemble of archetypal protagonists. The same "rocks," the same stratification of dyadic *mythemes*, keeps being thrust up out of the societal subconscious into the light of day. In fact, at this point she exclaims: "Damn, one of the samest of them just turned up again! I wish he'd leave me alone. The answer is still no," thereby announcing the arrival of Anteros and the commencement of another mythopoeic cycle.[39]

Lévi-Strauss is critical of what he takes to be Jung's misguidedly single-minded emphasis on the symbolic psychological significance of individual archetypal figures. For the French ethnologist, it is the combinations of

---

[38] Lafferty, "Continued," pp. 74-75.

[39] Ibid, p. 75.

mythological archetypes arranged across both synchro-diachronical axes that reveals the true structural signification of these archetypal thought-types. Lévi-Strauss goes so far as to "claim to show not how men think in myths, but how myths operate in men's minds" without their being fully conscious of the fact.

> It would perhaps be better to go still further and, disregarding the thinking subject completely, proceed as if the thinking process were taking place in the myths, in their reflection upon themselves and their interrelation. For what I am concerned to clarify is not so much what there is in myths (without, incidentally, being in man's consciousness) as the system of axioms and postulates defining the best possible code, capable of conferring a common significance on unconscious formulations which are the work of minds, societies, and civilizations chosen from among those most remote from each other. As the myths themselves are based on secondary codes (the primary codes being those that provide the substance of language), the present work is put forward as a tentative draft of a tertiary code, which is intended to ensure the reciprocal translatability of several myths. This is why it would not be wrong to consider this book itself as a myth: it is, as it were, the myth of mythology.[40]

This approach to archetype finds a parallel in Lafferty's own unique appropriation of the Jungian archetypes, for as he memorably explains, the archetypes are not thought-patterns that one harbors in the mind, but rather they are mythopoeic structures that we each inhabit and exemplify, so that—as Lévi-Strauss asserts—it is not that we think in archetypically mythological ways, but on the contrary the structured and structuring mythic thought-patterns that think through us.

---

[40] Lévi-Strauss, *The Raw and the Cooked*, p. 12. See also Thomas Shalvey, *Claude Lévi-Strauss: Social Psychotherapy and the Collective Unconscious* (Amherst: University of Massachusetts Press, 1979), p. 12.

Moreover, Lafferty links this understanding of mythopoeic archetype to the *ad hoc* combinatorial techniques of the *bricoleur* that many of his works evince.

> We will not lie to you. This is a do-it-yourself thriller or nightmare. Its present order is only the way it comes in the box. Arrange it as you will.
>
> Set off the devils and the monsters, the wonderful beauties and the foul murderers, the ships and the oceans of middle space, the corpses and the revenants, set them off in whatever apposition you wish. Glance quickly to discover whether you have not the mark on your own left wrist, barely under the skin. Build with these colored blocks your own dramas of love and death and degradation. Learn the true topography: the monstrous and wonderful archetypes are not inside you, not in your own unconsciousness; you are inside them, trapped, and howling to get out.[41]

In effect, what Lafferty is doing here is alerting us to the true nature of archetypal mythopoesis, and inviting us to participate in his *bricolage* technique of combining and recombining *mythemes* in order to formulate our own mythic narratives. And all the while, Lafferty slyly yet knowingly leads us into the structural semiosis of the work itself, so that rightly understood, it can be read as a synchro-diachronical text that at once codes and decodes itself.

While the engine of the mythopoeic narrative is the primal binary opposition encapsulated in a *mytheme*, the function of the myth is not merely to acknowledge that contrariety, but also to attempt to resolve or overcome it, for "mythical thought always works from the awareness of oppositions to their progressive mediation."[42] This attempted resolution is traced out along the diachronic axis of the myth as narrative. The central purpose of a mythological narrative

---

[41] R.A Lafferty, *The Devil Is Dead* (New York: Avon Books, 1971). p. 9.

[42] Lévi-Strauss, "Structural Study of Myth," p. 440.

is to "provide a logical model capable of overcoming a contradiction," but—as Lévi-Strauss quickly acknowledges—this is an often "impossible achievement," as happens to be the case in "Continued On Next Rock," where the primary "contradiction" proves to be irresolvable. As a consequence, a "theoretically infinite number of slates" or strata will be generated out of this unresolved conflict, "each one slightly different from the others. Thus, myth grows spiral-wise until the intellectual impulse which has originated it is exhausted." It is for this reason that a myth's narratological progression resides in the temporal order, and therefore its iterations or growth across time manifests as a "continuous process," whereas its essential dyadic structure "remains discontinuous" or synchronously located in the atemporal vertical axis.[43] In "Continued On Next Rock," Lafferty presents the Magdalen/Anteros opposition as a synchronous dyad, while chronicling its spiraling development over a series of stratilogical variations. Moreover, each of these variations is presented in a different language, for as Lévi-Strauss indicates, while separate iterations of a *mytheme* will be produced within a given societal matrix, each with its own distinctive modes of expression, nonetheless the synchronous nature of the dyad will ensure its reciprocal translatability across different language-culture complexes. So, for example, Anteros' unrequited courtship of Magdalen is traced in a number of texts or "love poems" in a variety of languages: Nahuat-Tanoan glyphs, Anadarko-Caddo hand-talk presented as a formalized system of pictographs, Kiowa picture writing, and finally in a "deformed" alphabetical script resembling modern English. This synchro-diachronical schematization also begins to explicate some of the spatio-temporal particularities of the story. The "peculiar fluting" of the broken chimney is "almost like a core sample," a longitudinal section that cuts like a "lightning bolt through the whole length" of the rock formation and exposes its stratification.[44] In stark contrast to the rock outcrop is an adjoining mound that is excavated to

---

[43] Ibid, p. 443.

[44] Lafferty, "Continued," p. 73.

reveal a surprising variety of archaeological finds that are temporally anomalous, defying any pre-established logic of the way cultural artifacts are supposed to evolve over the course of centuries. In fact, many of these artefacts have been arranged in a cross-sectional manner, each grouping of bones, flints, beads, etc., set in a kind of transverse patterning that allows for a synchronous analysis. These disconcerting discontinuities lead one of the anthropologists in the story to proclaim that "Archaeology is made up entirely of anomalies . . . rearranged to make them fit in a flukey pattern. There'd be no system to it otherwise."[45] To put this in terms which Lévi-Strauss may have used, we could say that the spatio-temporal disposition of material artifacts only discloses a meaningful pattern to the observer when the codes or rules (i.e., its signifying structure) according to which the observed system of relations amongst the artifacts was produced is decoded.[46]

Beyond their archaeological content, the rock and the mound continue the symbolism of oppositional pairings, to the extent of assimilating paradigmatic idioms identified with each of the main protagonists with these topological features.

---

[45] Ibid, p. 79.

[46] For further elucidation on how structuralism's attempt to conceptualize the world in terms of relationships between things rather than in terms of the things themselves can inform the science of archaeology, see M. Alison Wylie, "Epistemological Issues Raised by a Structuralist Archaeology," in *Symbolic and Structural Archaeology*, ed. I. Hodder (Cambridge: Cambridge University Press, 1982), pp. 39-45; David B. Small, "Toward a Competent Structuralist Archaeology: A Contribution from Historical Studies," *Journal of Anthropological Archaeology* 6 (1991), pp. 105-121; Robert Preucel, "Structuralism and its Archaeological Legacy," in *The Oxford Handbook of Archaeological Theory*, ed. A. Gardner, M. Lake, and U. Sommer (Oxford Handbooks Online, Scholarly Research), Online Publication Date: September 2014: http://www.oxfordhandbooks.com/view/10.1093/oxfordhb/978 0199567942.001.0001/oxfordhb-9780199567942-e-013, and Boris Wiseman, "Lévi-Strauss and the Archaeology of Perceptible Worlds," *Yale French Studies* 123, Rethinking Claude Lévi-Strauss (1908-2009), ed. R. Doran (2013), pp.166-186.

For example, the top of the up-thrust chimney rock is associated with the mythological "sky bridge" of various native cosmologies, a celestial realm symbolically linked to the heavenly stars and the darkness of night. Indeed, when Anteros uses dynamite to dislodge fragments of the chimney rock formation, the explosion

> Sounded as if the whole sky were falling down in them, and some of those sky-blocks were quite large stones. The ancients wondered why fallen pieces of the sky should always be dark rockstuff and never sky-blue clear stuff. The answer is that it is only pieces of the night sky that ever fall, even though they may sometimes be most of the daytime in falling, such is the distance. And the blast that Anteros set off did bring down rocky chunks of the night sky even though it was broad daylight. They brought down darker rocks than any of which the chimney was composed.[47]

In a dramatic thematic counterpoint, Anteros is associated with overtly telluric imagery. He is the "digging man" and the mound he expertly excavates is already honeycombed with telltale artefacts that he himself—or perhaps one of his earlier archetypal manifestations—placed in the earth. He is identified with the vast mineral treasure hidden in the hidden entrails of the world, he is "rich in all ways" with the fecundity of the soil, as displayed in the abiding cyclical movements of birth, death, and rebirth, and which is given fleshly form in his very person as an untamed chthonic sexuality that is at unmistakable symbolic variance with the pure, powerful, and yet ultimately unfruitful elysian heights that Margaret exemplifies. "You fear the earth, you fear rough ground and rocks," one of Anteros' pictographic poems declares, "you fear moister earth and rotting flesh, you fear the flesh itself, all flesh is rotting flesh." But, the archetypal earth-man's unearthed peroration continues,

---

[47] Lafferty, "Continued," p. 77.

> If you love not rotting flesh, you love not at all. You believe the bridge hanging in the sky, the bridge hung by tendrils and woody vines that diminish as they go up and up till they are no thicker than hairs. There is no sky-bridge, you cannot go up on it. Did you believe that the roots of love grow upside down? They come out of deep earth that is old flesh and brains and hearts and entrails, that is old buffalo bowels and snakes' pizzles, that is black blood and rot and moaning underground. This is old and worn-out and bloody Time, and the roots of love grow out of its gore.[48]

Anteros recognizes himself in the roaring and rutting of wild animals that he totemically incarnates by turns as a deer, turtle, and badger—a creaturely, uncanny enfleshment that leads in turn to a series of almost sacrificial deaths at Margaret's insistence, and in which his bestial flesh is quasi-ritualistically given as food to the other characters. For Lévi-Strauss, such totemic images function as a complex classificatory system that can be employed by the savage or *bricoleur* mind to both "establish increasingly minute differences," or to "encompass reality in increasingly broad oppositions."[49] In either case, the signifying animal is used as a "conceptual tool with multiple possibilities for detotalizing or retotalizing any domain, synchronic or diachronic, concrete or abstract, natural or cultural."[50] In this instance, Lafferty"s

---

[48] Ibid, p. For further meditations on the chthonic aspects of Lafferty's mythopoeic imagination, see Daniel Otto Jack Petersen, "Oh The Deep Dimensionality of Swamps! Notes Toward an Anatomy of the Laffertian Muck-Monstrous," in *LaffCon 1: The World's First and Only R.A. Lafferty Conference* (Ktistec Press, 2016), pp. 35-38.

[49] Wiseman, *Lévi-Strauss, Anthropology and Aesthetics*, p. 39.

[50] Lévi-Strauss, *Savage Mind*, pp. 148-149: "... in none of these cases can the animal, the 'totem' or its species be grasped as a biological entity: through its double character of organism-that is, of system-and of emanation from a species-which is a term in a system-the animal appears as a conceptual tool with multiple possibilities for detotalizing or retotalizing any domain,

bestial invocations serve to "totalize" the Margaret/Anteros dyadic antithesis in such a way that it encompasses not only figures from the animal kingdom and attendant hunting and culinary processes, but expands the symbolic contrariety at the center of the myth to the whole of the natural world itself, including both the terrestrial realm and the celestial sphere.[51]

> I cry out with big voice like a bear full of mad-weed, like a bullfrog in love, like a stallion rearing against a puma. It is the earth that calls you. I am the earth, woolier than wolves and rougher than rocks. I am the bog earth that sucks you in. You cannot give, you cannot like, you cannot love, you think there is something else, you think there is a sky-bridge you may loiter on without crashing down. I am bristled-boar earth, there is no other.[52]

Anteros is adamant that the inexorable mythopoeic logic of this tale can only end in a grand reconciliation of irreconcilables or in tragedy, there are no other options, as the forces of nature play out their inexorable climactic role.

> You will come to me in the morning. You will come to me easy and with grace. Or you will come to me reluctant and you be shattered in every bone and member of you. You be broken by our encounter. You be shattered as by a lightning bolt striking up from the earth. I am the red calf which is in the writings. I am the rotting red earth. Live in the morning or die in the morning, but remember that love in death is better than no love at all.[53]

---

synchronic or diachronic, concrete or abstract, natural or cultural."

[51] In *The Raw and the Cooked, Mythologiques* vol. 1, Lévi-Strauss explores the mythopoeic significance of binary cooking techniques in considerable detail.

[52] Lafferty, "Continued," p. 86.

[53] Ibid.

Quite significantly, the culmination of this process unfolds in a misty haze, for as Lévi-Strauss has explicated at some length, in aboriginal mythopoetics fog occupies a symbolic halfway point between the two opposing poles of earth and sky; it is a symbolic phenomenon that is at once disjunctive and conjunctive, a "mediating term conjoining extremes and rendering them indistinguishable," or which comes between dyadic pairs "to prevent them growing closer."[54] In the creation accounts of some Amerindian tribes, at the dawn of creation a primordial fog united the earth and sky while simultaneously confusing and uniting light and darkness, a confounding mist that only dispersed with the appearance of the visible sun. Thus fog can act either as an agent of confusion and blindness, or as a means of erasing boundaries and reconciling or transcending primeval polarities. The final scene in "Continued On Next Rock" commences with a similarly mist-muddled sunrise: "The sun had come up a garish gray-orange color through fog;" and in this beclouded light the "chimney rock looked greatly diminished in its bulk (something had gone out of it) and much crazier in its broken height . . . It was as if something were coming down from the chimney, a horrifying smoke; but it was only noisome morning fog."[55] The foul morning mist presages a number of cataclysmic events: the collapse of the chimney stone, the apparent disappearance of Anteros and Magdalen, and the discovery of one final piece of writing, a concluding section of text found amidst the "amnesic and wit-stealing fog," apparently composed in modern English, yet "deformed," with some key linguistic element missing.[56] As already indicated, the mythopoeic miasma that covered the primordial soil may operate as an agent of antipodal

---

[54] Claude Lévi-Strauss, *The Naked Man, Mythologiques* vol. 4, trans. J. and D. Weightman (Chicago: The University of Chicago Press, 1990), p. 398. See also Magnus Course, "Of Words and Fog: Linguistic Relativity and Amerindian Ontology," *Anthropological Theory* 10: 3 (2010), pp. 247-263.

[55] Lafferty, "Continued," p. 87.

[56] Ibid, p. 88.

resolution, but just as often it functions as an instrument of chaos and final dissolution, as it proves to be in this instance, for out if it emerges "the bristled-boar earth reaching up with a rumble . . . a lightning bolt" striking upward "out of the earth," accompanied by an "explosion and roar." And with that blast:

> The dark capping rock was jerked from the top of the chimney and slammed with terrible force to the earth, shattering with a great shock. And something else that had been on that capping rock. And the whole chimney collapsed about them.
>
> She was broken by the encounter. She was shattered in every bone and member of her. And she was dead.[57]

Magdalen's violent demise by means of this chthonic discharge of electricity is dyadically accompanied by the simultaneous uncovering of a statue from the bowels of the earth, a portrait of Anteros, fashioned "life-like in basalt stone," his face contorted, "sobbing soundlessly and frozenly," his shoulders "hunched with emotion. The carving was fascinating in its miserable passion, his stony love unrequited. Perhaps he was more impressive now than he would be when he was cleaned. He was earth, he was earth itself."[58] The repetitive pattern of proffered and rejected love is left intact in the unsettled denouement. In the end, the binary contrariety of anteros/anti-eros which constitutes the *mytheme* remains unresolved, laying the groundwork for further attempted resolutions along the diachronic axis in a theoretically infinite number of variations upon this primordial duality, already anticipated in the "dark broken rocks" that bear a cryptic final message which must be read and decoded before its meaning is once again lost. We are left "studying a stratum" that hasn't "been laid down yet, reading a foggy future" which will undoubtedly unfold according to

---

[57] Ibid.

[58] Ibid. pp. 88-89.

an all-too-familiar yet unanticipatedly novel structural configuration.[59]

III

Weren't you talking about somebody shutting the door of the pavilion, and we would be caught in spite of a hundred doorless doorways?[60]

Come to the door. Look at every clock you can see. Are they not all stopped?[61]

My antipodal ghost. We're just alike only a world apart.[62]

All ghost appearances are time trips.[63]

---

[59] Ibid, p. 89.

[60] R.A. Lafferty, *The Elliptical Grave* (Weston, Ontario: United Mythologies Press, 1989), pagination not available

[61] R.A. Lafferty, "The Six Fingers of Time," in *Nine Hundred Grandmothers*, Ace SF Special, Series 1 (New York: Ace Books, 1970), pp. 43-73, at p. 56

[62] R.A. Lafferty, *The Devil Is Dead*, p. 160.

[63] R.A. Lafferty, "Bank and Shoal of Time," in *A Spadeful of Spacetime*, ed. F. Saberhagen (New York: Ace Books, 1981), pp. 187-213, at p. 198.

In Other Days at Other Doors May We Be Otherwise Redressed and In the Dimness Put To Rest the Ghosts of All Our Metaphors

So far, we have attempted to open the hidden meaning of Lafferty's door by first providing a conceptual precis of the bricoleur's methodology, then examining that method at work in the structure of a narrative displaying many elements of a bricolage aesthetic. Now we will endeavor to allow the collage images on this door to disclose their own compositional inner logic. As we have seen, the *bricoleur* creates with whatever materials are found at hand, and in the visual arts certain techniques and movements have come to be associated with this creative point of view: outsider art, folk art, naïve art, junk art, primitivism, intuitive art, marginal art, *art singulier*, *art brut*, *neuve invention*, visionary environments, *découpage*, combine painting, assemblage, *bricolage*, montage, and *papier collé* or collage. Many bricoleur practitioners are self-taught artists with no formal training and work outside the boundaries of the art market and the mainstream art world, although professional artists in the modernist and post-modernist avant-garde have appropriated and developed several of these methodologies.[64] Perhaps the most common

---

[64] Cf. William Chapin Seitz, *The Art of Assemblage* (New York: The Museum of Modern Art/Garden City, NY: Doubleday and Company, Inc., 1961); Thomas P. Brockelman, *The Frame and the Mirror: On Collage and Postmodernism*, Philosophy, Literature, and Culture (Evanston, IL: Northwestern University Press, 2001); Fine, Gary Alan Fine, *Everyday Genius: Self-Taught Art and the Culture of Authenticity* (Chicago: University of Chicago Press, 2004); Brandon Taylor, *Collage: The Making of Modern Art* (New York: Thames & Hudson, 2006); Greg Bottoms, *The Colorful Apocalypse: Journeys in Outsider Art* (Chicago: University of Chicago Press, 2007); Leslie Umberger, *Messages & Magic: 100 Years of Collage and Assemblage in America* (Sheboygan, WI: John Michael Kohler Arts Center, 2008); David Maclagan, *Outsider Art: From the Margins to the Marketplace* (London: Reaktion Books, 2009); David Banash, *Collage Culture: Readymades, Meaning, and the Age of Consumption* (Amsterdam and New York: Rodopi, 2012).

feature in many such techniques is the taking of portions of ready-made texts, images, and materials and reassembling the fragments into new compositions upon a flat surface. This is the very essence of collage, and bears very close resemblance to mythopoeic *bricolage*. Indeed, for Lévi-Strauss, collage is nothing other than the "transposition of 'bricolage' into the realms of contemplation."[65] In other words, the adaptation and implementation of the *bricoleur's* compositional strategy to the production and experience of visual imagery.

The origins of collage as a medium can be traced back to a tradition of folk artistry, a long "tradition of homespun collage creations that date back centuries but are most commonly found in the domestic scrapbooks and novelty creations of thousands of anonymous collagists of the nineteenth century," which were rarely displayed "and almost always made for private use and pleasure, were created out of whatever material was at hand," including such quotidian objects as "photographs, stamps, illustrations and text from books, newspapers, or other printed matter."[66] These items, which are not natural materials, but which are already culturally mediated can be spliced and recombined so as to transfer reference from the impersonal realm of mechanical mass production to the personal domain of aesthetic creation. As such, "collage is founded on a paradox"—for it presents "a 'world' composed of competing and interlocking worlds."[67] Indeed, collage requires that the spectator attend to an agglomerated multitude of such visual worlds, yet these worlds are not "always easy to trace or identify discretely," since one may be able to "identify some discrete components" utilized in the composition, but once these elements are used in a collage," they resonate with each of the other elements

---

[65] Claude Lévi-Strauss, *The Savage Mind*, p. 30.

[66] See David Banash, "From Advertising to the Avant-Garde: Rethinking the Invention of Collage," *Postmodern Culture* 14:2 (2004), pp. 1-41. See also Marjorie Perloff, "The Invention of Collage," in *Collage*, ed. J.P. Plottel, New York Literary Forum 10-11 (New York: New York Literary Forum, 1983), pp. 5-47.

[67] Brockelman, *The Frame and the Mirror*, p. 37.

and with the new whole. Each new element contributes another magnitude of resonances, producing more and more possible readings."[68] If there is language to the way in which collage components are spliced together to form new sentences, then each of these elements must be seen as both text and context. As Bert Mallet-Prevost Leefmans explains, the interrelation between the parts of the collage "reciprocally control the significances of these parts and produce, through the very linking process, those emergent qualities that are functions of the 'gaps' between the elements."[69] Another way of explicating this relationship is to describe it in terms of signifier (the cut out and affixed visual elements themselves), and the signified (the referent, or that for which the signifier stands), which as we have already seen, embodies a creative tension between the representational and the signifying dimension at the heart of any verbal or visual modes of communication. The individual elements that constitute a collage carry over a series of descriptive signifiers from their original context, but they become bearers of new signification precisely by being placed in relation to other such signifiers, and this re-contextualizing boundary or "gap" between them becomes the "site of a series of formal operations, the locus of a mytho-poetical calculus."[70] Hence, as we have already explored in some depth, these elements are constituted as signs in an operational semiotic structure that contain a newly significant content that transcends their original mimetic features. As Leefmans explains, it is the semiotic "leaps across these gaps" that constitute "the action, the dynamic," the very meaning of the new work of art.[71]

---

[68] Amy K. Kilgard, "Collage: A Paradigm for Performance Studies," *Liminalities: A Journal of Performance Studies* 5:3 (2009), pp. 1-19; at p. 3.

[69] Bert M-P. Leefmans, "*Das Unbild*: A Metaphysics of Collage," in *Collage*, ed. J.P. Plottel, pp. 189-227; here at p. 193.

[70] Cf. Wiseman, *Lévi-Strauss, Anthropology and Aesthetics*, pp. 88-89.

[71] Leefmans, "*Das Unbild*," p. 193.

Of course, this process of creation through the re-contextualized juxtaposition of already culturally mediated elements is the paradigmatic methodology of the *bricoleur*, the process of *bricolage* whereby events and objects at hand are put together in structured sets, and by such means converted into a system of signification that displays the inherent creative tensions between its constitutive mimetic elements and its significatory structural function. As a result, these image-sets can be simultaneously perceived as both a representational system and an exploration of the semiotic potentialities of that system of sign relations:

> These gaps, these bondings, transform the elements they link but at the same time become autonomous and significant in themselves—and they are gratuitous in that they are neither caused nor limited by any laws but those of the imagination as it is affected by its associations. It is thus the "content" of the gap that becomes the source and the power of the new.[72]

Figure 4. Lafferty's Door, upper third section. Photo © 2016 Andrew Ferguson. Used per CC-BY-4.0 license.

---

[72] Ibid.

The work of art discloses itself as we assimilate its signification, and in the process that dynamic interplay of the constitutive and constituting elements, of signifier and signified, itself emerges from the structured and structuring process of juxtapositioned relationality. That is to say, as the artwork progresses towards new significatory forms, the "emergent properties of their systems will determine the structures through which they may be elucidated."[73] In a mythopoeic narrative, it is the unfolding iterations of primal dyadic polarities which acts as the agent of change towards new forms of signification along the diachronic axis; in a collage, it is the sensory and conceptual traversal of that signifying gap, which at once separates and conjoins the distinctive visual elements, that drives the aesthetic experience of the viewer to uncover novel meanings in the resonant space between the images. In effect, the audience is asked to participate in the semiotic process of creation through which the *bricoleur* arranged these constitutive compositional elements in patterns of emergent signification.[74] As Lévi-Strauss explains, the aesthetic out-

---

[73] Ibid, p. 196.

[74] It is interesting to note that according to Boris Wiseman, Lévi-Strauss is himself a "collage artist of sorts" and his vast four-volume work, the *Mythologiques*, is a "mythopoeic creation in the sense that they are an assemblage of citations whose meaning, once the citations have been reassembled by Lévi-Strauss, has been transformed. Put differently, Lévi-Strauss is like a film editor who has been given film segments to put together (the myths) and has ended up creating with them a very personal work. According to this view, the real inventor/author of the system of Amerindian mythology is Lévi-Strauss himself. Although, evidently, he is not the inventor of the individual myths that make up the system, in putting together his own particular combinatorial arrangement of mythical elements (his means of cracking the code of myth) Lévi-Strauss has constructed his own version of Amerindian mythology, a vast collage of citations, whose meaning he has reinvented in order to tell us another story that is contained in latent form, as his theory would have it, in its indigenous matrix. What can be perceived in such a reading of this work is the story of an impossible quest for a lost time, a golden age prior to the 'death of myths', when structures

come is the result of a "union between the structural order and the order of events, which is brought about within a thing created by man and also in effect by the observer who discovers the possibility of such a union through the work of art."[75]

With these conceptual prolegomena in mind, we can turn our attention to Lafferty's bewilderingly "kaleidoscopic" assemblage. Focusing on the top third of the door reveals nothing more than an initially confusing pageant of seemingly disparate images (See Fig. 4). Yet after further inspection one can discern that the images are arranged in a series of rows and columns, which can be deciphered both vertically and horizontally. This should put us in mind of the two-fold synchro-diachronical structure of mythopoesis, which can also be read in a sequence diagonally across the transverse axis and also synchronously or up and down the vertical plane. Moreover, as we saw, myths analyzed in this way evince a characteristic configuration of layers which emerges as three-dimensional strata, by means of which this symbolic reiteration of signifying stratification may be scanned "left to right," "top to bottom," and "front to back." So, depending on the spectator's point of view, as the eye traverses the span of the pictorial plane, the horizontal assemblage of images could, in turn, elicit the idea of motion through chronology, such as in a montage sequence of unspooling film frames, or the temporal unfolding of comic strip panels; while the vertical juxta-positioning of concatenated illustrative elements might very well simultaneously invoke the notion of a cross-sectioning of congealed geomorpho-logical sedimentation, the chronotopic arrangement of musical notations within a written score, or perhaps the hierarchical gradation of discrete unit points of information on a graph. In other words, the rows and columns can be read as either a permanently given constant or as an historical, enacted event.

---

had not yet lost the battle with seriality and the meaning of the world we inhabit was yet to be destroyed by History and a conception of time as a succession of events;" *Lévi-Strauss, Anthropology and Aesthetics*, pp. 198-199.

[75] Lévi-Strauss, *Savage Mind*, p. 25.

Figure 5. Lafferty's Door (Detail of Fig. 4). Photo © 2016
Andrew Ferguson. Used per CC-BY-4.0 license.

Upon focusing our gaze more closely, a smaller section of
the upper portion of R.A. Lafferty's door demonstrates how
the over-all matrix of synchronous/diachronous relations is
operative in any given sub-region of the composition (See Fig.
5). Here we encounter a column of *korai* or archaicized female
forms, synchronously arrayed in such a manner that they
suggest a series of variations on a theme: the archetypal
woman, each feminine figure framed with rectilinear

regularity by no less archaic machinery on one side, and color re-productions of various still life paintings on the other. To all intents and purposes, the mechanical and the natural have been carefully juxtaposed so as to suggest two antipodal regions of imaginal symbolization mediated by the primordial figure of the exemplary woman in the central pillar—a visual analogue for what Lévi-Strauss recognized as one of the most basic pairings, nature against culture (nature : culture)— which in turn lies at the very heart of the creative process: the movement of (natural) objects into the sphere of (cultural) signification, and a concomitant apprehension of properties in those objects "which are normally concealed" and yet "are the very properties" that those objects have in "common with the structure and functioning of the human mind."[76]

For Lévi-Strauss, the fundamental dichotomy between these two conceptual realms, and their potentially fruitful reconciliation, are inextricably intertwined with questions of sex and sexual difference. Indeed, in his analysis of kin relations and mythology, one of the recurrent mythological tropes deals explicitly with the problematics of exogamous kinship, the complex rules for the matrimonial exchange of females outside of the tribe in order to build larger networks

---

[76] Georges Charbonnier, *Conversations with Claude Lévi-Strauss* (London: Jonathan Cape,1969), p. 125: "The two things are not contradictory to the extent that the promotion of an object to the rank of sign, if it is successful, must bring out certain fundamental properties which are common both to the sign and the object, i.e. a structure which is evident in the sign and which is normally latent in the object, but which suddenly emerges thanks to its plastic or poetic representation, and which furthermore allows a transition to all sorts of different objects. . . There is a two-fold movement: an aspiration of nature towards culture, that is of the object towards the sign and towards language, and a second movement which, through such linguistic expression, allows us to discover or perceive properties of the object which are normally concealed and which are the very properties it has in common with the structure and functioning of the human mind." Cf. Paul Heyer, "Art and the Structuralism of Claude Lévi-Strauss." *The Structurist* 12 (1972-73), pp. 32-37.

of social organization.[77] Succinctly put, women are the basis for the kind of cultural formation that fosters technological innovation and the economic exchange of goods and services, in addition to being a source of inspiration for a significant amount of artistic production, the development of complex religious rituals, and the elaboration of the mythopoeic imagination itself.[78] In Lévi-Strauss' view, this dynamic reveals a fundamental structure of reciprocity as both the catalyst and system of creative engagement with the "other"—and whether that encounter is with a natural or human form of alterity, the "relation of reciprocity is for Lévi-Strauss inconceivable outside a clear distinction between self and nonself, a difference that is at once ontological, logical, and ethical, as well as perfectly embodied in systems of kinship, social classification, and in the complex narrative forms we call myths."[79] It is an encounter that is always inherently dichotomous, and thus always potentially conflictive, but which is an imperative dynamic, since it promises the possibility of avoiding destructive sorts of individual, familial, societal, and cultural incestousness through the agency of gift-giving as the paradigm of all productive exchanges.[80] Yet such encounters with alterity not

---

[77] See Claude Lévi-Strauss, *The Elementary Structures of Kinship*, Revised edition, trans. J.H. Bell, J.R. von Sturmer, and R. Needham (Boston: Beacon Press, 1969).

[78] Cf. Žarana Papić, "The Opposition Between Nature and Culture as a 'Natural' Definition and Interpretation of Sexual Difference—Lévi-Strauss' Projection of the Origins of Culture as a Social Contract Between Men," *Ženske Studije* 1 (1995), pp. 155-196.

[79] Marcel Hénaff and Robert Doran, "Living with Others: Reciprocity and Alterity in Lévi-Strauss," *Yale French Studies* 123, p. 63-82, at p. 62.

[80] The foundational character of reciprocity, and the logical rules for such exchanges, leads Lévi-Strauss to assert that there are three interrelated "mental structures" evident in all human societal manifestations: "the exigency of the rule as rule; the notion of reciprocity regarded as the most immediate form of integrating the opposition between self and others; and finally,

only reveal a constant pattern of structuring reciprocity, but also recurring structures of dominance, inequality, violence, exploitation, and destruction where the process of reciprocal recognition fails.[81] To take but one example, the violently unresolved Anteros/Magdalen dyad in "Continued on Next Rock" illustrates the primordial necessity of reciprocity, and the innately perilous character of such potential exchanges, but also the destructive repercussion when there is a failure to overcome the antinomies of otherness.

The mythopoeic logic of reciprocity and creative relationality as a form of symbolic exchange therefore adumbrates mythmaking as a "methodological tool in the spiritual, conceptual structuring of the human world and in its practical, historical and cultural construction."[82] And as we have observed, in Lafferty's narrative these reciprocating antipodal *mythemes* reveal their structural logic by their very articulation. In other words, the diachronic development of the plot traces out the underlying narratologically synchronous organization of reciprocating conceptual polarities (See Fig. 3). In Figure 5, as in the rest of the door, we have distinct visual elements, let us call them *iconomemes*, that function in much the same manner as the individual reciprocating mythic components of the story. To be more

---

the synthetic nature of the gift, i.e., that the agreed transfer of a valuable from one individual to another makes these individuals into partners, and adds a new quality to the value transferred." *The Elementary Structures of Kinship*, p. 84.

[81] However, the law of reciprocity by its very nature contains an ethical precept: "This law is not that of the mere circulation of goods or commerce: it is that of the risk of generosity—specific to the gift/counter-gift structure—and of agonistic reciprocity—knowing how and when to give in return. The social relation is neither an assemblage of isolated individuals nor a movement of members of a group regulated only by institutional logics, it is essentially a relationship between agents who meet and confront one another as different and autonomous, who must negotiate their constitutive alterity, and who know how to oblige one another to do so through reciprocal constraints." Hénaff and Doran, "Living with Others." p. 81.

[82] Papić, "The Opposition Between Nature and Culture, p. 156.

precise, the juxtaposition of *objets trouvés*, or found images, works by simultaneously recalling their original settings while creating new sorts of meaning in those indeterminate boundaries or mimetic gaps between *iconomemes*. Like mythological thought (*mythemes*), these *iconomemes* function like instruments of reciprocal gift-exchange that reside half-way between "percepts and concepts," and thus function as signs or "operators" that "represent a set of actual and possible relations."[83] Which is only another way of saying that they demarcate the locus of reciprocal mythopoeic exchange where "the signified turns into the signifying and vice versa."[84]

---

[83] Lévi-Strauss, *Savage Mind*, p. 18: "The elements of mythical thought similarly lie halfway between percepts and concepts. It would be impossible to separate percepts from the concrete situations in which they appeared, while recourse to concepts would require that thought could, at least provisionally, put its projects (to use Husserl's expression) 'in brackets'. Now, there is an intermediary between images and concepts, namely signs. For signs can always be defined in the way introduced by Saussure in the case of the particular category of linguistic signs, that is, as a link between images and concepts. In the union thus brought about, images and concepts play the part of the signifying and signified respectively.

[84] Ibid, pp. 20-21: "Images cannot be ideas but they can play the part of signs or, to be more precise, co-exist with ideas in signs and, if ideas are not yet present, they can keep their future place open for them and make its contours apparent negatively. Images are fixed, linked in a single way to the mental act which accompanies them. Signs, and images which have acquired significance, may still lack comprehension; unlike concepts, they do not yet possess simultaneous and theoretically unlimited relations with other entities of the same kind. They are however already *permutable*, that is, capable of standing in successive relations with other entities – although with only a limited number and, as we have seen, only on the condition that they always form a system in which an alteration which affects one element automatically affects all the others. On this plane logicians' 'extension' and 'intension' are not two distinct and complementary aspects but one and the same thing. One understands then how mythical thought can be capable of generalizing and so be scientific, even though it is still entangled in imagery. It too works by analogies and comparisons even

Figure 6. Lafferty's Door (Detail of Fig. 5). Photo © 2016 Andrew Ferguson. Used per CC-BY-4.0 license.

This process of structural icono-mimesis in Lafferty's visual work becomes somewhat more evident when we turn to an area immediately to the left of the "*korai* column" and concentrate on one of the still life paintings located there (See. Fig. 6). In this detail, we see a cut-out reproduction of Paul Gauguin's *Te Tiare Farani (The Flowers of France)* from 1891, which currently resides at the Pushkin Museum of Fine Arts in Moscow. When Gauguin went to Tahiti in 1891, he expected to find nature in an unspoiled Edenic state, but what

though its creations, like those of the 'bricoleur', always really consist of a new arrangement of elements, the nature of which is unaffected by whether they figure in the instrumental set or in the final arrangement (these being the same, apart from the internal disposition of their parts): 'it would seem that mythological worlds have been built up, only to be shattered again, and that new worlds were built from the fragments' (Boas 1, p. 18). Penetrating as this comment is, it nevertheless fails to take into account that in the continual reconstruction from the same materials, it is always earlier ends which are called upon to play the part of means: the signified changes into the signifying and vice versa." See Hal Foster, "Savage Minds (A Note on Brutalist Bricolage)," *October* 136 (Spring 2011), pp. 182–191.

he first encountered in the capital city of Papeete was a fully Europeanized colonial outpost with only a few small remnants of authentic Maori society.[85] Moving to the remote village of Mataiea, Gauguin immersed himself in the still extant native culture and began to formulate a highly personalized syncretistic iconography that mixed elements from both Christian and Maori visual traditions, along with his own idiosyncratic understanding of the workings of *la pensée sauvage*.[86] Gauguin chronicled his first foray to Polynesia in *Noa*, a written account that is part autobiography, part travelogue, and part ethnographic report, but whose ultimate function is an attempted aesthetic reconciliation of the seemingly irreconcilable distinctions between such notions as savagery and civilization, nature and culture, primitivism and modernity. Gauguin's primary path into pre-colonial society was his *vahine* or young native wife Teha'amana, called Tehura in *Noa*, who teaches him about the Maori pantheon, cosmogony, language, and mythopoetics:

> In the evening we have long and often very grave conversations in bed. Now that I can understand Tehura, in whom her ancestors sleep and sometimes dream, I strive to see and think through this child, and to find again in her the traces of the far-away past which socially is dead indeed, but still persists in vague

---

[85] Cf. Bengt Danielsson, *Gauguin in the South Seas*, trans. R. Spink (London: George Allen & Unwin, 1965).

[86] See, for example, Nancy Perloff, "Gauguin's French Baggage: Decadence and Colonialism in Tahiti," in *Prehistories of the Future: The Primitivist Project and the Culture of Modernism*, ed. Elazar Barkan and Ronald Bush (Stanford, CA: Stanford University Press, 1995), pp. 226-269; and Philippe Peltier, "Gauguin: Artist and Ethnographer," in *Gauguin Tahiti*, ed. G.T.M. Shackelford and C. Frèches-Thory (Boston: MFA Publications, 2004), pp. 47-65. Perloff's essay highlights the destructive encounter between European civilization and Maori alterity in nineteenth-century French Polynesia, and also points towards troubling elements of interpersonal exploitation in Gauguin's problematic relationship with his native *vahine* "other."

memories. I question, and not all of my questions remain unanswered.

Perhaps the men, more directly affected by our conquest or beguiled by our civilization, have forgotten the old gods, but in the memory of the women they have kept a place of refuge for themselves. It is a touching spectacle which Tehura presents, when under my influence the old national divinities gradually reawaken in her memory.[87]

As the narrative indicates, it is the woman, Tehura, who mediates the nature of Maori life to Gauguin, and in turn Gauguin strives to form a productive synthesis of native and European elements In the painting *Te Tiare Farani* the artist has captured some of the perils and promise of this exchange. On the left, two native Tahitians are depicted, a pensive young man with a hat and a smiling woman. Both are garbed in European clothes, indicating they are at least partly assimilated into foreign French culture, but the man's expression in the face of this enculturation is apparently negative, while the female's countenance radiates a certain welcome gladness. The floral arrangement that dominates the right side of the canvas also exemplifies a somewhat ambivalent polarization. The placement and depiction of the vase on the table is reminiscent of the work of Gauguin's Post-Impressionist mentors, such as Paul Cézanne, Edgar Degas, and Édouard Manet, but the flowers already evince the painter's encounter with the vivid tropical efflorescence on display in the unspoiled island precincts, and this pictorial indecisiveness suspended as it were halfway between the newly found natural glory of Tahiti and a nostalgically evoked past still partway tethered to European civilization, is only further heightened by the fact that the Gauguin has chosen to depict blooms from his native French homeland in this native setting.[88]

---

[87] Paul Gauguin, *Noa Noa*, trans. Otto Frederick Theis (New York: Nicholas L. Brown, 1920), p. 90.

[88] See Anna Barskaya, *Gauguin*, Great Masters (London: Sirocco, 2004), p. 64. Lafferty seems to highlight this connection

Clearly, Gauguin's picture visualizes the at times fraught interplay of nature and culture and captures a transitional point of mediation between binary poles of meaning. Lafferty's canny placement of this cut out, caught at once between its original art historical meaning and its newly contextualized signification in the collage as a whole, can be seen to function along both synchro-diachronical axes. Recapitulating Lévi-Strauss' insight that the signifying process unfolds out of an oppositional dynamic, Gauguin's position within the composition simultaneously represents the foundational binary conflict between nature and culture in a fixed manner, and also facilitates its icono-mimetic unfolding as a dynamic sequence. Thus, looking once more at Fig. 4, perhaps we can now venture a provisional interpretation of the row of female figures directly below Gauguin's painting, along with the horizontal row of male figurines at the bottom of the section of archaic machineries on the right, as figurative iterations of a primeval dyadic polarity (nature : female :: culture : male), imagined both as a diagrammatic schema of this perennial mythic-poetic logic, and its ongoing evolution in a series of mediated transitional time-frames.[89]

by placing a still life by Paul Cézanne directly below the Gauguin reproduction, cf. Fig. 5.

[89] Nonetheless, a woman, because of her unique mediating qualities, has one foot in each of the antipodal conceptual regions. "In short, we see once again some sources of woman's appearing more intermediate than man with respect to the nature/culture dichotomy. Her "natural" association with the domestic context (motivated by her natural lactation functions) tends to compound her potential for being viewed as closer to nature, because of the animal-like nature of children, and because of the infrasocial connotation of the domestic group as against the rest of society. Yet at the same time her socializing and cooking functions within the domestic context show her to be a powerful agent of the cultural process, constantly transforming raw natural resources into cultural products. Belonging to culture, yet appearing to have stronger and more direct connections with nature, she is once again seen as situated between the two realms." Sherry B. Ortner, "Is Female to Male as Nature Is to Culture?," *Feminist Studies* I: 2 (1972), pp. 5-31, reprinted in *Woman, Culture, and Society*, ed. M. Z. Rosaldo and L. Lamphere (Stanford, CA:

Stanford University Press, 1974), pp. 68-87, here at p. 80. We see the intermediacy of the archetypal woman in Lafferty's placement of the *kore* figures at the median point between the representations of natural fecundity and technological regimentation. "[W]oman's intermediate position may have the implication of greater symbolic ambiguity . . . Shifting our image of the culture/nature relationship once again, we may envision culture in this case as a small clearing within the forest of the larger natural system. From this point of view, that which is intermediate between culture and nature is located on the continuous periphery of culture's clearing; and though it may thus appear to stand both above and below (and beside) culture, it is simply outside and around it. We can begin to understand then how a single system of cultural thought can often assign to woman completely polarized and apparently contradictory meanings, since extremes, as we say, meet. That she often represents both life and death is only the simplest example one could mention;" Ibid, p. 85. This contradictory polarization is evident in Lafferty's portrayal of Magdalen in "Continued On Next Rock," where she paradoxically embodies both the attraction and the repulsion, the potentiality and the rejection, the eros and anti-eros of sexuality. For other critiques of Lévi-Strauss' view of women, see, among others, Julia Kristeva, *Desire in Language: A Semiotic Approach to Literature and Art*, European Perspectives Series, trans. L.S. Roudiez (New York: Columbia University Press, 1980); and idem, *Powers of Horror: An Essay on Abjection*, European Perspectives Series, trans. L.S. Roudiez (New York: Columbia University Press, 1982); Luce Irigaray, *This Sex which is Not One*, trans. C. Porter and C. Burke (Ithaca, NY: Cornell University Press, 1985).

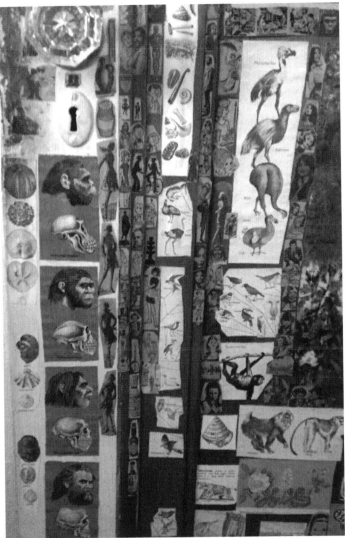

Figure 7. Lafferty's Door. Photo © 2016 Andrew Ferguson.
Used per CC-BY-4.0 license.

This sort of spatio-temporal transitioning is a central motif of another portion of the Lafferty's door (See Fig. 7). In this section, located below the door-knob and keyhole, Lafferty has arranged a motley group of images in vertical columns. Among them we see a series depicting hominid and early human evolutionary lineages (Australopithecine, Paranthropus; Neanderthal, Homo sapiens); various bird taxonomies; a grouping of extinct avian species (Phorusrhacos, Diatryma, Moa, Dodo); a tropical Mandrill (Mandrillus sphinx), member of the Cercopithecidae family of primates; sundry illustrations of marine and terrestrial fauna and flora as found in the fossil record, etc. This odd assortment of pictures can be at least partially ascribed to Lafferty's fascination with the natural world, his largely self-taught familiarity with the biological sciences, and his affinity for animals.[90] However, there is more to be discerned here in this collage of "older recensions" as Lafferty refers to previous iterations of the human evolutionary tree. To begin with, the process of speciation works both ways, backwards and forwards, and therefore they often also coexist with future instantiations of the evolutionary process. Indeed, Melchisedech Duffey, John Solli, or Finnegan as he is known at other times, as well as other characters are embodiments of these atavistic iterations. "I am of a different blood than I had believed," Finnegan confesses, "there is an old animal in me, and it begins to take me over. I doubt if I am human in the accepted sense. I'm of another recension."[91] It is said that they still "exist as pure elites in isolated regions of the earth; that another recension of them hide in the human blood stream as in caves or underground rivers, and that these periodically . . . produce authentic Neanderthal primordials."[92] In fact, it is *Homo sapiens* who should be rightly considered as nothing

---

[90] Cf. Daniel Otto Jack Petersen, "Valery's Really Eyes and the Parade of Creatures; Or, Lafferty's Animal Fair Comes to Town; Or, You Are a Pig Made Out of Sticks," *Feast of Laughter* 2 (2015), pp. 21-51.

[91] Lafferty, *The Devil Is Dead*, p. 94.

[92] Ibid. p. 183.

more than an evolutionary sport, a contingent mutation, "contingent, conditional, temporary, makeshift and improbable in our species . . . badly conceived and badly put together."[93] The Xauens, the immediate ancestors of the human lineage bred and a new species was born that "passed all the highly developed apes in an instant" . . . yet according to older theories of evolution, no "species can change noticeably in less than fifty thousand years." But the example of Xauenanthropous demonstrates that a species can "change in between three and nine months, depending on the direction traveled."[94]

In his speculations regarding spontaneous evolutionary leaps or mutations Lafferty may seem to anticipate some of the more recent ground-breaking work in paleo-biology that has overturned now outdated notions of phyletic gradualism with that of punctuated equilibrium, which posits prolonged periods of genetic homeostasis disrupted by rare yet dramatically rapid rates of evolutionary change.[95] But Lafferty's narrative not only highlights the fluidity and instability of monophyletic groups during phases of dynamic mutational change, it also addresses the phenomenon of instantaneous speciation by hybridization, a process that at least theoretically indicates that many organisms could very well be a "member of one species during one part of their lives and a member of one or more different species in subsequent parts of their lives," and the vexing problem that this sort of multiple speciation raises within biology regarding the very existence of diachronic species, since such hybridization would tend to reduce species to nothing more than synchronic

---

[93] R.A. Lafferty, "Ginny Wrapped In The Sun," in *Nine Hundred Grandmothers*, Ace SF Special, Series 1 (New York: Ace Books, 1970), pp. 29-42, at 31.

[94] Ibid, p. 39.

[95] This novel theory in evolutionary biology was first presented in a landmark paper by Niles Eldredge and Stephen J. Gould, "Punctuated Equilibria: An Alternative to Phyletic Gradualism," in *Models in Paleobiology*, ed. T.J.M. Schopf (San Francisco: Freeman, Cooper & Co., 1972), pp. 82-115.

individuals with a given set of genetic characteristics as instantiated in discrete frames of time.[96] Certainly, Lafferty, with his notion of contingent mutation via meiosis, an "incredible, sudden and single mutation; one that has been misunderstood both as to effect and direction," appears sympathetic to G.K. Chesterton's earlier assertion that the emergence of *Homo sapiens* cannot be ascribed to the cumulative effect of a slow accretion of genomic variations (i.e., phyletic gradualism), but can only be understood in temporal terms as a radically discontinuous form of instantaneous speciation.[97] "There is nothing even faintly suggesting" a step-by-step process whereby the human mind developed out of previous evolutionary stages, "it was not and it was; we know not in what instant or in what infinity of years." According to Chesterton, all that we can say is that "something happened; and it has all the appearance of a transaction outside of time. It has therefore nothing to do with history in the ordinary sense. The historian must take it or something like it for granted; it is not his business as a historian to explain it. But if he cannot explain it as a historian, he will not explain it as a biologist."[98]

Interestingly enough, for Chesterton the emergence of a unique new species, mankind, is only made manifest by

---

[96] Cf. David N. Stamos, *The Species Problem: Biological Species, Ontology, and the Metaphysics of Biology* (Lanham, MD: Lexington Books, 2003), p. 265.

[97] Lafferty, "Ginny," p. 32. An analogous process of meiotic hybridization, with intriguing results regarding the possible role of interspecific hybridization in species differentiation, the exchange of genetic material between species, and the viability of parthenogenetic reproduction, has been observed in some organisms under laboratory conditions; see, for example, J.G. van der Beek and G. Karssen, "Interspecific Hybridization of Meiotic Parthenogenetic *Meloidogyne chitwoodi* and *M. fallax*," *Phytopathology* 87:10 (1997), pp. 1061-1066. Cf. P. S. Soltis, "Hybridization, Speciation and Novelty," *Journal of Evolutionary Biology* 26:2 (2013), pp. 291–293.

[98] G.K. Chesterton, *The Everlasting Man* (New York: Dodd, Mead & Co., 1925), p. 22.

artistic creation, such as the Upper Paleolithic art preserved in caves at Altamira, Lascaux, and Chauvet-Pont-d'Arc, where the motions of the various animals depicted on the walls also captures the distinctive gesture of the artist. "Art is the signature of man," it evincing that "somehow or other a new thing had appeared in the cavernous night of nature, a mind that is like a mirror. It is like a mirror because it is truly a thing of reflection. It is like a mirror because in it alone all the other shapes can be seen like shining shadows in a vision."[99] The creative human mind reflects upon creation, and within that reflection the mirror reflects itself. Or, better yet, that uniquely human act of reflection is both a structured and a structuring process, so that the perspective from which the world is reflected by the mind that mirrors also gives us a perspectival glimpse into that glass, the mirroring mind itself. A mind that does not merely give us a mimetic representation of the world, a bare reflection, but which rather imbues that reflected world with meaning, by transforming the objects that it depicts into bearers of signification. A significatory function ratified by the work of the structuralist archaeologist and paleontologist André Leroi-Gourhan, who traced the chronological development of parietal art across 20,000 years of history, but also investigated the structural patterns of visual signification evident in the images in terms of the types and frequencies of the animals depicted on the cave walls, along with the relational juxtapositions among these painted figures, to indicate how these figurative sequences signified along both synchro-diachronical axes.[100] While Leroi-Gourhan's interpretative analysis of the binary complementary oppositions in Upper Paleolithic art (e.g.,

---

[99] Ibid, pp. 16; 18.

[100] See André Leroi-Gourhan, "Le symbolisme des grands signes dans l'art pariétal paléolithique," *Bulletin de la Societé Préhistorique Française* 55 (1958), pp. 384–398; idem, *Les Religions de la préhistoire (Paléolithique)*, Mythes et religions 51 (Paris: Presses Universitaires de France, 1964); idem, "The Evolution of Paleolithic Art," *Scientific American* 218:2 (1968), pp. 59-70; idem, "The Religion of the Caves: Magic or Metaphysics?" trans. A. Michelson, *October* 37 (1986), pp. 6-17.

bison : male :: horse : female) remains contested, what is undoubtedly true is that what we find here is a complex symbolic language arranged along a dyadically structuring logic of the sort identified by Lévi-Strauss as paradigmatically mythopoeic.[101]

---

[101] Cf. Annette Michelson, "In Praise of Horizontality: André Leroi-Gourhan 1911-1986," *October* 37 (1986), pp. 3-5; Claude Lévi-Strauss, "Nous avons lui et moi essayé de faire à peu près la même chose," in *André Leroi-Gourhan ou les Voies de l'Homme: Actes du colloque du CNRS, Mars 1987*, ed. L. Bernot (Paris: Albin Michel, 1988), pp. 201–206; Margaret W. Conkey, "The Structural Analysis of Paleolithic Art," in *Archaeological Thought in America*, ed. C. C. Lamberg-Karlovsky (Cambridge: Cambridge University Press, 1989), pp. 135-154; Françoise Audouze, "Leroi-Gourhan, a Philosopher of Technique and Evolution," *Journal of Archaeological Research* 10:4 (2002), pp. 277-306; Frédéric Joulian, "André Leroi-Gourhan, Claude Lévi-Strauss, la question de l'unité de l'hommeet de l'évolution," in *André Leroi-Gourhan, L'homme tout simplement: Mémoires et postérité d'André Leroi-Gourhan*, Travaux de la Maison Archéologie & Ethnologie, René-Ginouvès 20, ed. P. Soulier (Paris: Éditions de Boccard, 2015), pp. 85-101. Leroi-Gourhan extended this structural methodology beyond the parietal context, until the 1950s, he employed a more traditional "stratigraphic procedure of excavation, making a vertical cut into the earth layers in order to trace the evolution from one stage—or layer—to the next. When he began his series of revolutionary excavations at Pincevent, France, in 1964, he perfected the planographic method, which consisted of making a horizontal cut in order to study the fossil remains of one time period alone. By replacing a comparative method with one that isolated a single layer of remains, he triggered a paradigmatic shift in the approach that archeologists would take to prehistoric materials from that moment on. Of course, this methodological shift presupposed and fortified a hermeneutic one: Of importance to Leroi-Gourhan and his followers was less the determination of a chronology for layered sets of remains than a deepened understanding of the interrelations among the remains found at one level and situated within one temporal frame. Leroi-Gourhan's 'privileging of synchronic over diachronic in relational analysis of cultural texts' does indeed characterize the Saussure-inflected structuralist enterprise, as Annette Michelson has noted. But this synchronic, relational attitude produced far more than a stereotypical structuralist reading of visual 'texts;' it also gave

In the short story "In Deepest Glass" Lafferty posits that figurative art originated during a more archaic period of pre-history, during the time of the "older recension" or Neanderthals, yet this newly emergent imagery already possesses the power to signify, although Lafferty points out that the particular artistic medium, stained glass, employed by his highly speculative Neanderthals, was by and large not manufactured by them, the "stained glass was rather something that happened to them as an intuitive people."[102]

But the Neanderthal days were times of great volcanic activity. The air was full of chromatic, windborne acids which settled into picture-forms with the frost and which remained after the frost had evaporated, strong and colorful etched pictures. These airborne acids suffused the glass with red and blue, yellow and green, dun and gray, violet and orange pictures, pictures of wooly rhinoceros and bison, of horse and mammoth, of lions and lambs, of deer with Neanderthal deer-herders, of gentle dire-wolves and grinning sabre-toothed cats, of landscapes and cluttered rivers and ice cliffs and piles of rock and snow mixed; and of many, many of the Neanderthal people. All of the things had heraldic aspects to them,

---

birth to 'paleoethnography,' a method for interpreting prehistoric artifacts and traces that emphasizes not only internal, pictorial or syntactic relations but also the techniques—and the gestural routines of human bodies—that must have been employed in order to forge them;" Carrie Noland, "Inscription and Embodiment: André Leroi-Gourhan and the Body as Tool," *Agency and Embodiment: Performing Gestures/Producing Culture* (Cambridge, MA: Harvard University Press, 2009), p. 96. As we have seen, a similar paleo-ethnographic methodology, with both sequentially diachronic and relationally synchronic dimensions, is evident in Lafferty's "Continued On Next Rock."

[102] R.A. Lafferty, "In Deepest Glass," in *The Berkley Showcase: New Writings in Science Fiction and Fantasy, Vol. 4*, ed. J. Silbersack and V. Schochet (New York: Berkley Books, 1981), pp. 49-61; here at p. 49.

and yet all were full of fluid life. They were rich, they were golden, they were magic.

These pictures were drawn on and in the glass windows, but the Neanderthals did not draw them physically. Perhaps, to some extent, they drew them mentally, did outline the sorts of pictures which they desired the living spirits of the weather, the Living Spirits of the World, to draw for them. Some of the Living Spirits of the World were surely the Neanderthals themselves.

And these stained glass windows did have spirits *imprisoned* in them, some of them willingly, some of them unwillingly. Even when handling a small fragment of this old glass one can feel a spirit or spirits inhabiting it. (In a later Arabian tale, the Genie was really imprisoned in flat glass, not in a glass bottle as a mistranslation gives it.)

The whole history of Man and His Friends was contained in the deep glass pictures of the Neanderthals. This was the pristine stuff from the beginning.[103]

It is important to note once more that Lafferty clearly reiterates that the cave-dwellers did not create the glass artwork physically; in fact, the stained glass may be best thought of as natural manifestations of subconscious mental concepts and unconscious dreams. Or, perhaps, one could more purposefully say that they are the innate thought structures through which the Neanderthals imaginatively perceive, semiotically process, symbolically order, and materially construct their environment. In these opening passages Lafferty seems to be providing a mythological account of the very origins of mythopoeic thought, with his Neanderthal stained glass arguably a mirror-view upon the inner workings of a primordial thought-process, which is already not only thinking through myths, but as Lévi-Strauss would have it, is a mind through which myths themselves are

---

[103] Ibid, p. 50.

thinking.[104] Moreover, if this is indeed an introspective glimpse at these nascent myths' own "reflection upon themselves and their interrelation"—a product as much of the structured natural world of volcanos and wind-borne acidic ash as the structuring human mind which mirrors it—then the artwork produced out of this sort of inner reflection could be seen as a kind of projective embodiment, through the resulting medium of stained glass, of the mythopoeic imagination itself working in us. As Lafferty goes on to say, the stained glass windows "have spirits imprisoned in them," since they already instantiate a proleptic (synchronous) haunting of man by the mythopoeic Spirits of the World, those spectrally archetypal spooks of Lafferty's "Ghost Story" (the putative title of Lafferty's grand, unfinished—indeed unfinishable—meta-fiction encompassing all of his stories, written and unwritten, dreamt and undreamt) that potentially (diachronously) contains, like the mythic Neanderthal glass, the "whole history of Man and His Friends."[105]

---

[104] Wiseman, *Lévi-Strauss, Anthropology and Aesthetics*, p. 198: "The *Mythologiques* expound a method of analysis, and at the same time a general theory of creation. A theory of mythical creation *and a theory of Lévi-Straussian creation*. While the *Mythologiques* are on one level about a process that occurs in the outside world (the genesis of Amerindian myths), they also reflect an inner process of imaginative creation or re-creation. The one is understood through the other. The *Mythologiques* should therefore also be read as a description of Lévi-Strauss's own inner experience of the creative act required of him by the study of myths." In an analogous fashion, we too can perhaps also see "In Deepest Glass," along with the rest of Lafferty's oeuvre as a reflection upon the author's own inner process of imaginative creation and re-creation.

[105] "It seemed, until I thought of it a bit, that I had written quite a few novels, and many shorter works, and also verses and scraps. Now I understood by some sort of intuition that what I had been writing was a never-ending story and that the name of it was 'A Ghost Story.' The name comes from the only thing that I have learned about all people, that they are ghostly and that they are sometimes split-off. But no one can ever know for sure which part of the split is himself. 'Is this myself, right here and now, or is this the ghost?' is a question that most people, from some

Figure 8. Lafferty's Door, lower section. Photo © 2016 Andrew Ferguson. Used per CC-BY-4.0 license.

Returning now to the initially confusing iconography in Figure 7, we can more readily discern some relational visual patterns, including Lafferty's older and newer recensions in a column to the left, and the rows and columns of both archaic and modern-day flora and fauna, visually reminiscent of the verbal bestiaries and herbiaries Lafferty had already enunciated in his Neanderthal tale. Put in conjunction with the broader area of images to the right (See Fig. 8), we can discern a variety of taxonomic complexity fully as rigorous as the phylogenetic branching of present-day biological cladistics, or the elaborate groupings of prehistoric animals detected by Leroi-Gourhan in any number of Paleolithic cave complexes. As we saw before, for Lévi-Strauss there is an inextricable link between the creative endeavor and the

---

shyness, do not ask themselves nearly often enough." R.A. Lafferty, "AN ESSAY EXPLAINING THE ALTERNATE ENDINGS OF THE BOOK ARGO In the Course of Which I'm Obliged to Explain The Detailed Workings of The World Itself," Postscript to *More Than Melchisedech: Argo* (Weston, Ontario: United Mythologies Press, 1992), no pagination.

classificatory processes that underlie both the work of the scientist and the "savage mind." In his discussion of totemism, he had pointed out that the different animals species represented in totemic art were used as a means to formally encode differences between various clans and tribes, and thereby establish a form of social classification. Moreover, these totemic schemas can be employed to establish either more minute classificatory differentiations, by breaking down the animals into their constituent parts, or expanding the system of codification to the level of species of animal kingdom, so that it can potentially classify any "domain, synchronic or diachronic, concrete or abstract, natural or cultural."[106] This ability of totemic encoding to increase or decrease its symbolic scope "enables the 'primitive' scientist to cast a conceptual net over any aspect of reality. The work of art construed as a 'modèle reéduit'–construed as a 'mediator' between humanity and the world –appears to work in a similar way to these classificatory systems."[107] In other words, it is precisely the capacity of such schema to detotalize or retotalize any conceptual domain in both synchro-diachronic axes across the nature/culture divide, which links these sorts of classificatory systems to Lévi-Strauss' understanding of art as a *compendium mundi* or symbolic microcosm of the world.

In later portions of "In Deepest Glass" Lafferty goes on to envision a second great era of Neanderthal-like stained glass in a future where "billions of new glass illuminations" appear in "red and blue, yellow and green, in all the colors and hues and shades and intensities." Once again the glass images are full of "heraldic animals and of heraldic people," but now "(without losing their heraldic element) they were real people, often recognized, always vital."

> There were landscapes, there were cities in minute detail, there were all sorts of machinery and equipment, there were buildings and activities. It was not at first realized just how many activities were

---

[106] Lévi-Strauss, *Savage Mind*, p. 149.

[107] Wiseman, *Lévi-Strauss, Anthropology and Aesthetics*, p. 39.

depicted in the pictures. The "Living Spirits of the World" always lean over backwards to avoid the charge of spiritualizing in their pictures, and yet there were spiritual elements also; they could not be avoided. Again, and to a greater extent than in either of its preludes, the amazing artistry was effected by the "Living Spirits of the World:" but now some of those spirits were human and some were not; some of them were material and some were not; some of them were conscious and some were not; some of them were alive, and some of these "living spirits" were dead. What had happened, what was happening, was an Epic that was much too large to comprehend in a moment or a decade. But the epic quality was not appreciated by the commonalty. The majority of the people didn't want their windows cluttered up with pictures that cut down on the light and the view. And they didn't like the paranatural elements in some of the stained glass. Many folks found it disquieting to discover, on rising in the morning, that all the dreams they had dreamed during the night were pictured in detail on their windows, and all the dreams of their wives and children and dogs too.[108]

This passage contains an account of the retotalizing process that any work of art undergoes in order to function as a medium, a process which must commence with an attempt to comprehend the world that the artwork is endeavoring to mediate as an ordered totality, an organizational function that parallels the ultimate aim of any act of classification itself. In another narrative Lafferty speculates that the cave-painters at Lascaux evoked the animals into life in the very act of painting them; it is only when the animals are given *names* and thus classified semiotically within a broader conceptual arrangement that they can be perceived as existing—the creative act is originary in both an epistemic and ontological manner:

---

[108] R.A. Lafferty, "In Deepest Glass," pp. 53-54.

What happened in the cave art days of Lascaux was the "Naming" of the Animals. The paintings were the namings, or at least they were an aspect of the namings. It must be understood that this was concurrent with the creative act. The depicted animals were absolutely new then. If the paleozoologists say otherwise, then the paleozoologists are wrong. The men also were absolutely new then.

Some, perhaps all, of these cave paintings were anticipatory: the paintings appeared a slight time before the animals themselves appeared. My evidence for this is subjective, and yet I am as sure of this as I am of anything in the world. In several cases, the animals, when they appeared, did not quite conform to their depictment. In several other cases, owing I supposed to a geodetic accident, the corresponding animals failed to appear at all.

It is certain that this art was anticipatory and prophetic, heralding the appearance of new species over the life horizon. It was precursor art, harbinger art. It is certain also that this art contained elements of effective magic; it is most certain that the species were of sudden appearance. The only thing not certain is just to what extent the paintings were creative of the animals. There is still fluid mystery about the mechanism of the sudden appearance of species. The paleontologists cannot throw any light on this mystery at all, and the biologists cannot. But the artist can throw light on it, and the psychologist can. It is clear that a new species appears, suddenly and completely developed, exactly when it is needed.[109]

Lafferty will go so far as to posit that the mythopoesis originates with the animals of the primordial past, "All of the real original stories, all of the best stories, were first told by the animals." The older recension, the "'Old People'" or the "'Red-Boned People'" all "understood the speech of the

---

[109] R.A. Lafferty, "Dorg," in *Lafferty in Orbit* (Cambridge, MA: Broken Mirrors Press, 1991), pp. 185-192; at p. 188.

animals, and the 'New People', the Cro-Magnons, did and do not. Really it was the case that the animals would still speak when in the company of the Neanderthals; but they would pretend an inability to speak when in the company of the Cro-Magnons." Indeed, to this day they "still pretend this inability when in the company of the 'New People.'"[110] This ability to comprehend the totemic language of the natural world placed the mythopoeic arts at the center of pre-historic society. Indeed, as Lafferty also points out, this conceptual invocation of the animals concurrently invokes human culture into existence, "men also were absolutely new then," that is, there is no true humanity—no myth-making humans—until humanity begins to arrange the phenomenal world mythopoetically. So in "In Deepest Glass" the new stained glass works encompass both the realm of nature as well as a multitude of human sociocultural manifestations, for as Lévi-Strauss points out, "classificatory schemes . . . allow the natural and social universe to be grasped as an organized whole," containing not only human but also non-human subjects, both living and dead, and even paranatural objects from the land of dreams.[111]

---

[110] R.A. Lafferty, "Through the Red Fire or, the Hidden Truths about Story-Tellers Dredged up from the Unconscious of One of Them," in *It's Down the Slippery Cellar Stairs*, Drumm Booklet 14 (Polk City, IA: Chris Drumm, 1984), pp. 21-24, at p. 22. Lafferty further contends that "We story-tellers are still here, and we still belong to the old 'red-bone people', though few of us are full-bloods. Many or most of us do not know in our conscious moments that we belong to an 'Old People', but it is so. We are desirous of continuing our story-telling trade for we know no other." In other words, the great storytellers who continue the mythopoeic tradition, including presumably Lafferty himself, embody the reality of hybridity.

[111] Lévi-Strauss, *Savage Mind*, p. 135. He goes on to point out that "What is significant is not so much the presence - or absence - of this or that level of classification as the existence of a classification with, as it were, an adjustable thread," which gives the classifier, "the means of 'focusing' on all planes, from the most abstract to the most concrete, the most cultural to the most natural, without changing its intellectual instrument;" p. 136.

This totalizing imperative coincides with the reality that no work of art is ever a fully organized or finished totality comprehending the whole of the world. Each act of re-totalization is an attempt to render the world within the contingent margins of a provisional *compendium*. Just as the classificatory schemas of the scientist are posited in order to be tested, so every attempt to comprehend the world mytho-poetically is subject to revision and recreation. "Totalization is not equal to closure. The process of understanding is inherently related to a dynamic whereby acts of totalization are attempted and then undone, by those who have attempted them, or by others. The construction of meaning is inseparable from its opposite as the metaphor of bricolage illustrates amply."[112] The totalizing strategies utilized in *bricolage* do not close down enquiry, rather they are an ongoing series of speculative explorations, in keeping with the combinatorial methodologies of the *bricoleur*, whose transformational logic continually fashions new meanings, new significations, by recombining older forms of cultural and personal knowledge and experience. "What the *bricoleur* does when he/she reassembles the components of one object to create another is bring to light another set of possible relations between those components... In Lévi-Strauss' aesthetic theory, it is what the artist does when he/she creates a new version of the world that is a new combinatorial variation of it."[113] If Lafferty's stained glass imagery conveys

---

[112] Wiseman, *Lévi-Strauss, Anthropology and Aesthetics*, p. 45.

[113] Ibid. Lévi-Strauss stresses the combinatorial openness of the *bricoleur*'s relationship to his objects, in this case images, since each one "represent a set of actual and possible relations; they are 'operators' but they can be used for any operations of the same type." This openness allows for a potentially limitless array of new meanings that may be construed from the endlessly re-arranged objects/images in order to construe new forms of signification out of older material, and this is due to unique nature and function of signs. "Now, there is an intermediary between images and concepts, namely signs. For signs can always be defined in the way introduced by Saussure in the case of the particular category of linguistic signs, that is, as a link between images and concepts. In the union thus brought about, images

an immensely varied "Epic that was much too large to comprehend in a moment or a decade," then its meaning cannot be comprehended in any one *compendium mundi*, but only continually signified through an equally varied series of creations and re-creations, a continuous process of detotalization and retotalization, with each new combination revealing some new facet of its total meaning. Like Lafferty's "Ghost Story," an inconclusive epic chronicling the deeds of archetypal animate and inanimate entities and their collective unconscious dreamings, Lafferty's door is an unsettled imaginal epic.[114] A *bricolage* whose sum total of signification is

---

and concepts play the part of the signifying and signified respectively. Signs resemble images in being concrete entities but they resemble concepts in their powers of reference. Neither concepts nor signs relate exclusively to themselves; either may be substituted for something else," *Savage Mind*, p. 18. Also see Edith Wyschogrod, "The Logic of Artifactual Existents: John Dewey and Claude Lévi-Strauss," in *Crossover Queries: Dwelling with Negatives, Embodying Philosophy's Others*, Perspectives in Continental Philosophy (New York: Fordham University Press, 2006), pp. 449-463.

[114] On more than one occasion, Lafferty explained that all his fiction is "one very very long novel ... a ghost story that is also a jigsaw puzzle. And the mark of my ghost story is that there is a deep underlay that has never attained clear visibility, never attained clear publication." This description is found in "Sometimes I'm asked how many novels I've written..." a two page manuscript draft fragment and list of novel titles, Series II (Writings), Box 22, Folder 23 of the R.A. Lafferty papers in the Department of Special Collections and University Archives, McFarlin Library, University of Tulsa; undated, p. 1. Lafferty also indicated that this process of continuous re-structuring was even more of a necessity in our present time, "an unstructured era of post-musical music, post-artistic art, post-fictional fiction, and post-experiential experience. We are, partly at least, in a post-conscious world," R.A. Lafferty, "The Day After The World Ended," in *It's Down the Slippery Cellar Stairs*, pp. 34-39, at p. 36. As a result, the task of the creatively reconstructive *bricoleur* who reassembles the ruins of past civilizations into a thriving new culture is even more important: "the question to be asked of everyone is 'If you are not right now making a world, why aren't you?'" This vitally important essay is reprinted in this issue of

not to be found any one image, or set of images, but in the multiple possible combinations of images, and the manifold signifying "gaps," the semiotically rich boundary spaces between variable sets of images, successively available to the spectator's mind. Consequently, Lafferty's verbal/visual masterworks raise the perennial question of "whether there might not be a sequence and pattern to the Masterworks." A vexing query indeed, for the "question, 'Is there a design in the Great Epic of the acid-stained windows?' was on par with the old question, 'Is there a design in the universe?' And the same sort of people and computers who had always roared a thunderous 'No!' to the one question now roared it to the other."[115]

As Leroi-Gourhan's paleo-anthropological work indicates, Lévi-Strauss' research into *bricoleur* methodologies reinforces, and our own analysis confirms, in Lafferty's door collages we have a dynamically recombinant set of mythopoeic transformations, a synchro-diachronic configuration laid out in visual terms across both spatio-temporal axes, an unavoidable confluence, since any events occurring in time or in space inevitably presuppose each other. Space is the setting for all interactions, and because a setting involves not just a distribution of discrete events in distinct time frames, but their co-ordination with other coterminous events, and with features of the locus within which they all take place, therefore "such co-ordination always involves time as well as space." Moreover, the "connection between these" is the conditional possibility for the "means of the repetition," whether it be thematic, visual, conceptual, or verbal, which give such phenomena their "definite 'form'" across the unfolding of the temporal order[116]

Feast of Laughter.

[115] Lafferty, "In Deepest Glass," p. 55.

[116] Anthony Giddens, *Social Theory and Modern Sociology* (Stanford, CA: Stanford University Press, 1987), p. 144. In the context of relativistic physics, time cannot be separated from space since the observed rate at which time passes for an object is always depends on the object's trajectory and velocity relative to the observer. For further elucidation see Robert DiSalle, "Space

As we have explored at some length, in Lévi-Strauss' estimation the grammar of mythopoeic creation functions much like other human forms of discourse, including visual communication. Each discourse evinces two constitutive elements: *langue*, the synchronous, atemporal structure, or combinatorial rules of a discourse, and *parole*, the diachronic instantiations of those ahistorical linguistic rules as a series of combinations across time in a succession of locations. In addition, Lévi-Strauss argues that *parole* operates in "non-reversible time" i.e., as a specific combinatorial instance or event in a distinct slice of linear time in a particular place, and which is perforce unidirectional, since chronometric time cannot be turned back. Whereas *langue* belongs to what Lévi-Strauss designates as "reversible time," since this aspect of discourse encompasses the synchronous or ahistorical structures of mythopoeic thought itself, and thus exists simultaneously in the past, present, or future.[117] History's participation in the ahistorically present reiterations of mythopoeic logic manifests the reversibility of the temporal order: "reversible time is time as repetition, temporality as reproduction."[118] On a similar note, Lafferty's meditations upon the eccentric structure of his endlessly recursive "Ghost Story" concludes (or begins) with an admonition regarding the inherent spatiality of temporal events:

> An event is like a box or other geometrical object . . . and it should be pretty much the same no matter which side it is viewed from. Let us say that we look at it from the south side (that is the past), or from the

---

and Time: Inertial Frames," in the *Stanford Encyclopedia of Philosophy*: http://plato.stanford.edu/entries/spacetime-iframes/

[117] See Lévi-Strauss, "Structural Study of Myth," pp. 430; 432; 443-444.

[118] Giddens, Ibid: "Reversible time, in a culture with clocks, is as it were symbolized by the clock that goes backwards. For however much a culture might be dominated by modes of strict time-regulation, day-to-day life remains geared to the repetition of events and activities."

east side (that is the present), or from the west side (that is an alternative . . . present), or from the north side (that is the future). The event will look a little bit different from these various viewpoints, but not much. You must not reject one view of it when you come to another view. They are all equally parts of it.[119]

All of this serves to indicate that objects and events in mythopoeic space-time are located in a uniquely mediatorial site that partakes of both the ordinary features of chronometry (diachrony) as well as partaking in certain attributes more characteristic of the eternal (synchrony). As created beings, humans already reside in the *metaxy*, an ontological middle ground betwixt temporal contingency and the necessity of eternal existence. The mid-way point between the synchronal and the diachronical is aeviternity, a temporal mode of in-betweenness that bestrides the material and the spiritual realms.

For Lafferty, following Aquinas and the Christian tradition, humans are torn between their physical and non-corporeal selves, "with one foot in the temporal flux of measured motion, and the other in the unchanging duration of God's eternal *esse*.[120] There are multiple aeviternal manifolds, one corresponding to each individual and to every set of relations, since the *aevum* is the arena where the spatio-temporal drama of existence is played out, particularly at the dangerous boundary-edge where the devouring present meets a future fraught with possibility. As Lafferty vividly illustrates in his Argo Cycle, it is in this "narrow interval" or "series of intervals removed out of time and held apart," a "mixture of future and past and present" where all possible "nows" are eschatologically present to each other, and are thus open to an

---

[119] Lafferty, *More Than Melchisedech: Argo*, no pagination.

[120] Gregorio Montejo, "Aeviternity: R.A. Lafferty's Thomistic Philosophy of Time in the Argo Cycle," *Feast of Laughter* 1 (2014), pp. 102-114.

especially radical form of contingency, which Melchisedech Duffey and his fellow chronic Argonauts inhabit as they traverse across the oceans of time, that perilous conflux of synchronicity and diachronicity called aeviternity, upon the Argo (See Fig. 9) the barque that sails "Forward into time or sideways in time . . . Into the future or into the present."[121] What happens "if one is too eager and crosses this leading edge? The world ends, for that person, for that while.

> If this thin line is crossed, then one is out in the narrow interval of unreality. It's a chancy though flexible place there.
>
> Melchisedech Duffey and his history had come up to the absolute present time, and then had gone a thumb's width beyond that, Duffey and his nimbus had gone into the future then? No, they had gone into the shattering state of contingency. It was a fracturing of reality. And it was a fracturing of Melchisedech Duffey.[122]

---

[121] Lafferty, *More Than Melchisedech: Argo*, no pagination.

[122] Ibid.

Figure 9. Lafferty's Door, "the Argo" (Detail of Fig. 8). Photo © 2016 Andrew Ferguson. Used per CC-BY-4.0 license.

On Lafferty's telling, Melchisedech and his cohort on the Argo are fractured persons haunted by their own multiple incarnations along the aeviternally contested time-steams. In point of fact, Duffey's spatio-temporal splintering seems to recapitulate a disjunctive and re-combinatorial process akin to the method of *bricolage* where, much as on the Argo, juxtaposed subjects who subsist as both synchronic essential forms and successive contingently diachronic material instantiations of themselves, inhabiting both the fluid yet mechanical and abstractive *chronos* of sequential movement, as well as the opportunely significant and semiotically rich time of *kairos*, that moment when eternity breaks into and transforms history and thereby renders time meaningful.[123]

---

[123] See John E. Smith, "Time, Times, and the 'Right Time'; Chronos and Kairos," *The Monist* 53: 1 (1969), pp. 1-13; Karl Rahner, "Theological Observations on the Concept of Time," in *Theological Investigations, vol. 11, Confrontations 1*, trans. D. Bourke

Because of the iso-morphism of space-time, the mechanical hinging of discrete points of chronometric time can be mapped onto the *khora*, a conceptualization of space as an abstract area rather than a concrete place—a receptacle, an extension, an interval between being and non-being that provides a "space" for physical things to potentially be, but only once they have been deterministically located, and their trajectories plotted out in relation to all the other objects contained within this khoraic space.

The equivalent relation to *kairos* as a redemptive period of emergent change is the *topos*, a place organized by praxis rather than a mere space within which practices can be undertaken. It is the locus of reversible time, a topology of recapitulated language, ritualized action, mythopoeic reiteration, and sacred redemption.[124] It is the structural condition for the possibility of creation, a creative activity which itself opens up spatial possibilities for further creation, the "*topos* or location of the unconscious, and also of all of the *limbi* or border lands."[125] This site is initially "unadorned and unconscious flat-land," and thus "subject to change; but the changes are very contingent for a long time," for only when a *topos* has acquired sufficient ornamentation, it is blessed, or it is cursed. If it is blessed, it becomes one of the Holy Lands;"

(London: Darton, Longman and Todd/New York: Seabury Press, 1974), pp. 288-308; Anna-Teresa Tymieniecka, "Life's Primogenital Timing: Time Projected by the Dynamic Articulation of the Onto-Genesis," *Analecta Husserliana* 50 (1997), pp. 1-22; Hans Rämö "An Aristotelian Human Time-Space Manifold: From *chronochora* to *kairotopos*," *Time & Society* 8:2 (1999), pp. 309-328; Joseph Bracken, "A New Look at Time and Eternity," *Theology and Science* 2 (2004), pp. 77-88.

[124] Christopher Roberts, "Entropy, Sacrifice and Lévi-Strauss's Dismissal of Ritual," *Method and Theory in the Study of Religion* 23 (2011), pp. 326-350 criticizes Lévi-Strauss for not fully understanding the centrality of ritual repletion and sacrifice as constitutive elements of a semiotically significant network of relational mythopoeic structures.

[125] R.A. Lafferty, *The Three Armageddons of Enniscorthy Sweeney*, in *Apocalypses*, Futorian Science Fiction (Los Angeles: Pinnacle Books, 1977), pp. 189-374; at p. 256.

yet, even in their "first form, the lands are not quite flat. There are the ledges from which the statuary stones are quarried"—we see here once again the notion that the unconscious is a topography that can be archeologically excavated and its exposed stratification studied—and there "are also the "clay-pits from which the red adam-clay is taken and from which Pan-Therium came. But the *topos* still maintains the appearance of flatness or of stepped flatness."[126] This "Pan-Therion or Pan-Therium," is identified as the "All-Animal, the prototypical animal. He is the cool-fever-flesh from which all others diverge. He is the composite . . . and the generating force. He is the red-clay which is clay-flesh. He is also the Dream-Master." In Lafferty's mythopoeic protology, the Pan-Therion is a demiurgic creator whose dreams, a series of oneiric eructations ("My belched dreams become creatures as soon as they acquire flesh") which bring forth creation into existence (very much as a topology, during the course of time, will extrude its topographical features) in a conspicuously piecemeal manner; which is to say, it is constructed in a characteristically *bricolage* fashion. This "*topos*, this unadorned and unconscious flat-land, is subject to change; but the changes are very contingent for a long time," so, for example, if "hills are wanted, they are dragged in on skids by creatures pulling them with ropes. If mountains are required, they are rolled in on wheels or log rollers. This is analogous to the geological mountain-bringing process. The mountains always come in on easy-flowing extrusions that are really wheels or rollers of magma."[127] As such, the Pan-Therium is the prototypical *bricoleur*, as well as a paradigmatically totemic figure, at once an archetypal Panther but also the shape-shifting figure of an exemplary *ur*-beast, an amorphous "pre-creature" whose inherently multivalent animalism is the unclassifiable source of classification itself, and thus the primal structuring pattern for semiotically ordered existence itself:

---

[126] Ibid, p. 257.

[127] Ibid.

Many mythologies say that it was the Bear who made the world. Yet, there is no contradiction there. The Bear is one of the very strong elements in the Pan-Animal. This primordial dream-master beast is in fact the "Bearcat" who appears both in the Prophet Elias and in Mark Twain and who is found in the common expression of today "Boy, is that ever a Bearcat!" It is Pan-Therium, the Bearcat that is in the beginning. It's the flesh that is the red grass. It belches the dreams out of its stomach and they battle for supremacy, whether they shall survive as "Worlds," or not survive at all.[128]

Lafferty's elaboration of space and time in these passages, and in various portions of his Argo cycle, would seem to suggest a recurring pattern of mythopoeic transformations formulated as an analogical relationship of antinomies: *chronos : khora :: kairos : topos*. In other words, time *(chronos)* as a diachronically mechanical measure of before and after is to space *(khora)* as a conceptually empty container wherein stabile objects are fixed and measured, as time *(kairos)* as synchronously relational and structurally meaningful is to space *(topos)* as the locus of creative and redemptive praxis. Moreover, this is no mere affiliation of static dyadic pairs, but rather the juxtaposing of dynamically related terms and functions, with the indication of a possible inversion of the terms and functions in the second dyad—which holds the promise of a transformative resolution of the opening antipodal opposition—already present in a vestigial manner in the original opposition.[129] This transformation is inherent

---

[128] Ibid, p. 256.

[129] Lévi-Struss formulated this transformative process thus: fx(a) : fy(b) :: fx(b) : fa-1(y) in "Structural Study of Myth," p.p. 442-443; however, there is no universally accepted interpretation of how precisely he meant this formulation to work. In my own use of this formula, I have consulted the following secondary sources: Mark S. Mosko, "The Canonic Formula of Myth and Nonmyth," *American Ethnologist* 18:1 (1991), pp. 126-151; Alaine Côté, "The Set of Canonical Transformations Implied in the Canonical Formula for the Analysis of Myth," in *The Double Twist: From Ethnography to Morphodynamics*, Anthropological

to mythopoesis, since the function of mythic thought is not merely to recognize contrarieties, but to surmount them, for as we have seen, "mythical thought always works from the awareness of oppositions to their progressive mediation."[130] As always, the attempted resolution commences with an oppositional pair, here *chronos* and its conceptual antipode *khora*, reifying diachronicity and synchronicity, the systematic calculation of discrete links along a ceaseless concatenation of deterritorialized processual events, over against the flattened horizon of an indivisible point where all objects are precisely located by being rendered simultaneously present. In this formulation, however, the second antipodean dyad is not a simple repristination of the first set of contraries. Rather, the logic of mythopoesis dictates that a myth's unfolding will include an attempt at resolution through which the elements of the first dyad will be transmuted through the expression of a dynamic element by means of an inversion or permutation of elements in the second. Hence, in this instance, the concept of space (*khora*) will be able to serve as a mediating function between opposite terms once it undergoes the sort of topographical inversion that allows it to become the sort of place (*topos*) where empty time (*chronos*) can successfully transition into a meaningful structure of temporal vectors (*kairos*). Or, as Lafferty expresses it in *The Three Armageddons of Enniscorthy Sweeney*, the flat land where a "few flat panthers and bears and bearcats, flattened as if melted down to the flatness of pancakes," are "draped limply over the folded and stepped flatness of the land," must acquire "sufficient ornamentation" if it is to be redeemed, if it is to be rendered in all its meaningful depths. "If it is blessed, it becomes one of the Holy Lands. If it is cursed, we don't know what it becomes," although we could speculate that such a flat world would remain trapped in an endless cycle of unchanging and

---

Horizons, ed. P. Maranda (Toronto: University of Toronto Press, 2001), pp. 199-221; Jack Morava, "Une interprétation mathématique de la formule canonique de Claude Lévi-Strauss," *Cahiers de L'Herne* 88 (2004), pp.216-218.

[130] Lévi-Strauss, "Structural Study of Myth," p. 440.

thus meaninglessly repetitive motion.[131]

> This permutation is necessary . . . to, account for structural patterns in which the final result is not merely a cyclical return to the point of departure after the first force has been nullified but a helicoidal step, a new situation different from the initial one not only in that it nullifies it but also because it consists of a state which is more than a nullification of the initial. . .To put it metaphorically, the inverse of, say, a loss which expressed the actual impact of a negative power is not only a loss nullified or recuperation, but *a gain.*[132]

Now, the conceptual terms in these sorts of mythopoeic formulations of inverted mediation are often embodied in fantastic characters or cosmological figures, and the potentially mediatorial or redemptive functions are exemplified in the mythic actions undertaken by these symbolic agents. As a matter of fact, this is exactly the kind of formalized process of inversion that Lafferty describes in his explication of how he came to write "Continued On Next Rock," particularly when he says that he started out by turning the architectonics of his narrative "upside down and backwards," and thereby "involuted the idea of time (making all things contemporary or at least repeating)," thereby also turning the "system of values backwards, trying to make the repulsive things appear poetic . . . . trying to set anti-love up as comparable to love"—for, after all, even the "flattest thing you can imagine has to have at least two sides;" in fact, "it can have many more"—and after that, merely letting the terms, in this case the "characters that had been generated by this action," fulfill their dynamic functions; i.e., let the elements of

---

[131] Lafferty, *The Three Armageddons of Enniscorthy Sweeney*, pp. 256-257.

[132] Pierre Maranda and Elli Köngäs-Maranda, *Structural Models in Folklore and Transformational Essays,* Approaches to Semiotics 10 (The Hague: Mouton De Gruyter, 1971), pp. 26-27.

the mythopoeic logic "work out their own way."[133] The main reason that the primal dichotomy in "Continued On Next Rock" remains unresolved at its denouement is due to the fact that Margaret remains stubbornly unchanged, and thus fails to function as a truly mediating factor. Her actions are part of cyclical rather than a "helicoidal" pattern, but for all that we cannot dismiss her trajectory as nothing more than a vicious circle. The eternally opposed poles of that dyadic pairing will continue to unfold across time, and hence a "theoretically infinite number of slates" or mythopoeic strata may be eventually generated, "each one slightly different from the others," which is why an unresolved myth will grow "spiral-wise until the intellectual impulse which has originated it is exhausted."[134] Nonetheless, effective mediation requires a crucial inversion of terms and functions by an intentional agent, in this case a mythopoeic actor capable of turning things "upside down and backwards."

> Duffey was one of those rare persons who might be able to impose topological inversion on the world. This was possible both mathematically and psychically. This would be bringing about the case that the world was contained in Duffey and not Duffey in the world. Many of us in this discipline have known about such possibilities, and we have even recognized several momentary happenings of it.[135]

---

[133] Lafferty, "How I Wrote 'Continued On Next Rock,'" pp. 19-20

[134] Lévi-Strauss, "Structural Study of Myth," p. 443.

[135] R.A. Lafferty, *More Than Melchisedech: Tales of Chicago* (Weston, Ontario: United Mythologies Press, 1992), p. 109.

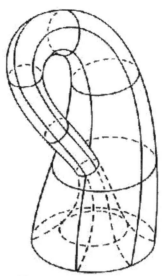

Figure 10. Klein bottle.

The captain of the Argo is one such actor who embodies this inverting principle, but he is not the only one, Finnegan is also a "double *phougaro* or funnel, the link between several different worlds," one of those characters "who have verifiable existence in at least two of those worlds," certainly Finnegan "himself believed that he was subject to topographical inversion; he believed that one of the worlds was always interior to him and another one exterior, and that they sometimes changed their places."[136] In Lafferty's mind topological inversion seems to be inextricably intertwined with the notion of temporal permutation. Duffey, Finnegan, and the other chrononauts of travel on the Argo into the contested time-streams of a contingent future in order to affect the present, but their mission seems to be as much about reconstituting their fragmented personhood, as it is about changing troublesome temporal vectors. If the end-point of

---

[136] R.A. Lafferty, "Interglossia to *The Devil Is Dead*," *Is* 5 (1972), pp. 16-18; reprinted in *How Many Miles to Babylon* (Weston, Ontario: United Mythologies Press, 1989), pp. 1-2, here at p. 1.

the process of inversion is not merely a nullification of a previous state, but a gain, then the chrononaut's spatio-temporal fracturing and recombination signifies, in true *bricoleur* form, a re-creation, the sort of "ornamentation" that in time allows a *topos* to be blessed and become "one of the Holy Lands." Andrew Ferguson has identified this world-building imperative as a regnant theme at the very center of Lafferty's story-telling.[137] In analyzing this recurring protological structure of Lafferty's narratology, Ferguson finds it helpful to adapt and recast Paul Ricœur's notion of three paradigmatic moments of mimetic production, Mimesis$_1$, Mimesis$_2$, and Mimesis$_3$, or, prefiguration, configuration, and re-figuration, wherein time is humanized to the extent that it portrays temporal experience, in terms of typical Laffertian metaphors, such as the archetypal "ghosts" that haunt many of Lafferty's fictions, the "deep underlay" or ontic and semiotic bases of that work, and finally the "jigsaw puzzle" or constructive aspects—what I have identified as Levi-Strauss' elaboration of the *bricoleur* structure and mediatory strategies in Lafferty's mythopoetics. A structuring that, in Ricœur's words "carry the meditation past the same point a number of times, but at different altitudes,"[138] a mediating process that can perhaps be better understood in terms of emblematic *bricoleur* methodologies such as totalization, detotalization, and re-totalization, and the tell-tale mytho-poetically "slated" configurations that "seeps to the surface" as layered three-dimensional strata by means of a repetitive synchro-diachronic pattern of stratifications, in which can be read all three spatial dimensions "left to right," "top to bottom," and "front to back" as it unfolds in time.[139] Following some of the work on the phenomenology of

---

[137] Andrew Ferguson, "R.A. Lafferty's Escape from Flatland; or, How to Build a World in Three Easy Steps," *Science Fiction Studies* 41: 3 (2014), pp. 543-561.

[138] Paul Ricœur, *Time and Narrative*, Vol. 1, trans. K. McLaughlin and D. Pellauer (Chicago: The University of Chicago Press, 1984), p. 72.

[139] Lévi-Strauss, "Structural Study of Myth," p. 443.

narrative by Paul Ricœur, Ferguson identifies an analogous interrelationship between narratological "innovation and sedimentation," but acknowledges that the "precise mechanism that allows them to play, as it were, on the same field," but which—in Ricœur's own estimation—"constitutes the axis around which the various changes of paradigm through application are arranged,"[140] although Ferguson concludes that this topographical inversion or "deformation amounts to a *twist*, the result being neither circle nor spiral but rather a Möbius strip," so that a story moves successively upon its homeomorphic surface "through phases of innovation . . . and sedimentation . . . revealed here to be at once paradigmatic opposites and syntagmatic complements"—and it is this "twist" in the Möbius which allows the mimetic narratological spiral to "remain endless while also doubling back on itself."[141]

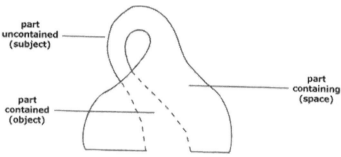

Figure 11. The topological structuring of the Klein bottle.

A Möbius surface has a definite orientation in space; that is, it can be produced either in a left- or right-handed form, all depending on the direction in which the form is twisted. If either a left- and right-oriented Möbius strip were constructed and then glued together in such a way that both are completely superimposed on each other, then a topological structure called a Klein bottle would result (See Fig. 10). As we

[140] Ricœur, *Time and Narrative*, Vol. 1, p. 70.

[141] Ferguson, "R.A. Lafferty's Escape from Flatland," p. 555.

can see, the Klein bottle has the same property of asymmetric one-sidedness as the two-dimensional Möbius strip, but embodies an added dimension that cannot be produced in a physical model of the bottle, since neither a left- nor right-facing Möbius strips can be superimposed on each other in three-dimensional space without tearing the surfaces. A topological form that "penetrates itself in a given number of dimensions can be produced without cutting a hole if an *added* dimension is available."[142] As the mathematician, artist, computer scientist, and speculative writer Rudy Rucker explains, if we were to imagine a species of "flatlanders" attempting to assemble a Möbius strip, since the reduced physical reality of these beings would be limited to two dimensions, when they tried to make an actual model of the Möbius, they would be forced to cut a hole in it, thereby compromising its topological integrity.[143] As Rucker further elucidates, since we have access to more than two dimensions, no such problem would arise for us. Rather, it is the attempt to create a three-dimensional Klein bottle that is problematic for us, since it is formed by passing one end of a tube through the side of the tube and joining it to the other end, thus necessitating a disruptive hole on its surface. Writer and visual artist Paul Ryan has anatomized the three basic topological features of the Klein bottle's structure as "part contained," "part uncontained," and "part containing" (See Fig. 11).[144] What at first appears as an uncomplicated case of topographical containment and uncontainment, is quickly problematized when we notice how the part contained opens

---

[142] Steven M. Rosen, *Topologies of the Flesh: A Multidimensional Exploration of the Lifeworld* (Athens, OH: Ohio University Press, 2006), p. 30. Also see Diego L. Rapoport, "Surmounting the Cartesian Cut Through Philosophy, Physics, Logic, Cybernetics, and Geometry: Self-reference, Torsion, the Klein Bottle, the Time Operator, Multivalued Logics and Quantum Mechanics," *Foundations of Science* 41 (2011), pp. 33-76.

[143] Rudolf v. B. Rucker, *Geometry, Relativity and the Fourth Dimension* (New York: Dover Books, 1977), pp. 52-55.

[144] Paul Ryan, *Cybernetics of the Sacred* (Garden City, NY: Anchor Press, 1974).

out at the bottom of the figure to form the "perimeter of the container, and how this, in turn, passes over into the uncontained aspect."[145] The three parts of this structure thus flow through the dimension of time into one another in an unbroken movement. Symbolized here in two dimensions is the process by which the reflected upon three-dimensional Kleinian object, in the very act of containing itself, is transformed into a four-dimensional inner-dimensional and trans-temporal event that does not compromise the bottle's structural integrity. Interestingly, Lévi-Strauss analyzed several myths in which a tubular object, such as a pipe features prominently, and in which the protagonist undergoes a series of unusual transformations: "(1) the hero's body enters a tube that contains him; (2) the tube formerly contained in the hero's body emerges from it; (3) the hero's body becomes a tube—something either goes in or comes out of it."[146] In other words, "the tube is first extrinsic, the intrinsic; the hero's body is first contained, then becomes a container," and this sequence establishes an analogical comparison: "the contained body is to the containing tube as the contained tube is to a container that is no longer a body but is itself a tube."[147] The hero, Lévi-Strauss concludes, has become a kind of Klein bottle; or, perhaps as Lafferty would designate it, a "double *phougaro.*" Even more fascinating, Lévi-Strauss then goes on to analyze several other Amerindian tales and discovers a Kleinian structure to the narratives, so that when they are diagrammed, their dyadic antipodes culminates in a spatio-temporal inversion of antinomies. That is to say, Lévi-Strauss' canonical formulation of mythopoesis can be given topographical expression as a four-dimensional Klein bottle.[148]

---

[145] Rosen, *Topologies of the Flesh*, p. 36.

[146] Lévi-Strauss, *The Jealous Potter*, trans. Bénédicte Chorier (Chicago: The University of Chicago Press, 1988), p. 162.

[147] Ibid, p. 163.

[148] Lévi-Strauss's friend, the psychoanalyst Jacques Lacan, later formulated a series of topological models of the human unconscious, including one based on the Klein bottle, in order to model the process of psychic disintegration and reintegration in

As our analysis of "Continued On Next Rock" has indicated, not only are Lafferty's narratological strategies similarly mythomorphic in the way that they unfold, but I would go further now and suggest that Lafferty's door seems to function in an analogously topographical manner to Lévi-Strauss' four-dimensional Kleinian mytho-poetics. The door's flat rectangular plane is the site where "time turns into space" a phrase from Richard Wagner's opera *Parsifal* ("Zum Raum wird hier die Zeit"), when the forest landscape in which the characters Gurnemanz and Parsifal are standing metamorphoses to be replaced by a wall of rock, and for a moment the two distinct *loci* are reciprocally conjoined in a spatio-temporal collage. As the critic James Burton points out, "What is normally possible only in a temporal sequence – a body occupying different places, different states, a person becoming someone quite different," mythopoeic praxis make "possible in space."[149] Significantly, Lévi-Strauss identifies this moment in Wagner as "probably the most profound definition that anyone has ever offered for myth."[150] If mythopoesis is, as Lévi-Strauss claims, the "site of that long-promised land where relief is to be found for the impatient, threefold awareness of a 'later' that has to be waited for, a 'now' that slips through the fingers, and a voracious 'yesteryear' that draws to itself, disrupts and collapses the future into a present already confounded with the past," then the "category of time revealed by the study of the myths is, in the last resort, that which the dreams themselves have always dreamed of. Time which is more than just regained," but rather time as the

---

his patients. The parallels with Finnegan as a spatio-temporally and psychically shattered "double phougaro" or human Klein bottle are suggestive. See Jacques Lacan, *The Seminar of Jacques Lacan Book XIII: The Object of Psychoanalysis*, trans. C. Gallaher (London: Karnac Books, 1994).

[149] James Burton, *The Philosophy of Science Fiction: Henri Bergson and the Fabulations of Philip K. Dick* (London: Bloomsbury, 2015), p. 187.

[150] Claude Levi-Strauss, "From Chrétien de Troyes to Richard Wagner," in *The View from Afar* (New York: Basic Books, 1985), p. 219.

merely chronometric "abolished" and time as all periods present to each other simultaneously and "alive for the benefit of the next" achieves, so that mythopoesis is the site of *kairos*, the *topos* of aeviternity, a reciprocation conjunction of the prior, the present, and the prospective, where all possible nows are ubiquitous to each other.[151]

Upon such topological flatlands the process of world-creation takes place, and the perpetual task of adorning this *topos* must be newly taken up again every day, a flatland built up out of provisional objects, discarded dreamscapes, proto-totemic beasts, and archetypal figures, each of these found elements fitted together in the piecemeal manner of a *bricolage* assemblage:

> At the present time there is a twelve year old boy in Figueras in Spain who paints this *topos*, this floor of the unformed and the unconscious every day. This is the uncluttered and primordial earth, and it looks like a mauve pavement. The twelve-year-old Catalan boy paints this landscape as inhabited by a few flat panthers and bears and bearcats, flattened as if melted down to the flatness of pancakes.[152] The flat beasts are

---

[151] Claude Lévi-Strauss, *The Naked Man*, p. 606.

[152] The Catalan boy from "Figueras" is a clear allusion to the Surrealist painter Salvador Dali, who was born in Figueres, in the province of Girona, Catalonia, Spain, in 1904. Lafferty identified himself as a particular sort of Surrealist: "I don't regard myself as a Surrealist in the sense of the *Surrealist Manifesto* published by Andre Breton in 1924. To me, that Manifesto is somewhat dated, being a recoil from World War I, and being too heavily Freudian. My own unconscious is more Jungian than Freudian. But if Breton hadn't staked claim to the name, I would probably call myself a Surrealist in the 'Remembrance of Things Within' sense, but not in the 'world of dream and fantasy joined to the everyday rational world, be coming 'an absolute reality, a surreality.' I suppose that I believe in another sort of surreality or super-reality, but it would have to be on a wider basis than the encounters of self and me. As often as not, it is my subconscious that supplies the rational element, and the exterior world that supplies the dream and fantasy feeling." Tom Jackson, "An

draped limply over the folded and stepped flatness of the land.

The paintings are of the early mornings, so shadows are thrown in contradictory directions from dawn and false-dawn (there is a selection-by-combat between them also). It is in the early mornings that these proto-beasts are as flat and limp as melted paper, for it is then that they have belched themselves empty of dreams. These dreams or eructations are painted as flying in the low air with their vulture heads and bat-wings, or canvas-and-strut wings.

This *topos*, this unadorned and unconscious flat-land, is subject to change; but the changes are very contingent for a long time. If hills are wanted, they are dragged in on skids by creatures pulling them with ropes. If mountains are required, they are rolled in on wheels or log rollers. This is analogous to the geological mountain-bringing process. The mountains always come in on easy-flowing extrusions that are really wheels or rollers of magma.

When a *topos* has acquired sufficient ornamentation, it is blessed, or it is cursed. If it is blessed, it becomes one of the Holy Lands. If it is cursed, we don't know what it becomes.

Even in their first form, the lands are not quite flat. There are the ledges from which the statuary stones are quarried. There are the clay-pits from which the red adam-clay is taken and from which Pan-Therium came. But the *topos* still maintains the appearance of flatness or of stepped flatness.[153]

Interview with R. A. Lafferty," *Lan's Lantern* 39 (1991): 49-53, at p. 52. Also, according to Lafferty, Dali, Gustave Doré, Hieronymus Bosch, and Finnegan all knew hell, and all of them "portrayed it authentically, but with a light touch;" *Promontory Goats* (Weston, Ontario: United Mythologies Press, 1988), p. 5.

[153] R.A. Lafferty, *The Three Armageddons of Enniscorthy Sweeney*, pp. 256-257.

Akin to the young Spanish boy in Figueras, Lafferty the demiurgic *bricoleur* assembles a recurrent aeviternal image by means of a stratifying series of reciprocation images, each found object a nexus of correlated interfaces. In this manner, Lafferty's door operates as a kind of time machine, much in the way that the Argo navigates the time-lashed seas of *More Than Melchisedech*. The door is at once both a composite spatio-temporal object, and the temporal event in which that spatial object manifests itself. It is simultaneously a door whose esoteric meaning demands to be "opened," as well as the incessant and potentially never-ending experience of opening that door, for the very reason that the door's design contains and mediates all the multiple ways in which it can ever be hypothetically "opened"—a liminal occasion that necessarily unfolds both forwards and backwards, for the act of "opening" has both anticipatory and retrospective aspects built into its very structure. Standing before Lafferty's door, symbolically displacing one of Duffey's chrononauts, the metaxic spectator likewise occupies a contested topographic boundary zone between re-contextualized and re-contextualizing time-frames. As the observer's eyes navigate across the signifying swells, breakers, and fluxes of this visual synchro-diachronic *aevum*, like Finnegan, momentarily we too are a "double *phougaro*," an enfleshed Klein bottle, which establishes a link "between several different worlds," as we experience a kind of topological inversion by allowing Lafferty' unfolding imaginal world to conceptually inhabit us. With every encounter, Lafferty invites the viewer/reader of these dynamically revelatory images to step into his creative role, and in the process of tracing and retracing its myriad mythopoeic paths, we protologically (re)construct the meaning(s) of this world again for the first time.

IV

> "Only prayer and fasting and virtual miracle will bring them when there are none," Duffey said. "I pray, I fast now for several minutes, but will they come? Open the auditorium doors and the corridor doors and the front and back door of the building. Then we will see."
>
> "But we are very careful to keep the doors closed," the little teacher said, "or things might get in."
>
> "I certainly hope that things will get in," Duffey said. Then he went into an intensity of concentration or prayer.[154]

The characteristic feature of the savage mind is its timelessness; its object is to grasp the world as both a synchronic and a diachronic totality and the knowledge which it draws therefrom is like that afforded of a room by mirrors fixed on opposite walls, which reflect each other (as well as objects in the intervening space) although without being strictly parallel. A multitude of images forms simultaneously, none exactly like any other, so that no single one furnishes more than a partial knowledge of the decoration and furniture but the group is characterized by invariant properties expressing a truth. The savage mind deepens its knowledge with the help of *imagines mundi*. It builds mental structures which facilitate an understanding of the world in as much as they resemble it. In this sense savage thought can be defined as analogical thought.[155]

> A new thing had appeared in the cavernous night of nature, a mind that is like a mirror. It is like a mirror because it is truly a thing of reflection. It is like a mirror because in it alone all the other shapes can be seen like shining shadows in a vision. Above all, it is like a mirror because it is the only thing of its kind.

---

[154] R.A. Lafferty, *More Than Melchisedech: Tales of Chicago*, p. 100.

[155] Lévi-Strauss, *Savage Mind*, p. 263.

Other things may resemble it or resemble each other in various ways; other things may excel it or excel each other in various ways; just as in the furniture of a room a table may be round like a mirror or a cupboard may be larger than a mirror. But the mirror is the only thing that can contain them all. Man is the microcosm; man is the measure of all things; man is the image of God.[156]

Conclusion: *Bricolage* as *Analogia Entis*

At its most basic, *bricolage*, much like the structuralist method itself, is nothing more than a "means of experiencing and understanding the world . . . as a system of relations."[157] *Bricolage* employs methods such as totemism in order to establish an "overarching classification system which organizes all experience into an integrated whole in terms of which one can locate anyone or anything relative to all other beings, things, events, and forces. It defines nature, the human place in nature, and any person's place in the natural and human order. Its logic is one of classification and analogy."[158] More than one person has noted the similarity of this classificatory methodology with medieval scholasticism's numerous "classification systems devised to impose order on the ever-expanding breadth of human knowledge" (*scientia*) and to demonstrate the "interconnectedness of its parts."[159] For example, Umberto Eco concludes his study of Aquinas' aesthetic theories with a brief comparative analysis of

---

[156] Chesterton, *Everlasting Man*, p. 19

[157] Wiseman, *Lévi-Strauss, Anthropology and Aesthetics*, p. 45.

[158] Paul E. Durrenberger and Dorothy Durrenberger, "Translating Gunnlaug's Saga: An Anthropological Approach to Literary Style and Cultural Structures," *Translation Review* 21/22: 1 (1986), pp. 11-20, here at p. 12.

[159] Joseph Dyer, "The Place of *Musica* in Medieval Classifications of Knowledge," *The Journal of Musicology* 24:1 (2007), pp. 3-71, at p. 3.

Thomistic and structuralist methodologies. Among the similarities between the two systems, Eco discerns a certain common concern with invariant epistemological schemas, as evinced by scholasticism's realist account of the active intellect's production of universal intelligible species, and structuralism's parallel study of linguistic universals in the mind which reaffirms the atemporal nature of the structures of the mind and a fixed order in the psyche. Eco finds an even more intriguing correspondence in Thomas' position that substantial forms persist through changes and therefore are always available to be rearranged in new configurations. For Aquinas, this is the case as well in cultural artefacts, which find their meaning in the structural relationship of such reconfigured conjunctions of elements, and always retain their ability for "rearrangement in new correlations, for disposal in an infinity of combinations." As Eco points out, this stance is remarkably similar to the structuralist conception of art as *bricolage*, or the selection of fragments or left-overs of previous cultural formations and re-deployment in new combinations, to be found in Lévi-Strauss.[160]

In addition, Eco adduces a way in which structuralism's characteristic concern with the synchronous and diachronous dimension discernible in all phenomena could be explicated in scholastic terms, with diachrony identified with the Aristotelian-Thomistic notion of *natura* understood as a principle of continuous motion, and synchrony as a static expression of its trajectory, the *essentia*, of that nature's unfolding diachronic dynamism across time, formulated "so that we may discern the state of it," and thereby analyze the structural "field of relationships of which the process consist."[161] Further parallels could undoubtedly be drawn between scholastic and structuralist modes of thought. For example, the Aristotelian-Thomistic distinction between form and matter, and its ineradicable hylemorphic confluence within all substances, could be fruitfully compared to the

---

[160] Umberto Eco, *The Aesthetics of Thomas Aquinas*, trans. H. Bredin (Cambridge: Harvard University Press, 1988), p. 219.

[161] Ibid, p. 221.

differentiation made within structuralism between *langue* and *parole*. The former conceived as a synchronous, atemporal structure or form; and the latter comprehended as the diachronic instantiations of that ahistorical structuring form in a series of materially contingent combinations across time and space.

However, the most singularly significant feature that joins the structuralist methodology of *bricolage* and the scholastic tradition together is their shared analogicity. In Aristotle we find some of the first and most enduringly influential accounts of analogy, that is, of how we may say that various things exist in a distinctive yet nonetheless corresponding manner to other things.[162] When addressing the problematic of how being can be predicated alike to a plurality of existential modalities, Aristotle responds by pointing out how diverse things that share a common denomination are related to one thing—that is, to a primary instance from which their different meanings are subsequently derived. So, according to Aristotle, analogousness designates a similarity of relation, a relational unity-in-difference, which in the case of substances, of things that exist, accounts for both their ontological sameness and distinction by positing an *analogia entis*, an analogy of being.[163] This is an analogy based on predication or categorization, since when something is said "to be" it is always said in combination with a predicate that catalogs the distinctive mode of that being; that is, one not only says that an existing

---

[162] E.g., "Everything which is healthy is related to health, one thing in the sense that it produces it, another in the sense that it is a symptom of health, another because it is capable of it. And that which is medical is relative to the medical art, one thing being called medical because it possesses it, another because it is naturally adapted to it, another because it is a function of the medical art. And we shall find many other words used similarly to these." Aristotle, *Metaphysics* IV, 2, 1003a35-1003b4.

[163] See M.-D. Philippe, "*Analogon* and *Analogia* in the Philosophy of Aristotle," *The Thomist* 33:1 (1969), pp. 1–74; Joseph Owens, *The Doctrine of Being in the Aristotelian Metaphysics: A Study in the Greek Background of Mediaeval Thought*, 3rd edition, revised (Toronto: Pontifical Institute of Mediaeval Studies, 1978).

entity shares in a common notion of being, but also indicates the particular nature of its distinctive manner of existence.[164] In other words, a substance is not merely described as existing, but is said to be a horse, or as a tree, or as human, just as something is said to be pale, or dark, or short, or tall, or healthy, or sickly, etc.

It is not hard to detect how this sort of analogical classification finds a close parallel in the totemic predication described by Lévi-Strauss, where species are employed as a means to not only formally encode differences between various clans and tribes, and thereby establish a form of social classification, but to establish either more minute classificatory differentiations, by breaking down the animals into their constituent parts, or expanding the system of predicamental codification to the level of speciation, so that it can potentially classify any existing social entity. Indeed, like the Aristotelian categories, totemic encoding empowers the *bricoleur* to cast a conceptual net of classificatory analogical relations over every aspect of reality. This dynamically analogous understanding of existence indicates that relationality itself is a primordial structural feature of every substance. In fact, in scholasticism, analogous relationality and substantiality go together as two distinct but inseparable modes of reality, for as Thomas Aquinas points out, being as substance, as existing in itself, naturally flows over into being as relational, as turned towards and related to other entities by its self-actuating and self-communicative activity. In sum, to exist truly is "to be" substance-in-relation.[165] As Daniel Otto

---

[164] Aristotle's categories, or predicamentals, enumerate all the possible kinds of things that can be the subject or the predicate of a proposition. Aristotle thereby locates every entity of human apprehension under one of ten possible existential categories: substance, quantity, quality, relation, position, time, posture, condition, action, and affection. Cf. John Ackrill, *Aristotle: Categories and De Interpretatione* (Oxford: Clarendon Press, 1963).

[165] See Gregorio Montejo, "'This Was More Than a Spectacle, More Than an Illusion, It Was a Communicating Instrument': R. A. Lafferty and Hans Urs von Balthasar on the Relational Form of Being," *Feast of Laughter* 2 (2015), pp. 52-73.

Jack Petersen has copiously demonstrated, Lafferty's work is replete with precisely the sort of Lévi-Straussian predicamental totemism, or Aristotelian analogically relational categorization, which aspires to enumerate and classify the almost inexhaustible existential variety and unfathomable ontic depths of animal entities within an all-encompassing categorial aesthetic.[166] As Petersen writes, these Laffertarian inventories could be easily expanded to include "geological formations, meteorological phenomena, flora (the guy loved to make lists of types of grass!)," or even cultural artifacts, such as mechanical equipment.[167] Also, alongside Petersen, one should note as well what Object-oriented ontologist Ian Bogost has referred to as *ontography*,

> a name for a general inscriptive strategy, one that uncovers the repleteness of units and their interobjectivity. From the perspective of metaphysics, ontography involves the revelation of object relationships without necessarily offering clarification or description of any kind. Like a medieval bestiary, ontography can take the form of a compendium, a record of things juxtaposed to demonstrate their overlap and imply interaction through collocation. The simplest approach to such recording is the *list*, a group of items loosely joined not by logic or power or use but by the gentle knot of the comma. Ontography is an aesthetic set theory, in which a particular configuration is celebrated merely on the basis of its existence.[168]

---

[166] Cf. Daniel Otto Jack Petersen, "The Epic of Man and His Friends; or, Slumming It With the Ontic Outcasts; or, May Our Eyes Be Big Enough To Take In the Nine Hundred Percent Gain in Everything!," *Feast of Laughter* 1 (2014), pp. 67-100.

[167] Daniel Otto Jack Petersen, "Valery's Really Eyes and the Parade of Creatures; Or, Lafferty's Animal Fair Comes to Town; Or, You Are a Pig Made Out of Sticks," *Feast of Laughter* 2 (2015), pp. 21-51, at pp. 21-22.

[168] Ian Bogost. *Alien Phenomenology, or What It's Like to Be a Thing*, Posthumanities (Minneapolis: University Press of

As described by Bogost, this type of categorization bears more than a striking resemblance to the *bricoleur*'s storehouse of analogously related heterogeneous materials, since the components of the set are not related to any particular project, but are rather the contingent result of all the occasions that have occurred to "renew or enrich the stock, or to maintain it with the remains of previous constructions or destructions;"[169] an assemblage, as Bogost explains, of distinct pre-existent forms that result in a new whole, "a compendium, a record of things juxtaposed to demonstrate their overlap and imply interaction through collocation," which, like mythopoeic bricolage, "builds up structured sets, not directly with other structured sets but by using the remains and debris of

---

Minnesota, 2012), p. 38.

[169] "The analogy is worth pursuing since it helps us to see the real relations between the two types of scientific knowledge we have distinguished. The 'bricoleur' is adept at performing a large number of diverse tasks; but, unlike the engineer, he does not subordinate each of them to the availability of raw materials and tools conceived and procured for the purpose of the project. His universe of instruments is closed and the rules of his game are always to make do with 'whatever is at hand', that is to say with a set of tools and materials which is always finite and is also heterogeneous because what it contains bears no relation to the current project, or indeed to any particular project, but is the contingent result of all the occasions there have been to renew or enrich the stock or to maintain it with the remains of previous constructions or destructions. The set of the 'bricoleur's' means cannot therefore be defined in terms of a project (which would presuppose besides, that, as in the case of the engineer, there were, at least in theory, as many sets of tools and materials or 'instrumental sets', as there are different kinds of projects). It is to be defined only by its potential use or, putting this another way and in the language of the 'bricoleur' himself, because the elements are collected or retained on the principle that 'they may always come in handy'. Such elements are specialized up to a point, sufficiently for the 'bricoleur' not to need the equipment and knowledge of all trades and professions, but not enough for each of them to have only one definite and determinate use. They each represent a set of actual and possible relations; they are 'operators' but they can be used for any operations of the same type." Lévi-Strauss, *Savage Mind*, pp. 17-18.

events."[170] Moreover, the structuring of such analogous sets proffers meaningful knowledge about the larger relational ordering of the world to the *bricoleur* by providing a language with which to endow the seemingly meaningless chaos or inscrutable mysteries of life with significance. Indeed, the symbolic world built out of such analogous webs of significatory *bricolage* can not only be known but also manipulated. Lafferty tells the curious story of Rambo Touchstone, a man who has covered every available wall surface of one of his rooms with cut-out pictures. "Oh, I have room for many more pictures in this room," Touchstone insists to his visitor Gifford Hazelman, "I can put them on any

---

[170] "This formula, which could serve as a definition of 'bricolage', explains how an implicit inventory or conception of the total means available must be made in the case of mythical thought also, so that a result can be defined which will always be a compromise between the structure of the instrumental set and that of the project. Once it materializes the project will therefore inevitably be at a remove from the initial aim (which was moreover a mere sketch), a phenomenon which the surrealists have felicitously called 'objective hazard'. Further, the 'bricoleur' also, and indeed principally, derives his poetry from the fact that he does not confine himself to accomplishment and execution: he 'speaks' not only *with* things, as we have already seen, but also through the medium of things: giving an account of his personality and life by the choices he makes between the limited possibilities. The 'bricoleur' may not ever complete his purpose but he always puts something of himself into it.

Mythical thought appears to be an intellectual form of 'bricolage' in this sense also. Science as a whole is based on the distinction between the contingent and the necessary, this being also what distinguishes event and structure. The qualities it claimed at its outset as peculiarly scientific were precisely those which formed no part of living experience and remained outside and, as it were, unrelated to events. This is the significance of the notion of primary qualities. Now, the characteristic feature of mythical thought, as of 'bricolage' on the practical plane, is that it builds up structured sets, not directly with other structured sets but by using the remains and debris of events: in French 'des bribes et des morceaux', or odds and ends in English, fossilized evidence of the history of an individual or a society." Ibid, pp. 21-2.

empty place at all, or in the white or unfilled portion of a larger picture. Pale skies are legitimate places to put them."[171] The similarities with Lafferty's own *bricoleur* activities is readily apparent:

> Being generally too poor to have statuary, and his apartment being too small for that sort of clutter, he had pictures, pasted-up pictures. He had more than ten thousand pictures pasted up on the walls of his studio room. Some were smaller than postage stamps; some were as much as a foot square; most were in between. The pictures were cut out of travel brochures and advertisements, out of catalogs, out of *Arizona Highways Magazine* and *Oklahoma Today* and *Gourmet*, from art calendars of former years, from Antiques journals, from all sources whatever.
>
> The doors, the jambs, the sills, the baseboards, the window framing, the mullions between the glass panes, and all wall space (whether hidden behind books and other things or not) were covered with pictures. "They make themselves known by their pervading influence even when they're hidden," Rambo said. It was an amazing clutter. But there was a muted blending as well as howling clashes of colors and arrangements and contrasts. There was some taste in the collection and assembly.
>
> "I'll rejoice when you don't have another square inch on which to paste another picture however small, Rambo," Gifford Hazelman crowed.
>
> "Don't say that, Gifford," Rambo begged. "When I have filled every available space, then I must die."[172]

---

[171] R.A. Lafferty, "I'll See It Done and Then I'll Die," in *The Man Who Made Models and Other Stories*, Drumm Booklet 18 (Polk City, IA: Chris Drumm, 1984), pp. 14-21, at p.14. I am grateful to Daniel Otto Jack Petersen for bringing this story to my attention.

[172] Ibid. pp. 14-15.

This last curious bit of superstitious belief, which leads Gifford to describe Rambo as a "fetish-worshiper," sets the narrative in motion and establishes the theme of the story, for it turns out that Touchstone is full of all sorts of seemingly credulous opinions regarding his mortality. Among other things, he thinks that if a spider finishes building a web in his apartment, or the Cow-Pokes win the pennant, of if he finishes reading a particular novel, or if he achieves a score of 99,999 points in a game of Crack-a-Stack, then he is surely fated to die. In an early essay entitled "The Effectiveness of Symbols" Lévi-Strauss explores the connections between shamanism in mythopoeic societies and the power of such symbolic belief-systems to bring about therapeutic results in a patient. In one shamanistic ceremony, a medicine-man chants a mythic song, largely consisting of a *bricolage*-like itinerary of ritualistically prescribed actions and a catalogue of monstrous mythological spirits who are linked to various physiological symptoms, which helps a mother through a difficult childbirth by means of its elaborate symbolism. As Lévi-Strauss points out, the shaman gives the woman's ailment significance within a larger mythopoeic narrative structure of spiritual warfare, so that when the narrative climaxes with a symbolic victory over the illness-signifying demons, the woman is encouraged to enter a psycho-somatic state wherein she is able to finally give birth. The analogous relationship between "monster and disease" is established by the shamanistic *bricoleur* healer,

> It is a relationship between symbol and thing symbolized, or, to use the terminology of linguists, between signifier and signified. The shaman provides the sick woman with a *language*, by means of which unexpressed, and otherwise inexpressible, psychic states can be immediately expressed. And it is the transition to this verbal expression—at the same time making it possible to undergo in an ordered and intelligible form a real experience that would otherwise be chaotic and inexpressible—which induces the release of the physiological process, that is,

the reorganization, in a favorable direction, of the process to which the sick woman is subjected.[173]

Levi-Strauss also discusses instances where such shamanistic practices can be used for dark purposes: to lay curses, induces illnesses, or even lead to death. Here, the process works in much the same way, for the shaman's dark magic only functions if he is able to successfully manipulate a set of symbols "through meaningful equivalents of things meant which belong to another order of reality," in order to bring about a desired effect.[174] As he goes on to speculate, in psychoanalysis "abreaction refers to the decisive moment in the treatment when the patient intensively relives the initial situation from which his disturbance stems, before he ultimately overcomes it," and, in this sense, Lévi-Strauss thinks that shaman could be considered a "professional abreactor." Yet, upon closer inspection, the shamanistic therapy appears to be

> The exact counterpart to the psychoanalytic cure, but with an inversion of all the elements. Both cures aim at inducing an experience, and both succeed by recreating a myth which the patient has to live or relive. But in one case, the patient constructs an individual myth with elements drawn from his past; in the other case, the patient receives from the outside a social myth which does not correspond to a former personal state. To prepare for the abreaction, which then becomes an "adreaction," the psychoanalyst

---

[173] Claude Lévi-Strauss, "The Effectiveness of Symbols," in *Structural Anthropology*, trans. Claire Jacobson and Brooke Grundfest Schoepf (New York: Basic Books, 1963), pp. 186-205, at pp. 197-198. Jacobson and Schoepf translated the words "signifiant" and "signifié," usually translated as "signifier" and "signified," with the somewhat misleading terms "sign" and "meaning." I have altered the translation to the more familiar and faithful rendering of "signifier" and "signified."

[174] Ibid, p. 200.

listens, whereas the shaman speaks. Better still: When a transference is established, the patient puts words into the mouth of the psychoanalyst by attributing to him alleged feelings and intentions; in the incantation, on the contrary, the shaman speaks for his patient.[175]

In other words, in the shaman's ritual "resistance is lifted in transference by an interpretation whose signifiers will reorganize the patient's symbolic universe."[176] This semiotic rearrangement or transference is only possible because of the ineradicable gap between the imaginary and images in all analogical thinking, a relational contingency between signifier and signified that had been noted as far back as Aristotle, who explicated a theory of signification that consisted of two relations. The first relation between symbolic articulation (*phone*) and conceptual meaning (*pathema*), and a second relation between the resulting word or image (*onoma*)—as a combination of symbol and meaning—and the object referred to or named (*pragma*).[177] In this schema, we should note that Aristotle demarcates between the *pathemata* or conceptualization of extra-mental objects in the intellect, what Lévi-Strauss will designate as the signified, and the contingent symbolic formulation, which coupled with the concept will give voice or representation to a thing in the world, the signifier. So, while the meanings of the *pragmata* are based on a like relation to things in reality and on the way that objects are perceived and visualized in the mind, their subsequent signification, the way that resemblance is designated or symbolized, always has an element of

---

[175] Ibid, p. 199. Cf. Jerome Neu, "Lévi-Strauss on Shamanism," *Man* 10:2 (1975), pp. 285-292, and Paul-François Tremlett, *Lévi-Strauss on Religion: The Structuring Mind*, Key Thinkers in the Study of Religion (London: Equinox, 2008), pp. 77-82, for critical appraisals of Lévi-Strauss' shamanistic theorizing.

[176] Markos Zafiropoulos, *Lacan and Levi-Strauss or The Return to Freud (1951-1957)*, trans. J. Holland, The Centre for Freudian Analysis and Research Library (London: Karnac Books, 2010), p. 48.

[177] Aristotle, *De Interpretatione*, 16a, 3–8.

arbitrariness, since the *phone* has no direct link to the signified object, but only a mediate connection as the result of its pairing with a concept in order for symbolization to occur.[178] Aquinas further elaborates upon the nature of this semiotic contingency when he elaborates an epistemological process modeled on Aristotle wherein the apperception of an object proceeds from an initial perception of a physical object to an abstractive phase where the essence of a thing is conceptualized in the intellect apart from its material instantiation. However, this is not the culmination of true knowledge, which is only within a second reflexive movement (*reflexio*) in which the intellect turns back to the thing perceived and proceeds to reconstitute the composite object. As we have already touched upon, for both Aristotle and Aquinas all objects in the world are *hylemorphic*; that is, composed of both a synchronous, essential structure or form, and a diachronically contingent and concretized material component, and in this concluding *reflexio* the mind not only "attributes qualities and properties to an object, but actuates a 'predication.'"[179] To be more exact, the intellect applies to its abstract conceptualization of a thing's essence a judgment as to the entity's determinative ontological modalities, it renders an analogical judgment as to how the object exists, and thereby establishes the thing's particularized *analogia entis*.[180]

---

[178] See Hans Arens, *Aristotle's Theory of Language and its Tradition: Texts from 500 to 1750*, Studies in the History of Language Sciences 39 (Amsterdam/Philadelphia: John Benjamins Publishing Company, 1984); Deborah K. W. Modrak, *Aristotle's Theory of Language and Meaning* (Cambridge: Cambridge University Press, 2001); Ludovic De Cuypere and Klaas Willems, "Meaning and Reference in Aristotle's Concept of the Linguistic Sign," *Foundations of Science* 13:3-4 (2008), pp. 307–324.

[179] Roberto Pellerey, "Thomas Aquinas : Natural Semiotics and the Epistemological Process," in *On the Medieval Theory of Signs*, Foundations of Semiotics 21, ed. U. Eco and C. Marmo (Amsterdam/Philadelphia: John Benjamins Publishing Company, 1989), pp. 81-105, at p. 98.

[180] Thomas Aquinas, *Summa Theologiæ* I, q.85, a.5: "The human intellect must of necessity understand by composition and

According to Thomas, it is at this crucial adjudicative juncture, when—to use Lévi-Straussian parlance—the signifier is associated with the signified in the mind, that error may enter into the epistemic process.[181] And it is exactly at this perilous site where Lévi-Strauss not only locates the work of signification, which he identifies as the locus of the *bricoleur*'s mythopoeic calculus, but also situates that semiotic topological space where shamanistic transference occurs. To an even greater extent than in therapeutic adreactions, the *bricoleur*'s shamanic manipulation of analogical signification can also modify the organism. There is a homologous relationship between objects and signification in both shamanism and in psycho-analysis, and a shared praxis that consists

---

division. For since the intellect passes from potentiality to act, it has a likeness to things which are generated, which do not attain to perfection all at once but acquire it by degrees: so likewise the human intellect does not acquire perfect knowledge by the first act of apprehension; but it first apprehends something about its object, such as its quiddity, and this is its first and proper object; and then it understands the properties, accidents, and the various relations of the essence. Thus it necessarily compares one thing with another by composition or division; and from one composition and division it proceeds to another, which is the process of reasoning." See Gyula Klima, "The Semantic Principles Underlying Saint Thomas Aquinas's Metaphysics of Being," *Medieval Philosophy and Theology* 5 (1996), pp. 87-141; John Deely, "The Role of Thomas Aquinas in the Development of Semiotic Consciousness," *Semiotica* 152: 1-4 (2004), pp. 75-139.

[181] Aquinas, *ST* I, q.85, a.6: "The intellect, however, may be accidentally deceived in the quiddity of composite things, not by the defect of its organ, for the intellect is a faculty that is independent of an organ; but on the part of the composition affecting the definition, when, for instance, the definition of a thing is false in relation to something else, as the definition of a circle applied to a triangle; or when a definition is false in itself as involving the composition of things incompatible; as, for instance, to describe anything as 'a rational winged animal.'"

Of stimulating an organic transformation which would consist essentially in a structural reorganization, by inducing the patient intensively to live out a myth—either perceived or created by him—whose structure would be, at the unconscious level, analogous to the structure whose genesis is sought precisely in this "inductive property," by which formally homologous structures, built out of different materials at different levels of life—organic processes, unconscious mind, rational thought—are related to one another.[182]

To be more precise, Lévi-Strauss posits that the shamanistic methodology is symbolically effective in these cases because of the analogousness between structures that organize the patient's thought world and the world itself and thus establishes the possibility of "organic modifications that can be deduced from a symbolic event. It can also help us rethink the opposite movement, from the organism to the symbolic."[183] Thus, for both good and ill, for either curative or injurious purposes, "the traumatizing power of those situations stems from the fact that at the moment when they appear, the subject experiences them immediately as living myth," and by this Lévi-Strauss means that the "traumatizing power of any situation cannot result from its intrinsic features but must, rather, result from the capacity of certain events, appearing within an appropriate psychological, historical, and social context, to induce an emotional crystallization which is molded by a pre-existing structure," and that in relation to the diachronic event, "these structures—or, more accurately, these structural laws—are truly atemporal"—which is to say synchronic—and these "structures as an aggregate form what we call the unconscious."[184] At least in this narrative, Lafferty seems to be operating under very similar theoretical

---

[182] Lévi-Strauss, "The Effectiveness of Symbols," p. 201.

[183] Zafiropoulos, *Lacan and Levi-Strauss or The Return to Freud*, p. 50.

[184] Lévi-Strauss, "The Effectiveness of Symbols," p. 202.

presuppositions when he shows how Gifford, rather than Rambo, is struck down by the seemingly arbitrary "fetishes" and admittedly silly rules of the symbolic game of Crack-a-Stack that Touchstone has been playing. Like the practice of *bricolage*, in which the *bricoleur* mytho-poetically recombines not only words and images but actions as well, Crack-a-Stack "teaches flexibility of mind and easy adjustment to events."[185] He plays the game with a set of "symmetrical five-sided dice," which are as "geometrically impossible" as a Klein bottle and which "give a person the vertigo just to see them roll about."[186] Rambo is the consummate analogical semiotician, an *ontographer* deftly manipulating the affiliations between signifiers and signifieds as he decodes and encodes the symbolic structure of existence for various "Adult Algebra" publications, sitting "for hours every day before his mathematical typewriter. And many moments, when the inspiration did not flow, he diverted himself by selecting and pasting up small pictures on the vanishingly empty areas of his room."[187] And consonant to the shamanistically mediated abreactional passage from one symbolic thought-world to another documented by Lévi-Strauss, in the end it is Hazelman who undergoes a semiotic transference at the hands of Touchstone, and becomes "so idea-ridden and so hooked on the fetish stuff that it had to kill him."[188] As Rambo admits, if "I don't die of fetish fulfillment, then I may die of some appalling disorder. I hate disorder, and there is something orderly about fetishes."[189] Which is to say, along with Lévi-Strauss, that the power of the fetishistic mythopoesis of the *bricoleur*/shaman resides precisely in its ordering structure and the way that this order mirrors the ontic structuring that it symbolizes. Despite its narratological slightness, "I'll See It Done And Then I'll Die" manages to indicate that at the

---

[185] Lafferty, "I'll See It Done and Then I'll Die," p. 21.

[186] Ibid, p. 18.

[187] Ibid, p. 15.

[188] Ibid, p. 21.

[189] Ibid, p. 18.

predicamental level the deep metaphysical and analogous interrelations of objects in the world are not only of profound conceptual import, but contain significant experiential, heuristic, and practical ramifications as well.

For Lévi-Strauss, the indeterminate nature of our analogical knowledge of the world is not a transitory condition, one which can be overcome as our scientific knowledge increases, but rather an insurmountable consequence of the gap between the signifier and the signified. This interval between the two, manifested as a kind of excess on the part of the contingent signifier over the objects that are signified is a structural, and thus "permanent condition, a necessary consequence of the redundancy of language over the world, destined to emerge at every new step forward in knowledge."[190] The excess is twofold, for Lévi-Strauss also recognizes an ontological excess of being over all possible existential signification, and this fact which "drives language to create whole series of new signifiers, which, however, due to the combinatory and creative character of language itself, constantly generate new excesses of signifier, in an ongoing and unstoppable circular process."[191] In fact, this led Lévi-Strauss to postulate the notion of an "excess of signifier" or "floating signifier" in order to account for the discontinuity of linguistic processes and the continuity of cognitive processes within all forms of analogical discourse:

> But everywhere else, and still constantly in our societies (and no doubt for a long time to come), a fundamental situation perseveres which arises out of the human condition: namely, that man has from the start had at his disposition a signifier-totality which he is at a loss to know how to allocate to a signified, given as such, but no less unknown for being given. There is always a non-equivalence or "inadequation" between

---

[190] Antonio Caronia, "Floating Signifiers," in *Aksioma* – the Institute for Contemporary Art in Ljubljana, Slovenia: aksioma.org/domestic_standing_ovation/pdf/caronia_floating_sig nifiers.pdf.

[191] Ibid.

the two, a non-fit and overspill which divine understanding alone can soak up; this generates a signifier-surfeit relative to the signifieds to which it can be fitted. So, in man's effort to understand the world, he always disposes of a surplus of signification (which he shares out among things in accordance with the laws of the symbolic thinking which it is the task of ethnologists and linguists to study). That distribution of a supplementary ration–if I can express myself thus–is absolutely necessary to ensure that, in total, the available signifier and the mapped out signified may remain in the relationship of complementarity which is the very condition of the exercise of symbolic thinking.[192]

For humanity there is an overabundant excess of signifiers in relation to the thing signified, and the mind divides and allocates this surplus of signification according to the laws of symbolic thought, so that there may be a complementarity, an equation established between signifier and signified. This is the birth of language: the attempt to analogously relate, categorize, and name the different parts of the cosmos, and this unbridgeable divide between signifier and signified, according to *la pensée sauvage*, is "reabsorbable only for the Divine Understanding." In other words, this inadequation at the very heart of every attempt at an analogous equation between language and things is, paradoxically enough, the necessary condition for the very possibility of signification itself. Without this gap there is no symbolic knowledge, and thus no human knowledge whatsoever, for human thought progresses only discursively, and only through the medium of analogy, primarily through a kind of semiotic *bricolage*. Yet, the system of signification only functions if the there is an ultimate transcendent source of

---

[192] Claude Lévi-Strauss, *Introduction to the Work of Marcel Mauss*, trans. F. Baker (London: Routledge and Kegan Paul Ltd., 1987), pp. 62-63. Cf. Jeffrey Mehlman, "The 'Floating Signifier': From Lévi-Strauss to Lacan," *Yale French Studies* 48, French Freud: Structural Studies in Psychoanalysis (1972), pp. 10-37.

thought wherein this inadequation is resolved and all things are perfectly known and signified, an omniscient "Divine Understanding" that sets the structural parameters for the free play of signifiers in relation to things signified, and thereby creates the possibility of analogicity itself.[193]

This expansion of predicamental analogy into the realm of hinting at a transcendent *analogia entis* bears a striking familiarity to some aspects of the Thomist tradition. Aquinas himself developed his understanding of analogousness beyond the realm of Aristotelian epistemology, since unlike the Greek philosophers, Thomas must account for the relation of the Christian Creator to his creation. For Aquinas, God is not merely the highest or most powerful instance in the order of essence, nor the greatest and most perfect being among other beings, but rather as the transcendent first universal principle of the *actus essendi* (act of existence), to which the created order, which participates in being by dint of its creaturely status, must relate as to the first cause or prime analogate in a transcendental analogy that preserves the ever-greater ontic difference-in-unity between God and created things.[194] This insight was developed by later thinkers, perhaps most forcefully by Erich Przywara, who takes analogicity to have both noetic and ontological applications, so that analogy becomes a singularly rich and inclusive principle that enables us not only to predicamentally relate diverse types of reality in experience to each other, but also indicates that our total apprehension of being and becoming is directed beyond itself, since—as Lévi-Strauss will later point out—our knowledge of objects within the continuum of existence is never complete,

---

[193] Cf. Shalvey, *Claude Lévi-Strauss: Social Psychotherapy and the Collective Unconscious*, pp. 126-134.

[194] Reinhard Hütter, "Attending to the Wisdom of God— From Effect to Cause, from Creation to God: A Contemporary Relecture of the Doctrine of the Analogy of Being according to Thomas Aquinas," in *The Analogy of Being: Wisdom of God or Invention of the Anti-Christ?*, ed. T.J. White, O.P. (Grand Rapids, MI: Wm. B. Eerdmans, 2010), pp. 209-245. See Aquinas, *ST* I, q. 13.

but looks beyond itself to the fullness of reality.[195] The other crucial Thomistic insight which Przywara develops in conjunction with predicamental/transcendental analogy is a profound insight of the real distinction between essence and existence, which he uses in order to describe the metaphysical condition of the human being as created in relation to a Creator who is at once both intimately immanent to the creature yet also utterly transcendent. Indeed, it is the basis for his absolutely central yet somewhat cryptic notion of *Sosein in-über Dasein* (essence in-and-beyond existence), which stipulates that the human person as an actually existent being is not identical with his essence (*essentia*), but only tends continually to become identical to that essence during the course of its existence.

This definition of the human being as in actuality a dynamically developmental becoming derives in part from Aquinas' pivotal observation regarding the fundamental discontinuity between being as such and our particular mode of existence (*esse*). We are never in complete possession of existence itself nor of a total knowledge of being, and the realization of this essential finitude therefore requires a reference outside of essence to a trans-categorical notion of existence, of *esse* as a transcendental. In point of fact then, the relation between essence and existence in the human person is analogical, our human mode of being is itself an *analogia entis*. For Przywara, this means that we exist as an oscillation or suspended tension between two poles of thought and being that remains perennially open to what is beyond itself. Moreover, the creature is also suspended in an analogy

---

[195] Cf. Erich Przywara, *Analogia Entis: Metaphysics: Original Structure and Universal Rhythm*, trans. J. R. Betz and D.B. Hart (Grand Rapids, MI: Wm. B. Eerdmans, 2014). See also Niels C. Nielsen, Jr. "Przywara's Philosophy of the 'Analogia Entis,'" *The Review of Metaphysics* 5: 4 (1952), pp. 599-620; Thomas F. O'Meara, *Erich Przywara, S. J.: His Theology and His World* (Notre Dame, IN: Notre Dame University Press, 2002); John R. Betz, "Beyond the Sublime: The Aesthetics of the Analogy of Being (Part One)," *Modern Theology* 21: 3 (2005), pp. 367–411 and idem "Beyond the Sublime: The Aesthetics of the Analogy of Being (Part Two)," *Modern Theology* 22: 1 (2006), pp. 1–50.

between God as Creator and itself as created, since God is both that which is closer to the creature than anything, even itself, and yet at the same time infinitely distant from created being. In the end, the *analogia entis* is the analogous point, the metaxilogical suspended middle, of these two analogical relations: the intra-creaturely and the divine, not as a *tertium quid*, but as a description of a structure of intersecting rhythms, tensions, and movements at both the noetic and ontic levels of reality.[196] This expansive account of analogicity, of existence as comprised of a plenitude of entities, each of which actively presents itself to other real beings through its own distinctive *esse*, with its own set of characteristic self-manifesting and self-communicating actions, and which in turn receives the actions of other objects upon itself, so that collectively they belong to that almost infinitely interconnected structuring community of actualized things that is the analogically intelligible cosmos, had a lasting influence upon later Thomistically-inspired thinkers such as W. Norris Clarke and Hans Urs von Balthasar.[197] Balthasar's Przywarian analogicity, where the integrity, harmony, and splendor of beauty evinces itself in the very *esse*, or act of being whereby things participate in transcendent being, and in the process reveal the unlimited capacity of things for both self-communication and receptivity, is reflected in significant ways in Lévi-Strauss' structuralist paradigm of existence as an endless expanse of semiotic activity where signifiers and signifiers ceaselessly come together.[198] It is also the creative

---

[196] Cf, Przywara, *Analogia Entis*, pp. 119-124.

[197] For Clarke, see *Person and Being* (Milwaukee: Marquette University Press, 1993), and *The One and the Many: A Contemporary Thomistic Metaphysics* (Notre Dame, IN: University of Notre Dame Press, 2001). The literature on and by Balthasar is too vast to list here, but one possible starting point is Aidan Nichols, *A Key to Balthasar: Hans Urs Von Balthasar on Beauty, Goodness, and Truth* (London: Darton, Longman & Todd, 2011).

[198] Balthasar's aesthetic principles *vis-à-vis* Lafferty are explored in Montejo, "'This Was More Than a Spectacle, More Than an Illusion, It Was a Communicating Instrument,'" pp. 52-73. Based on a comparison of Lévi-Strauss' notion of floating

vision of R.A. Lafferty, who continuously creates analogical *topoi*, which, when they receive sufficient ornamentation, are blessed, and become one of the Holy Lands; and who warns us that we have lost the capacity for holy vision that enables us to see the rich mytho-poetically structured and interconnected patterns of significance in an increasingly meaningless flatland of our own devising (see Fig. 12).

Figure 12. Bricolage as Analogia Entis. Photo © 2016 Andrew Ferguson. Used per CC-BY-4.0 license.

> One of the things that has gone wrong is that you no longer recognize the spirit in things . . . The spirit of the Shaper, of course, is in everything, whether living or unliving, in every person, animal, plant, tree, pond, rock, house, factory. But your minds are not able to

signifiers and the overwhelming prevalence of linguistic structures in his work, Thomas Shalvey unequivocally declares that structuralism "is nothing else than a totally empiricized notion of the *analogia entis* prominent in pre-Cartesian scholasticism, through the Platonic notion of participation, and that, in this interpretation, Lévi-Strauss becomes a strange combination of Comte and Aquinas." *Claude Lévi-Strauss: Social Psychotherapy and the Collective Unconscious,* p. 130.

comprehend this. Once you saw a nymph in everything, every tree, every stream, every stone. At another time you saw an angel in each thing. Now you the lords do not see the spirit in anything at all. You are not holy enough to see the Shaper, not holy enough to see the angel, not even holy enough to see the nymph. Ah, most of you are not holy enough to see the stone.[199]

This work © 2017 Gregorio Montejo

Gregorio Montejo is a professor of Historical Theology at Boston College. His research interests include Thomas Aquinas, Christology, and Trinitarian Theology. Montejo is a member of the Catholic Theological Society of America and the Society of Biblical Literature. Most recently, he gave a presentation on "Re-imagining God's Apophatic Form: Aquinas, De divinis nominibus, and the Pauline Corpus" at Villanova University's Patristic, Medieval, and Renaissance Conference (PMR).

---

[199] R.A. Lafferty, "Animal Fair," in *Through Elegant Eyes: Stories of Austro and the Men Who Know Everything* (Minneapolis: Corroboree Press, 1983), pp. 81-103, at pp. 99-100.

"Here come the religious nuts again," Doctor Dismas said. "I may have to kill one of the fools if they keep coming back."

R. A. Lafferty, "Ginny Wrapped in the Sun"

Illustration © 2016 Anthony Ryan Rhodes

R. A. Lafferty and the Praise of Power

by Jonathan Braschler

Characters of spectacular qualities and abilities are a defining feature of large swaths of SFF. By way of example, Ender Wiggins is smarter than basically everyone else, Rand al'Thor is stronger, and Paul Atreides is a more talented mystic. Reading and writing about exceptional characters is one of the joys of SFF, but it's a risky joy. It can lead us into a trap which we might loosely call "the praise of power." For instance, one may get the sense that the story will vindicate and value our character because of his being the best in whichever activity he excels. Many people live that way, but they live badly. We call them "immature."

Most authors are thoughtful enough to at least partially avoid the trap. To continue with the same examples, Ender Wiggins is smart, but he's too good-natured to be puffed-up about it, and he's more worried about doing the right thing than being at the top of the game. Rand al'Thor is the most powerful, but he doesn't boast about it very much, and people of every ability have something valuable to contribute. Paul Atreides is perhaps the worst of the bunch; in his world everybody is always whispering in impressed and half-worshipful tones about whoever happens to have demonstrated some exceptional power or another, but the author has at least gone so far as to claim that he's attempting to undermine our hero myths, and nobody comes right out and brags about themselves unless the point is to laugh at them.

Every now and then, though, we find somebody who really likes the bragging. If all we knew about R.A. Lafferty was that he was a Christian with a philosophical bent, we might have been surprised to find out that he's one of those writers, since he practiced a religion which had eschewed the praise of temporary qualities so it could mandate the search for more lasting ones. But he really is more of a braggart even than Mr. Herbert. *Arrive at Easterwine* is an especially flagrant piece. Aloysius Shiplap is bragging about being especially bright. Valerie has more, well, I'm not really sure what she has, but she has more of it than any of the rest of them. Her husband is merely average, which is noted whenever he is mentioned. Epikt gives us the old run about humans being dumb and machines being smart. And we don't have time to describe Diogenes Pontifex, Gaetan Balbo, and the rest, who throughout the novel are busy proving or failing to prove their competence or foolishness in a variety of circumstances.

It would be too simple to look at Lafferty's attitude towards all this and call it "parody" or "subversion." Both are present in strength. But Lafferty is having too much fun to fall into merely that kind of thinking. He parodies his subversions and subverts his parodies, then runs them through the loop a few more times in case we still think we have our bearings. Because it's not just fun (and eminently worthwhile) to laugh at the puff-chested fool who imagines, rightly or wrongly, that he's stronger or smarter or a better director than Gaetan Balbo. For all its drawbacks, it's also fun (and eminently worthwhile) to be the puff-chested fool who imagines that he is, and to be a loud-mouth about it. "Whoever humbles himself like a little child..." Anyway, maybe he is only temporarily dumber. Maybe his power is locked away somewhere in the misty past. Maybe he is trailed by a remarkable set of invisible balloons. Maybe stupidity has qualities which we have not yet considered or tested. Hell, this time around he might actually beat the sucker.

This work © 2017 Jonathan Braschler

Jonathan is a factory worker and aspiring writer who lives in Arkansas. He was introduced to Lafferty's books by an insistent friend and has since become one of those insistent friends who's always trying to introduce people to Lafferty's books.

An Incidence of Coincidence
by Russell M. Burden

In his story "The Six Fingers" of Time, R. A. Lafferty expertly describes many occasions of coincidental circumstances especially in the lives of Doctor Mason's patients. It instantly brought to remembrance a time in my own life that left me wondering if a consortium of pit men were really pulling the strings.

In the beginning of the summer of 1998, I found myself at a rock and roll festival in Indianapolis, Indiana which was quite enjoyable. This was the last hurrah with my friends before I left for the rest of the school break. The emcee of the event was a man by the name of Matt. I thought he was a pretty cool guy and throughout the day he and I made light conversation with each other. We talked about this and that; nothing important. I did not mention my trip to him and at the end of the night we said our goodbyes.

The very next day I got on a plane and flew to Poland. My first two weeks were spent in Warsaw, Krakow, Auschwitz, and Poznan. I then found myself in a hostel in Zgierz that had one large open bathroom for all the guests. The shower stalls were nearly see through and the thought of a naked woman seeing me shower was just too much for this Midwest boy to take. It seems funny now as I recollect it but then it was very difficult for me.

I got settled in my room after having all this explained to me by a guy who looked at me like he was thinking, "Ugh, Americans!" I was so tired and hot from the bus ride that my need to feel fresh overrode my need for bodily discretion. I grabbed my towel and toiletries kit and headed towards the bathroom of my dignity's doom.

I noticed that my neighbor had the door open. I glanced in and saw Matt the emcee sitting on the bed. I saw my own flabbergasted expression and wide open eyes mirrored in him. We couldn't believe it. I still can't wrap my head around it but I learned then and there that the world is a small place and coincidences abound.

Russell Burden is a published author from Central Pennsylvania where he lives with his wife, three boys, a cat, and a turtle. His most recent story "Crash Test Dummy" was featured in Sanitarium Magazine Volume 43.

What is The Cranky Old Man From Tulsa Cranky About?

by Andrew Childress

We find it appropriate that a collection of R.A. Lafferty's non-fiction should be titled "Cranky Old Man From Tulsa." It's amusing, and it rings true. But why does it ring true? What is he cranky about? What's his problem, anyway? In all his philosophical fiction one senses a profound dissatisfaction with the world, whatever world it is, even the brightest and most developed of worlds, whether the Golden Astrobe of Past Master or the planned society of "The World as Will and Wallpaper." Yes, something is rotten in the state of Golden Astrobe, and in all other Lafferty worlds. What is it? Is it the triumph of neoliberalism? Capitalism run amuck? Or is it the foul stench of Communism? Have European intellectuals polluted society and destroyed decency?

No, no, no, and no. I want to suggest that Lafferty's attitudes might be better understood when we see that he can never be situated anywhere on the spectrum of our common political imagination in the American 21st century. In our common representation of political and intellectual positions there is a spectrum, far left to far right, and on each end die-hard ideologues caricaturize each other as The Bad Guys. Each end of the spectrum sets up a Manichaean universe where, like in *Star Wars*, we have the plucky Rebels versus the Evil Empire, a clearly defined arena with clearly defined bad guys and good guys. But Lafferty is neither right-wing nor left-wing, although he borrows some bugbears from each side. Like his Catholic compatriot Chesterton, his stance on matters political will never line up with that of any party in power; he violates shibboleths on both ends of the spectrum.

In America, the ideological right is nostalgic for the Reagan era and Soviet Russia because it's convenient to have a clearly evil left-wing figure, while the ideological left is nostalgic for the Roosevelt era and Nazi Germany because it's convenient to have a clearly evil right-wing figure. We are more comfortable when we can squint our eyes and fit the real world into the *Star Wars* schema of Rebels versus Evil Empire. Lafferty refuses this comfort, though. As Solzhenitsyn would have it, "the line dividing good and evil cuts through the heart of every human being. And who is willing to destroy a piece of his own heart?" Maybe Lafferty is. His dissatisfaction with the state of things is not subordinate to any political program to improve things. Lafferty identifies the object of resistance as a complex, not a unified entity, and as a spiritual reality, not a political party. Our political dualism is a system with right and left in which each side is opposed to the other and at times "resists" it; Lafferty represents an older dualism in which good and evil are opposed throughout the universe, mixed together everywhere and in constant opposition to one another. In his human characters and in their institutions, good and evil are marbled together; no man is pure.

So, what is he so cranky about? A world gone wrong, scattered and broken, as in Judy Thatcher's Epistle from "And Walk Now Gently Through The Fire." And a prevailing willful blindness to the wrongness, folks using the wrong brand of light, as in "The Emperor's Shoestrings." And yet, we can't help but notice the radiant joy in his fiction. Why is he so happy? Because he knows he is one of the many who has been wrangled "a second and better doom"; who has been blessed to be able to inhabit the scattered and broken world and "Rebuild, restructure, reinstitute, renew."

This work © 2017 Andrew Childress

Andrew Childress is working on a Master's degree in Information Studies and works at a company that makes machines to make machines. Before discovering Lafferty, he had the good fortune to be prepared for Lafferty by Jacques Maritain and Étienne Gilson, among others. He has spent most of the last four years between Arkansas, Texas, Belfast, and Palestine, and is now living happily in Austin with his wife.

Baby Talk
by Martin Heavisides

"A ridicule deferred is a ridicule lost forever."
  R.A. Lafferty

Last fall, a Toronto lawyer who works at one of the city's bigger firms asked for two weeks of paternity leave so he could help his wife settle into a routine with their newborn daughter. For that, he was mocked endlessly.

"So," his male colleagues would say, eyebrows cocked, "paternity leave, huh?"

"This tone suggested no true lawyer would ever do anything so sissified.

"It drove me nuts," says the lawyer, who asked not to be identified."

—Dave McGinn, *Nat Post*, Oct 16 '07

What follows is a balanced journalistic account of this issue as it works itself out in the contemporary marketplace. You know the drill: follow this example with one from a friendlier work environment, wing in a few more anecdotes and then bring on the sociological observation on how things are changing in the workplace and how further change might be managed. Give me the basic data and I could produce a dozen of these a day, so long as I could repress a constant urge to giggle. (Humour is strictly frowned upon in this sort of think piece, though a think piece without humour is like a rainstorm without water IMHO: it lacks a little something.)

It doesn't seem to have occurred to the lawyer—trapped in this anecdote like a fly in amber—that he had at least two responses available to him. The first was to maintain a dignified silence, firm in his own principles. In practice that seems to be out, since he was actually so infirm in his principles that this teasing "drove him nuts" as it would have on the school playground when he was three. In which case what he needs is a quiverful of barbed responses.

He could ask those teasing employees to tell him—quick, off the top of their heads—the names and ages of their children? What milestones in their children's development were they present for and which did they miss? First word, first step, little league, first school performance, first run-in with the law? Right, you were sort of obliged to take notice of that since parents, who on earth knows why, are held somewhat responsible in those cases if their children are not yet of age. Even if, as in your case, involvement was so minimal you could hardly have done or said anything to set them so seriously off on a wrong path. Your part of the joint enterprise was completed by your part in making them. And what's kept you a stranger to your children all these years? Ah right, all those thousands of extra billing hours in Millstadt v. Hagler, which has been in litigation more years than you can count on the fingers of both hands and is unlikely to be resolved in as many more. One or two colleagues whose hobby is literature have taken to calling it Jarndyce and Jarndyce and won't tell you why. Drives you nuts.

Certainly there's nothing the least bit sissy about a man all growed up whose life's work is resolving (or resolutely leaving unresolved) the endless hissy fits of corporations. Civilizations have been known to totter and fall over less. But do you never feel you've given over a little more of your heart and soul than—oh now please! the office is no place for that kind of blubbering.

Martin Heavisides is a contributing editor to Linnet's Wings *(most recently introducing a handpicked selection from the poetry of William Blake) and author of a novel,* Undermind. *One of his seven full-length plays,* Empty Bowl, *was given a live reading by The Living Theatre in New York and published in* Linnet's Wings *(Summer 2008).* Mad Hatter's Review, Gambara, *Cella's Round Trip,* Journal of Compressed Creativity, *and* FRIGG *are also among the sane and sensible journals that have accepted his work.* http://theevitable.blogspot.com http://movingpicturewrites.com

Ouch, My Foot!
by Kevin Cheek

From the department of shooting myself in the foot: Sharing my dimwitted approach to finding great deals on Lafferty books.

Over the last several years, I've been collecting a respectable number of Lafferty books. I blogged about it on Yet Another Lafferty Blog back in August of 2013, and since then I've added *Archipelago, Dotty, Episodes of the Argo, Four Stories, Grasshoppers & Wild Honey* - Chapters 1 & 2, *Half a Sky, Heart of Stone, Dear and Other Stories, How Many Miles to Babylon, Iron Tears, Lafferty in Orbit, Mischief Malicious (And Murder Most Strange), Snake in His Bosom and Other Stories, Tales of Chicago, The Back Door of History, The Early Lafferty, The Man Who Made Models, The Man With the Aura,* and most recently *The Man Underneath.*

I'm still lacking *Tales of Midnight, Argo, The Elliptical Grave, The Early Lafferty II,* and a couple of others. Can't find those for love or money, but I'll keep looking.

The method I've used to find these has been brain-dead simple: Every few weeks or so, I waste some time going through Biblio.com, Half.com, Amazon.com, eBay, AbeBooks, etc. searching for Lafferty books and sorting by lowest price first. Over the last 4 years, I've found some really great deals, like a copy of *Archipelago* for $28 (sorry, bad form to brag, but it's been almost two years and I'm still grinning over that one). It takes time, but once in a blue moon (or maybe less often) someone is letting go of some Lafferty at reasonable prices.

In addition, I've wound up in correspondence with some really great people who happen to be selling Lafferty books. For example, the man who sells books from an Amazon storefront called U-B-I-K is a tremendous fan of both Philip K. Dick and Lafferty, and he can speak brilliantly and at length about the writers. For example, he and I had a long email conversation comparing Lafferty's *Past Master* to Le Guin's

The Dispossessed. His comment is that they both got the message across in the end, but Lafferty has a whole lot more fun getting there. Another example would be the man who sold me a copy of *Dotty* at barely over cover price. He knew Ray Lafferty in Tulsa and received a box of books when Lafferty moved to the nursing home at Broken Arrow.

I realize that the more people who are searching like this, the more quickly the deals will disappear (hence my title). I think I am already seeing evidence of this—at least I am seeing those ridiculous deals appear less often—haven't seen one in almost a year. Still, I don't think the really great prices are driven by market forces so much as by individual sellers' ideas of what a fair price should be, market be damned.

Yes, I want to stumble on these deals myself, but more than that, I want as many people as possible to read Lafferty, Therefore, I recommend you do an obsessively comprehensive search at least once a month. It's rare, but occasionally the heavens open and drop into your lap the Lafferty book you need at a price you can afford.

This work © 2017 Kevin Cheek.

Kevin is a technical writer by trade and a Lafferty fan by nature. He edits Feast of Laughter *in his spare time and desperately wants you to read more Lafferty!*

Forked Lightning: Two Micro-essays
by Bill Rogers

On Re-reading Lafferty

So far, each Lafferty novel or story that I have picked up, I have read at least twice from beginning to end, with the exception of *Okla Hannali* which I reread in layers and waves which, taken together, probably compressed into about four readings. I haven't reread *Arrive At Easterwine* yet but am eager to do so because I know what normally happens on a Lafferty reread. The first read through is a barrage, an introduction to a visual vocabulary, the flourish of a peacock's tail prior to and apart from initial recognition of the bird. Here are the lab coats gathered around the core samples. Here are the elements and motion. Here the questions. Here the esoteric lists. Here the cast of characters, that quirky roll call. Once these elements are established in the reader's awareness the second read through is the string you pull that transforms the disparate geometry of a child's toy into the honest forms of say a duck or a bear, or the button you push that causes the shiny tin Christmas tree to open up its sides and reveal the spinning plastic Santa inside.

Shards

If there was ever a template for understanding Lafferty's stories I feel that he has shattered it and scattered it throughout all of them. Whether he intended it or not I believe he has left us a trail of shards that in sublime moments can profoundly reveal themselves to an unguarded reader. I believe that all of these flakings-off of his own Rosetta Stone vibrate at such a low frequency as to preserve the tensions in the stories they occupy. I feel the shards exist almost like secret hearts, hidden centers of the tales they occupy. I'm not even quite sure they can be separated from them. And I believe that, thanks to the internet archive of IF, I may have found such a shard in "Boomer Flats:"

> There is, however, a gap in the Magi set, due to the foolish dying of Arpad Arkabaranan. It is not of Scripture that a set of Magi should consist of only three. There have been sets of seven and nine and eleven. It is almost of Scripture, though, that a set should not consist of less than three. In the Masulla Apocalypse it seems to be said that a set must contain at the least a Comet, a Commoner and a Catfish. The meaning of this is pretty muddy, and it may be a mistranslation.

Bill Rogers, aka Giveawayboy, spends most of his time drawing and painting solo works or collaborating with his art partner in crime Revansj. The bulk of his days are steeped in tall tales, dreams and mythology. When he is not creating new drawings or paintings or writing poetry, he walks about in the barely known and re-enchanted landscape of Tampa Bay. Bill's first encounter with Lafferty's work was Annals Of Klepsis.

Twitterview with Michael Swanwick
by Stephen R. Case

This interview spontaneously generated on Twitter on January 21, 2016, prompted by the review of *The Best of Michael Swanwick* I wrote for my blog. In particular, I think his responses about his Catholicism and where to find other writings like Lafferty are interesting.

Stephen Case: Michael Swanwick is a hero [here is a review of his *Best of...* collection]: stephenrcase.wordpress.com/2016/01/21/the-best-of-michael-swanwick/

Michael Swanwick: There is a great deal in here for me to think about.

Stephen Case: Did I get anything right?

Michael Swanwick: You got a great deal right. "St Janis," e.g., was written immediately after reading "American Nights."

Stephen Case: Alright, what about "A Midwinter's Tale"? Am I right to hear the echoes of PEACE & FIFTH HEAD?

Michael Swanwick: Yes, in part. But more so Marc Chagall.

Stephen Case: Lovely. Two more questions if you don't mind. Still Catholic?

Michael Swanwick: there is no such thing as a former Catholic.

Stephen Case: Are you Catholic like Lafferty, Wolfe, Chesterton are/were? Meaningful question?

Michael Swanwick: Yes and no. Incidentally, there is a lay effort to make Chesterton a saint.

Stephen Case: And: what I find in you, Lafferty, Wolfe, and Gaiman (a bit), and what I try to create in my own work—where else can I find it?

Michael Swanwick: Too large a question. It's everywhere.

Stephen Case: Tautology! "Where can I find other expressions of bigness & reality of the world?" "Everywhere." But in excellent prose?

Michael Swanwick: Dear God, this is a golden age for prose. Okay, I'll give you one: Germaine Greer.

Stephen Case gets paid for teaching people about space, which is pretty much the coolest thing ever. He also occasionally gets paid for writing stories about space (and other things), which have appeared in Beneath Ceaseless Skies, Daily Science Fiction, Orson Scott Card's Intergalactic Medicine Show (forthcoming), and several other publications. His novel series First Fleet, *is available through Amazon. Stephen has a PhD in the history and philosophy of science from the University of Notre Dame and will talk for inordinate amounts of time about nineteenth-century British astronomy. He lives with his wife, four children, and three chickens in an undisclosed suburb of Chicago that has not yet legalized backyard chickens.*

Report from LaffCon1
by John Owen

> "Certainly dead men cast shadows. That's what history is about." -R.A. Lafferty

> "...all writers should be funny-looking and all stories should be funny." -R.A. Lafferty

LaffCon1 is over. We are grateful that so many people showed up and that so many people expressed so much joy. Thank you all for playing with us in the enormous shadow of Ray Lafferty.

Intelligent conversation does not need to be dull. I think that we were mostly successful in keeping things funny throughout the day. I know that we were mostly funny-looking, at least as evidenced in our group photo.

There has been a demand for the booklets. These booklets were made as thank you gifts for those who supported the con by being there. But there are many of you who could not be there for many good reasons. You have asked for the booklet. They are available now to be purchased at cost. As ever in Ktistec Press endeavors, we make no money on this. We have invested much and only hope for a return in many Lafferty fans continuing the conversation.

The booklet is still intimately tied to the con. It does not make sense apart from the con. Yet it can still be enjoyed as is. Specifically, the full color illustrations by Lissanne, Anthony, and Gregorio can be found in print nowhere else.

Look for it. Find it. Buy it. Search Amazon.com for *LaffCon1*.

What I ask is that, if you buy this booklet, you also buy a couple more titles by those talented individuals who have freely contributed to the booklet...

- *Chasing the Pheonix* by Michael Swanwick
- *Not So Much, Said the Cat* by Michael Swanwick
- *Speaking of the Fantastic II* by Darrel Schweitzer
- *Schweitzer MegaPack*

If you need a distraction from your concentrated Lafferty reading, these are the distractions for you.

#

We also have some audio!

There may be more eventually; Right now, we definitely have some good audio from the "Lafferty Studies" panel at LaffCon1. Search the LaffCon.org website for a link.

More than anything, all of us involved in "Lafferty Studies" hope for more and more participation. If you are reading Lafferty thoughtfully, we want your contributions.

Please, please, please. Continue reading Lafferty. Please, please, please. Write about Lafferty. And when you do, send those written submissions to *Feast of Laughter*.

Or, even better, start your own Lafferty journal. Shut us down completely.

We welcome any and all complementary and competitive research. All that we care about is that R.A. Lafferty's work is preserved and understood and brought forward into the future.

There is still much work to be done.

- Monday, June 6, 2016

John Owen comes home each evening to the golden cliché: the u.n.d; the p.h.; and l. and u.w.; and the e.c. (eight more would have been too many). Just to live is a happy riot. He is well known in the future for having created LaffCon, our universally acknowledged benevolent Galactic Governing Body (blessed be the conventioneers). On all of the planets, his name has become a byword for any grand success achieved based on wild enthusiasm coupled with poor planning and lack of any applicable skill set. John blogs infrequently about R.A. Lafferty at failingevenbetter.blogspot.com

Portrait of LaffCon1 as the Cranky Old Men from Tulsa

R. A. Lafferty and the New Wave
by Michael Swanwick

Laffcon1 was held in the Mercer County Library in Lawrenceville, New Jersey, on Saturday. Something like forty people attended, almost all of them exceptionally knowledgeable on the subject of the life and works of R. A. Lafferty.

It's hard to say what was the best part of the day. Possibly the presentation (by Gregorio Montejo, I think; my notes are a mess) on "Lafferty and the Visual Arts," which, on the strength of a single closet door, all that survives of Lafferty's collage art, made the case for Lafferty as an outsider artist. (Albeit not your usual outsider artist.) Or maybe Andrew Mass's early selection from the documentary movie he's making about Lafferty. It was heartening to see how much was being done to preserve the memory of the man and his works, and how high the quality of the work was.

The chief item I was on was a panel on "Lafferty and the New Wave." We didn't settle the question of exactly what Ray's relationship with the New Wave was then. But on reflection, I decided that it was relatively — for Lafferty, anyway — straightforward.

Ray definitely didn't identify himself with the New Wave and disliked most of the work published under that heading. But most of his readership did identify him with it. So how did an extremely religious autodidact and self-characterized grumpy old man (I should mention that everybody who met him thought he was very sweet) find himself in that position?

Context is all. The New Wave coincided roughly with what we like to call "the Sixties," a period which, confusingly enough, began midway through the decade and extended well into the Seventies. There was, among the young, a widespread rejection of old values, old ideas, and old ways of doing things. People were looking for new ideas, new ways of seeing things, new ways of doing things. A lot of what the New Wave writers were up to was trying to provide exactly those. And also new ways of telling stories.

Well, it turns out that new ideas and new ways of telling stories are pretty rare. But Lafferty had both. So the seekers found him. And even after he carefully and repeatedly explained that not only was he not a member of the Counterculture (as it was then called) but thought its very existence was evil, they continued to revere him.

Because he was the real thing. We were all looking for visions and he was a visionary. That was, and is, far more important than whether he had the same politics as his readers.

This work © 2016 Michael Swanwick

Michael Swanwick is the multiple-award-winning author of such books as Stations of the Tide, Gravity's Angels, *and* The Iron Dragon's Daughter. *He has been a Lafferty admirer, fan, and supporter for longer than many of his readers have been alive. He was the guest of honor at the first LaffCon this June, and has graciously allowed us to reprint his report on the event. His newest collection,* Not So Much, Said the Cat, *is just out from Tachyon Publications.*

Viva Lafferty!
by Rich Persaud

Playing cops and robbers we do not have time for. We are running a little magazine in the Quarter of New Orleans with the simple aim of restoring the world. That is all we can do. The other things we cannot do. If we restore the world, then the other things will already be done.

We will have no more cryptic extracts from the classified files. We will not look for taints on anyone just because he happens to be a snake or a devil. We will not mistake the mask for the face. This red caricature is not the face of the thing; it is only one of its masks, not the most important one, not the most dangerous one.

We will work for the Church in the dismembered World, and we will restore the World. That is the way it will be. —R.A. Lafferty, *Archipelago*, 1979

"If a thing is worth doing, it is worth doing badly." —G.K. Chesterton, *What's Wrong With The World*, 1910

In 2016 A.D., humans have seen touch screens respond in milliseconds, web pages display within one second, binge-beckoning-video stream on demand, electronic books download in seconds, cars arrive in mappable minutes and text messages ricochet for hours, yet the World responds to acts of creation with glacial indifference.

To attend an R.A. Lafferty conference is to leave behind responsive simulacra, to travel slower than light, to commit your physical presence and meld with consciousness drawn to literature beyond category. At the spark of aura, emotional voice and facial expression, Worlds touch and twirl among the words of a master. Responsive distractions fade under the light of creation.

After decades of discovery in used bookstores, Lafferty's words are increasingly available in print and electronic media. If easier to acquire, Lafferty's stories are no easier to grasp. What moves fans to delve beyond his words? Will new readers seek pilgrimages of initiation in place of used bookstores? Can Lafferty's slow-food stories compete with sub-second simulacra?

Although sales rarely matched Lafferty's commitment to his Worlds, he steadily immortalized his vision into a tapestry of stories, replete with arrival and departure points for all. What motivated Lafferty to write two hundred short stories and thirty-two novels, while he was understood by so few? Why does any human seek to restore Worlds that are decades beyond their zenith?

I was moved to preserve Lafferty's words by their coherence within and beyond my grasp. Lafferty's body of work felt alive and mysterious and true. Though I understood only portions, they opened previously invisible doors. His work was not an end, but a reminder of what might still be possible. If humans saw that once, I may see it yet, then seek beyond.

For centuries preceding 1969, Catholic churches celebrated the Latin Mass[1], until the Vatican II council[2]. Lafferty was not supportive of the change: "I am a Roman Catholic of what is considered an old-fashioned sort."[3] In an unpublished novel, Lafferty's characters, "... formed the 'Let-It-Alone-Dammit-Society'. They would try to prevent the

---

[1]   Wikipedia, "Tridentine Mass," https://en.wikipedia.org /wiki/Tridentine_Mass

[2]   Wikipedia, "Objections to the Second Vatican Council," https://en.wikipedia.org/wiki/Second_Vatican_Council #Objections_to_the_council

[3]   R.J. Whitaker, "Maybe They Needed Killing & The Importance of Happiness," in *Cranky Old Man from Tulsa: Interviews with R.A. Lafferty* (Weston, Ontario: United Mythologies Press, 1990). This interview is also reprinted in the current issue of *Feast of Laughter*.

dismantlers from dismantling the Church and the World."[4]

In Laffertian time where wisdom is proven over centuries, decades are stepping stones to restore Worlds. Operating in New York City since 1866[5], the Church of the Holy Innocents began providing daily Latin Mass in 2009, four decades after Vatican II. In 2016, Manhattan's St. Patrick's Cathedral offered its first Latin Mass in two decades[6]. Rev. Fr. Donald Kloster wrote:

> The Traditional Latin Mass (1962 Missal) is a venerable Mass with a 1650 year heritage dating back to the reign of Pope Damascus in the 4th century. The Latin language reverses the punishment of the Tower of Babel, giving the Catholic Church a true universal bond that transcends language barriers.[7]

Outside the literary world, three decades after the 1985 introduction of a computer designed for creativity, the 2016 documentary film *Viva Amiga* was released:

> From the creation of the world's first multimedia digital art powerhouse, to a bankrupt shell sold and resold into obscurity, to a post-punk spark revitalized by determined fans. *Viva Amiga* is a look at a digital dream and the freaks, geeks and geniuses who brought

[4] R.A. Lafferty, *Deep Scars of Thunder*, unpublished, https://hieronymopolis.wordpress.com/2012/12/13/r-a-laffertys-parable-on-the-conciliar-revolution-from-his-unpublished-manuscript-deep-scars-of-thunder/

[5] Church of the Holy Innocents, "History," https://shrineofholyinnocents.org/about/

[6] Archdiocese of New York, "Traditional Pilgrimage & Latin Mass at St. Patrick's Cathedral, Nov 14, 2016," https://archny.org/events/traditional-pilgrimage-latin-mass-at-st-patrickapos-s-cathedral

[7] Church of the Holy Innocents, "Latin Mass" (video), https://shrineofholyinnocents.org/latinmass/

it to life. And the Amiga is still alive.[8]

The Amiga is one of many fallen visions of computer Worlds. Those who lived those visions can be proud of modern computers, yet disappointed in today's distance from their glimpses of the sublime. They can see that more was possible, no matter what this World has since chosen. They can restore and nurture their glimpses, then seek beyond.

For nearly three decades, the independent Les Amis Café (1970-1997) operated a block from the University of Texas in Austin, before being replaced by Starbucks. In 2005, the documentary film *Viva Les Amis* was released:

> *Viva Les Amis* looks at one local café as an example of a national trend: The loss of the mom and pop shop ... During the 1970's, a counterculture of hippies, musicians, mimes, and protesters flocked to the café. In the 1980's, punk rock dominated the landscape ... Viva Les Amis explores how a local place contributes to the culture and identity of a city ...[9]

These remembrances of tradition are not contests with modernity. They are quests to root modernity on proven foundations, so we can have confidence in the structures from which we reach for more. To remember the greatness of what has come before, is to hold modernity to the highest standards of possible Worlds, to restore and extend all of our glimpses into the sublime.

Viva Latin Mass! *Viva Amiga*! *Viva Les Amis*! *Viva Lafferty*!

P.S. Lafferty fans are invited to make a pilgrimage of discovery on June 10, 2017 to the Mercer County Library in Lawrenceville, New Jersey, U.S.A, for the world's second R.A. Lafferty conference. You may leave with more questions than

---

[8] Viva Amiga, 2016, https://amigafilm.com

[9] Viva Les Amis, 2005, http://www.vivalesamis.com/synopsis .aspx

answers, but you will know that everyone in attendance has found an element of Lafferty's work worthy of restoration. For more information, visit http://laffcon.org

Holy Innocents, NYC Photo© 2017 Rich Persaud CC-BY-4.0

This work © 2017 Rich Persaud
Rich Persaud created www.ralafferty.org to introduce new readers to Lafferty's works. He encourages Lafferty fans to explore the multiple worlds and TIMELINES of the 2009 TV series Fringe. *He thanks* Feast of Laughter *contributors and S. for literary inspiration.*

LaffCon Memory
by Alan Reid

Delaware and Raritan Canal State Park
Photograph © 2016 Alan Reid

A Laffcon1 personal episode: One of the first Lafferty stories mentioned that day, as part of a "first story read" thread, was "Narrow Valley." Well I read "Narrow Valley" first at age thirteen or so. I also did lots of camping and hiking at that age, in a seemingly lost pastoral New Jersey.

Now only a few hundred feet away across highway US 1 from the meeting rooms of Laffcon, is the Delaware and Raritan Canal State Park. Forty four miles long, 500 feet wide, it crosses New Jersey unseen. I walked and canoed the whole thing a few times as a kid, before it became a park. Kids were wilder then. But that day, I had not been to the canal in forty years or more. So while at the conference, I skipped the free lunch. I walked across the highway, north to Carnegie Street, and stepped onto the towpath of the canal.

I was in my narrow valley, bucolic and superficially the same as my memory. I watched the water flow. I ate Honeysuckle flowers. Eventually I noticed the progression and invasive species in the undergrowth lining the towpath, but the shamanist aspect was unchanged. I was in a magic place, at least for me. I walked a couple miles then hoofed it back to the conference.

So this is part of what I think Lafferty was writing about in that particular story. I showed partner Lissanne the canal later in the day. She loves it, but as a new thing, not a kid's secret garden.

Born at about the time transistors were invented. Alan is a compulsive bibliophile and autodidact from New Jersey. He works nights and prefers home cooked meals.

I rolled a three. Dead man Captain John said that he had a seven. I put a dollar bill in his bony hand when it came up. I shivered when I touched its bones. I was never meant to play games with a dead man.

R. A. Lafferty, "Gray Ghost: A Reminiscence"

Illustration © 2016 Anthony Ryan Rhodes

New Dimensions: R.A. Lafferty Introductions
by Robert Silverberg

[*New Dimensions* was an anthology of original speculative fiction edited by Robert Silverberg from 1971 to 1981. When it first appeared, there were a number of other SF anthology series on the market, among them *Orbit*, *Infinity*, *QUARK/*, and *Universe*, but it outlived most of these other titles. Silverberg introduced a number of new authors in *New Dimensions*, and the series became known for its promotion of experimental speculative fiction of the highest caliber, including the work of R.A. Lafferty.]

Raphael Aloysius Lafferty is very much a law unto himself, sitting out there in Oklahoma and writing the damnedest stories, stories that a practiced hand can spot as Lafferty products by reading no more than five words. He soars, he cavorts, he leaps and prances, while at no time do his fingers leave the keyboard of his typewriter. And as a result we get novels like *Past Master* and *Fourth Mansions,* and short stories such as this one, which extrapolates the current craze for consciousness-expanding chemistry into a characteristically unique Laffertyesque extravaganza.

Introduction to "Sky," *New Dimensions 1* (1971)

This is a story about a schlemiel, to use a word probably not too often heard in Raphael Aloysius Lafferty's home town of Tulsa, Oklahoma. The schlemiel story is a genre I always thought I'd avoid if I were an editor, for it has seemed to me that stories about losers, twerps, dullards, and schnooks would be of interest only to an audience of losers, twerps, dullards, and schnooks, at best, and no such people would be reading anything I edited. Well, never mind all that R. A. Lafferty is a cunning and tricky writer, and—as can quickly be seen—the schlemiel he creates for us here is of an extraordinary sort.

Introduction to "Eurema's Dam," *New Dimensions II* (1972)

The luminiferous Lafferty, a writer who charts his course without reference to the familiar constellations of the skies known to you and me, bubbles forth once more, doing his own extraordinary thing. Editorial comment seems superfluous: enter his universe if you can, and good luck to you there.

Introduction to "Days of Grass, Days of Straw," *New Dimensions III* (1973)

Lafferty? Lafferty? He's that Oklahoma troll who's been bamboozling us for years with his indescribable and impossible stories. (Who but Lafferty would write a story whose main characters are a ghost, a sawdust-filled doll, and an Australopithecus?) His work has been published all over the lot, though he's best known outside the science-fiction world for his powerful novel of the American Indians, *Okla Hannali*. An issue of *New Dimensions* wouldn't be complete without him.

Introduction to "Animal Fair," *New Dimensions IV* (1974)

R. A. Lafferty had a story ("Sky") in the first *New Dimensions*, another ("Eurema's Dam") in the second, one more ("Days of Grass, Days of Straw") in the third, and I think several more farther along the way. All of them are lovely idiosyncratic pixyish fables, sinewy and lilting, and since I had arbitrarily chosen to include only one story by each author in this collection, I picked "Eurema's Dam" above the other Laffertys at my disposal mainly because it had won a Hugo (in 1973, at Toronto). I am not all that awed by stories that win awards, nor all that scornful of those that don't—among those that didn't win in 1973, though they were on the final ballot, were Russ' "When It Changed," which I had rejected, and Silverberg's "When We Went to See the End of the World," which I had written—but Lafferty's feat of winning a Hugo for "Eurema's Dam" deserves some commemoration. Virtually all Hugo-winning stories are first published in science-fiction magazines or in paperback anthologies, cheap and easily available to a wide segment of the electorate. But *New Dimensions II* had appeared only in an expensive hardcover edition that had sold perhaps 6000 copies. (The paperback reprint did not emerge until long after the awards had been handed out.) How, given that handicap, Lafferty's story had ever reached enough people to get the required number of votes, I have no idea. Yet it won, just beating out my own story. I will not pretend that I would not have preferred it the other way around; but I was undilutedly delighted that so fine and special a writer as Lafferty had carried off his first trophy with a story I had published.

Introduction to "Eurema's Dam," *The Best of New Dimensions* (1979)

This work © 2017 Robert Silverberg

Robert Silverberg is one of the most prolific authors in Science Fiction, with more than one hundred works of fiction, as well as more than seventy SF anthologies edited or co-edited by him. Among his most notable books are the novels Thorns, To

Live Again, Tower of Glass, Son of Man, *the Nebula award winning* A Time of Changes, The World Inside, The Book of Skulls, Dying Inside, The Stochastic Man, Shadrach in the Furnace, Lord Valentine's Castle, Star of Gypsies, *and* Roma Eterna. *Several pieces of Silverberg's short fiction, including "Hawksbill Station," "Passengers," "Good News from the Vatican," "Born with the Dead," "Sailing to Byzantium," and "Gilgamesh in the Outback," have also won Nebulas. The Science Fiction and Fantasy Writers of America made him its 21st SFWA Grand Master in 2004.*

Scribbling Giant: An Introduction to R. A. Lafferty and *East of Laughter*
by Gene Wolfe

[This essay was originally published with the title "Scribbling Giant" as an afterword to Lafferty's novel *East of Laughter* (Bath, UK: Morrigan Publications, 1988), pp. 177-191; and subsequently reprinted, with a few small additions, as "An Introduction to R. A. Lafferty and *East of Laughter*" in the journal *Quantum: Science Fiction & Fantasy Review* 36 (Spring, 1990), pp. 10-13.]

The great temptations are to compare Lafferty to David Lindsay and Jorge Luis Borges; I name them temptations because there is so much more to Lafferty than that. So let me begin by saying that he is undoubtedly a creature of genius in the only true and original meanings of those words. (Lafferty is not, of course, himself a genius in the decadent modern sense—an infant savant of thirty or fifty, like the German genius of whom I recently read who desires to subject himself to a surgical procedure to have his indeterminable intelligence reduced. He is far too wise for that.)

A genius—the real thing—is a monopresent spirit, that is to say, a spirit capable of animating only one person, place, or thing at the same instant; it is this genius that supplies its fortunate possessor with those distinguishing peculiarities of insight, knowledge, and—as it were—style. And though it may survive him, he cannot long survive it. To quote the excellent John Cuthbert Lawson, of Pembroke: "One word of caution only is required before we proceed to the consideration of the various species of genii not yet described. It must not be assumed that all genii, on the analogy of the tree-nymphs, die along with the dissolution of their dwelling-places; the existence of the genius and that of the haunted object are indeed always closely and intimately united, but not necessarily in such a manner as to preclude the migration of the genius on the dissolution of the first abode into a second. The converse proposition however, that any object could enjoy prolonged existence after the departure of the indwelling power, may be considered improbable.

"The genii with whom I now propose to deal fall into five main divisions according to their habitation. These are first buildings, secondly water, thirdly mountains, caves, and desert places, fourthly the air, and fifthly human beings."

Socrates, as we know, had such a spirit, which he called his daemon; its place was with him, but though he left this world long ago, his spirit is not yet wholly dead. He was a man of genius, and so is Lafferty.

Thus it will come as no surprise to you to be told that he is unrecognized, except by you, Les Escott, Chris Drumm, me, and several thousand other people. And it will do none of us any good at all—as it will certainly do Lafferty none—to rush about in the corridors of power shouting, "There is a cranky old man in Oklahoma who is possessed of a tutelary spirit! He is surely the greatest man in the world, possibly the greatest man in the entire United States, and conceivably the greatest man in Oklahoma!" I have tried it, and it does not work; the sole good thing that happened as a result of it was that an unfledged (now there's a significant expression, though you will not know it as such, having not yet begun *East of Laughter*) girl editor had me to lunch to talk about a miserably bad book she had just bought from an unbearably attractive blonde. I was able to hornswoggle her into sending me a xerox of the manuscript, and thus I became at no cost the possessor of about ten pounds of first-rate white paper, blank on the better side. Some benefit from that may yet appear—though not, I fear to Lafferty, and certainly not to the blonde.

He is of course an Irishman. I have assumed all along that you knew it, because it is the one thing the general reader (you probably thought yourself no more than a colonel; but it is in my power to promote you, General, and I have just done so) does know about him. Pedants, to be sure, insist that he cannot be an Irishman because he was, as the popular song has it, Born in America—and he lives in Tulsa. In this case as in so many others it is the popular feeling that is correct; and indeed there is nothing more characteristic of the true Irishman, and particularly the Irish writer of genius, than that he does not live in Ireland. See for example Lord Dunsany, George Bernard Shaw, James Joyce, and many others.

Lafferty is also an American, just as Mr. Dooley was, and there is no contradiction there. Saint Brandon (of whom you have just read) discovered America long before Columbus, as did an entire collection of miscellaneous Vikings and Phoenicians, Chinese, Japanese, Portuguese fishermen, and a baseball team from Cleveland; thus it is quite allowable to be both American and Irish—or a resident of Minnesota, for that matter.

There is a Lafferty story that should be better known than it is, however. I don't mean a short story, of course—*all* of those should be much better known than they are, and if I were to begin making a list of favorites I would use up most of the space allotted to me and drive you crazy, since you would then have to shake down all the book dealers of the world to find them. No, I mean a story about Lafferty himself, a story I am assured is true. It is simply that at twenty he was told by a writing teacher that he should not write until he was at least twenty years older.

And he believed this person, quit, and returned to writing at forty. Few of us follow our teachers' instructions quite so literally as that—and to be frank, I think that there are very few teachers whose instructions deserve it. Possibly it was literal-mindedness that got Lafferty his genius in the first place. The kind of people who pontificate about writers are awfully fond of saying that all the good ones have some sort of kink, something about their thinking—right or wrong—that takes an odd and unexpected turn. But it seems to me that the truth lies nearer the opposite pole, that all or at least most great writer possess a directness, a habit of looking certain things straight in the face, that seems oddly angled to the rest of us only because we are so accustomed to peering at life and love, death and much else out of the corners of our eyes.

For example, let's take the young, handsome, fair, smiling, incredibly urbane, bright of feature and open of soul young man covered with blood who is discovered in Roderick Outreach's room immediately after Roderick's murder.

Oh, didn't I tell you that *East of Laughter* is a murder mystery? Well, it is, among other things.

This young man reminds us very much of a very similar figure who appears so mysteriously in the first chapter of David Lindsay's *A Voyage to Arcturus*. You may recall that Mr. Backhouse the medium, who "dreams with open eyes," is on the point of producing his apparition in the bogus Egyptian temple prepared by Mrs. Trent, when the butler announces the arrival of two more guests: "Mr. Maskull, Mr. Nightspore."

> Everyone turned round. Faull rose to welcome the late arrivals. Backhouse also stood up, and stared hard at them.
>
> The two strangers remained standing by the door, which was closed quietly behind them. They seemed to be waiting for the mild sensation caused by their appearance to subside before advancing into the room. Maskull was a kind of giant, but broader and more robust of physique than most giants.

And so on. Notice that there is a very slight suggestion that these two may in fact be apparitions Backhouse has produced. He has several times insisted on beginning at nine o'clock; and it is at nine, just as he is ready to begin, that they appear. Note that Maskull is a giant. You have just made the acquaintance of another, Atrox Fabulinus. (His name means "terrible liar." I will leave the name of Lindsay's giant to you.)

Since I am about to tell you where Lindsay went wrong—and Lafferty right—at some length, it is only fair to Lindsay that I first tell you what was right about him; but though there was a great deal of it, I'm going to keep it brief and not attempt a balanced evaluation.

Lindsay was a mystic of no mean vision. He really did see, and see quite clearly, things of great importance of which most of us are no more than vaguely aware; furthermore he could make *us* see them. In these respects—and they are as fundamentally significant as any things concerning a writer can be—he was very like William Blake. On Tormance, a world circling, Arcturus, Maskull undergoes weird physical changes that both reflect and intensify the emotions and sensations with which he must grapple—a third arm for violence, for example. To the best of my knowledge Lindsay invented this device, and I know of no other writer who has used it successfully.

Now let us return to Backhouse's séance.

While a concealed orchestra plays Mozart, ectoplasm rises from the floor of the fake temple. The body of a handsome young man materializes, and when Faull, the owner of the London house where all this is taking place, squeezes its flaccid hand, the body comes to life—or at least appears to do so.

As Maskull tries to question it, Krag (a stranger) bursts into the room. He is "a thick, shortish man, with surprising muscular development and a head far too large in proportion to his body. His beardless yellow face indicated ... a mixture of sagacity, brutality, and humor."

Krag wanders around for a minute or two making mysterious rude remarks, then:

> Humor vanished from his face, like sunlight from a landscape, leaving it hard and rocky. Before anyone realized what he was doing, he encircled the soft, white neck of the materialized shape with his hairy hands and, with a double turn, twisted it completely round. A faint, unearthly shriek sounded, and the body fell in a heap on the floor. Its face was uppermost. The guests were unutterably shocked to observe that its expression had changed from the mysterious but fascinating smile to a vulgar, sordid, bestial grin, which cast a cold shadow of moral nastiness into every heart.

I don't suppose that any single paragraph can give us the key to any writer of note— but this one comes very, very close to it. It is absolutely central to understanding Lindsay, and the most essential element, the key within the key as it were, is that word *vulgar*. Remember that Lindsay used it, and how it was used; we will be coming back to it.

Now let's see what Lafferty has to say in a rather similar scene in the book you have just read:

> Hilary Ardri was the first of them into the Sky Studio. And yet he faced immediately a man who was strange to him, a young, handsome, fair, smiling, incredibly urbane man, bright of feature, open of soul, and covered with blood. The outstanding things about him were that he was smiling and covered with blood.
>
> "Who are you?" Hilary demanded ... "Who are you, man? Caesar Oceano, Denis Lollardy, seize this man! It is all wrong about him! Leo, block the door to this Sky Room and be sure that nobody goes out!"
>
> "It's blocked, Hilary. Nobody gets out!" the boyish Leo Parisi swore.
>
> "The man is like quicksilver, Hilary," Caesar complained as they skirried and grappled and fought. "But we have him here now like a rat in a corner. We will –"
>
> The lights in the Sky Studio went out, and for a moment the starlight through the skylights and sides was not able to pick up the slack. One, two, three seconds. Then the lights came on again, and Mary Brandy had her hand on the switch. Caesar Oceano and Denis Lollardy were both stretched on the floor dazed, and the strange man was not in the room.

Caesar Oceano and Denis Lollardy, I should add, are the good guys.

Now the truly wrong thing about Lindsay was that he quite honestly believed that Krag was the good guy—that he would say that his scene and Lafferty's are more nearly parallel than they actually are, in other words. Krag's true name on Tormance is Surtur, on Earth it is Pain, and the key (as I said before) is in that single word *vulgar*—what it means, and what it has come to mean.

It is, by no very great leap, derived from the Latin word *vulgaris*, which according to my Latin dictionary means: common, general, ordinary, conventional, usual, everyday, commonplace, democratic, plebeian, and belonging to the masses. So that I can show you what all this means, please think of a dog. It can be your own dog, or the neighbor's dog that wakes you up in the middle of the night, or even a dog of the exceedingly well-bred sort who is called Mama's Hopeful Crusader or something of that kind, though he is "Pal" to his friends.

Scientifically, all these dogs we have just thought of are called *canis familiaris*, "familiar dog" and even "family dog," which indeed describes them pretty well. But a hundred years ago, they were not *canis familiaris* at all. (And yes, this *is* an example of evolution, the evolution of language.) In those benighted days, they were *canis vulgaris*, and Carolus Linnaeus, or whoever it was who gave them that name, did not in the least mean to insult them. He merely intended to say that Spot, Fido, Pal, and indeed all their grandchildren, nephews, and cousins, were what is commonly ordinarily, conventionally, usually, and democratically called a *dog*, that this was what the ordinary men and women who did not worry about scientific nomenclature meant when they said "dog."

Later, as I told you, the name had to be changed; and about half the social history of the last three centuries is tied up (like a dog that has run around and around the lamppost to which he is tied until his collar is strangling him) in the reason for that change.

Right about now, General, you're thinking that I'm getting us awfully far from Lindsay, and that we've been out of sight of Lafferty for at least a page. But you're wrong. Lafferty is a vulgar writer, in the old, original sense of that word. That, I suppose, verges upon being an outrageous statement; but I will go further. I will contend that the expression on the face of the murdered boy in Lindsay's scene—the exact "vulgar, sordid, bestial grin" which so horrified Mr. Faull and his distinguished guests, is precisely Lafferty's most characteristic expression, though not, of course, his only expression.

And to answer the question you now wish to ask me, Krag has indeed tried to murder Lafferty; and is trying still.

It has often been remarked that the grandfather and the grandchild are natural allies; but the reason has seldom been explained. It is simply this—that the grandchild represents the generation that must try to set right its parents' mistakes, and the grandfather that which came to maturity before they were made. So it is with Lafferty and us. Lafferty represents the old human sanity. He is the ambassador dispatched to the late Twentieth Century by Dr. Johnson and Benjamin Franklin, Socrates and St. Paul. And theirs was a conservative point of view that cannot be said to have been conserved, since the conservatives (most of all) have forgotten it. Theirs was a liberal point of view so wildly radical and revolutionary that no one in the past several centuries has dared set it free again. If I were to try to expound all of it in detail, it would require a thicker book than this one, and I would surely make a fool of myself twenty times over. But for the purpose that has brought you and me to these pages, the purpose of drawing some sort of sketch-map of the lands *East of Laughter*, it can be summed up in a sentence: It consisted of admitting at every point in all discussions and all actions that things are exactly what they in fact are.

That point of view, just for example, would never dream of confusing the freedom to speak of each individual citizen (which it thinks sacred) with the freedom of a ten or twenty-billion-dollar corporation (which it knows is invariably meretricious). It might well give up smoking—but it would do so not because it thought that smoking was a good thing, but because it thought it a bad one. It might give away money—but it would give it away not because it thought money a bad thing, but because it thought it a good one.

Lindsay represents the parental generation, if you will—the generation whose mistakes it is our most urgent business to abolish before they destroy us. For he felt, as I have said, that Krag was good. Much worse, he felt that Crystalman, he of the "vulgar, sordid, bestial grin" was evil. Krag represented the work that became labor, that became drudgery, and that at last became torment.

Before we return to that word "vulgar," let's talk briefly about "sordid," and "bestial," both can be disposed of fairly quickly. By "sordid," Lindsay meant "sexual." Nor did he have in mind some specific sexual peculiarity that he felt singularly reprehensible.

Vice is a monster of so frightful mien,
As to be hated needs but to be seen;
Yet seen too oft, familiar with her face,
We first endure, then pity, then embrace.

Pope's lines have been frequently quoted, but though there is truth in them, it is not often noted that an opposite process not infrequently occurs. Rejecting some vice, we reject it in milder and milder shapes until soon we are condemning something that has ceased to be a vice at all. For all vices, even the worst, are exaggerations—overdoings of some legitimate thing.

One of the best men I have ever known once became indignant at the sight of a pregnant woman and stated emphatically that such women should be kept from public view until their children were born. It was useless to point out to him, as I did, that the woman in question was married, that pregnancy was necessary or the continuation of the human race, and that motherhood has been highly honored at all times and in all places.

My friend had started, or so I imagine, by condemning the sexual abuse of children, or something of that kind. But he's not been content with condemning it; he had proceeded to milder and milder "sins" until at last he had come (like Lindsay) to consider sex in all its forms vulgar, sordid, and bestial. Even married couples, he felt, should earnestly pretend that nothing erotic took place between them. Since the pregnant woman we had seen had surely engaged in sexual intercourse, it was shameful for her to show herself in public. Thus my friend (and I repeat that he was a very good man indeed) had now reached the point of championing something that is clearly wrong—hypocrisy—to hide something that is clearly right.

That is the sort of mistake Lafferty never makes. He is on the side of the angels; and indeed, he is very frequently in the van of the angels. But he is never so far in the van as to be on the other side.

"Bestial" is a tricky word, because it is used so often to castigate things that real beasts seldom or never do. Bestial cruelty, for example, is in truth innocent cruelty; the cat that plays with an unfortunate mouse is largely and perhaps entirely unaware of the mouse's fear and suffering—she plays with it just as she would with a toy mouse or a ball of yarn. In this case, however, I think that Lindsay (who was a good writer though a poor stylist) uses bestial as it should be used: to mean "like a beast." He is saying that the dying man grinned as innocently and unself-consciously as a chimp—or a skull, for that matter.

None of Mr. Faull's guests would have grinned so, we can be sure; and Lindsay had been taught, and sincerely believed, that it was seriously wrong to grin in that natural way, like a boy in the street. But that, I think, is how Lafferty grins. His books are riotously cheerful because their author is. For all I know he may be happy at no other time, though I hope that isn't true; but when he writes he is filled with the kind of wild joy that makes men throw their hats into the air. And it shows.

"Vulgar" as I said, originally denoted something having to do with the people at large, the common people. (A similar but less marked corruption of "common" has also taken place). The distinction was less between the masses and the aristocracy than between what was common and what was unusual; but to grasp what happened to the word, we must understand what a real aristocrat (as opposed, say, to a plutocrat) has been during most of our history. The elementary Greek word *aristos* means *best*. Thus the Greek aristocrats were the 'best people,' just as we speak of the "first families of Virginia," and so forth. Most were rich (by Greek standards, which meant rich enough to keep a horse), but some were not. They were landowners, not successful traders or manufacturers, and though they might have houses in Athens or Thebes, aristocratic families were invariably country families; this pattern endured for most of the last two thousand years, and it is a great deal older.

Such aristocrats might be as good as Aristides or Cimon, or as bad as Alcibiades or Alcidas. But there was a particular way in which they were never good, and one in which they were never bad. Every few years some historian studying such people—who are virtually extinct in our time—makes a discovery; and it is always the same discovery.

He finds to his boundless surprise that both mentally and morally they were remarkably like the peasants they lived beside and exploited. The aristocrat might drip with pearls and the peasant with sweat, but the peasant would have glittered in much the same way, and the aristocrat would have sweated in much the same way, had their places been reversed. When a duke rode in golden armor through the Paris of the middle ages, he did it because he felt it was a splendid thing to do. When the peasant watching him cheered or jeered him, he did it because he, too, felt that riding through Paris in golden armor was splendid. If he hated his duke (as he often did) it was because he understood him; for we cannot really hate anything unless we understand it, and if we only *think* we understand it, we are actually hating something else. If the duke was contemptuous of his peasant, as he often was, it was because he understood his peasant equally well. The medieval church might teach the poor peasant that his duke was only a man, and teach the duke that his peasant was a man as well as he; but both of them knew something more—that the other was, in fact, the same *sort* of man.

Nor is that to be wondered at. In their isolated villas and chateaux, aristocrats lived surrounded, not by other aristocrats (who were in fact their rivals), but by their peasants. They had been raised by peasant servants; the men took peasant girls as mistresses, and their wives gossiped with peasant maids. An aristocrat might have better manners and even a better education (Alcibiades had been taught by Socrates, something few of our own statesmen can say), but they were very much alike under the skin. It would be astonishing if they were not.

Thus though the duke might be good, he could not be good in the prim and prissy fashion that we (often unjustly) associate with young clergymen—no man living as close as the duke did to pigs and horses, dogs and cattle, can be. He might renounce his dukedom for sackcloth and a vow of celibacy. But he did it not because he thought manors and women bad things, but be he thought holiness and abstention better things. Or (as sometimes happened) because he thought manors and women things too good for such a wicked wretch as he.

And though the duke might be very bad indeed, he could not be bad in the fashion of the British intellectuals in this book. He might make a naked grab for power, and in fact he frequently did. But though he might cut his king's throat and justify it with lineage or lances, he did not try to justify it by vague claims to a mysterious moral or intellectual superiority. He knew that his fellows understood him too well; he was, in the best senses of the word, too vulgar for that.

Of the way in which the new, unusual people, the people who are not vulgar, the successful traders and manufacturers, came to exist in numbers, you can read in just about any history of our age. (Indeed you'll be fortunate to find one that tells you much about anything else). They very definitely do not live in the midst of their sailors and factory workers. Instead, they commonly live among others like themselves, their customers and suppliers. And because their power is based not upon lineage or lances but on the most vulgar (their sense) thing of all, money, and because no one else understands them very well, they justify it by claims to a mysterious moral and intellectual superiority.

Now there really is dignity in labor and greater dignity in suffering. I feel sure many of the new people believe in them quite sincerely, and among other reasons because they are real. But they are also exceedingly convenient for the new people, who need to convince their sailors and workers that suffering and labor are good *in themselves*, which as a matter of fact they aren't. If I were to force you to pile stones for twelve hours a day, I would not be doing you a favor, and if I forced you to do it under the whip, I would be doing you even less of a favor. That is the old, plain thing all the people Lafferty represents understood perfectly well, but that Lindsay did not understand at all.

Lindsay believed (as millions of others believe today) that labor was a good thing regardless of its end, and even that the less rational purpose it had, the better it was. And similarly that suffering was good of itself, and useless suffering better. He believed them not for any mysterious morally superior reason, but because he had been taught to; and he had been taught to because it was to someone's economic advantage that he and a good many millions of others did.

May I tell you how Lindsay died? (If you're eating now, or drinking something, you'd better put it down.) His teeth killed him. They decayed and he suffered them to decay, faithful to Krag, until at last the septic condition of his mouth ended his life

And that, I think is enough about Lindsay, though it isn't nearly enough about Lafferty. Let us turn to Borges.

Lafferty (like Ellison and some other moderns) would be far more widely known if only he lived and wrote in some far-away place, preferably deep in the southern hemisphere; his art is one that our age accepts only in translation. I don't mean to say that Borges, Hermann Hesse, and the rest are bad writers—they're in fact very good writers and not infrequently excellent writers. I *do* mean to say that there are writers in Britain and America (and in all probability Ireland, Canada, and Australia) equally good and of the same sort, who receive less than a tenth the attention. Everyone knows, I suppose, that *The Painted Bird* was retyped with some such name as "Nancy Smith" and sent around to publishers in New York, all of whom rejected it immediately without comment. Which is not to say that *The Painted Bird* is a bad book—only that it is the sort of book no one wants today when it has been written by Nancy Smith.

I assume you have read Borges (everybody who reads has, I imagine) and have noticed that Borges himself is a character from a Borges story. Take this from "The Library of Babel," an obvious example: "The mystics claim that their ecstasy reveals to them a circular chamber containing a great circular book, whose spine is continuous and which follows the complete circle of the walls; but their testimony is suspect; their words obscure."

Upon reading that, who does not visualize Borges, the blind librarian, trailing the sensitive fingertips of one blue-veined hand along the library shelves, wandering narrow corridors in stacks that were for him forever wrapped in night and wondering whether this new place to which he had taken himself was not the old place from which he had been taken an hour before?

Or this, from "An Examination of the Work of Herbert Quain,"

The worlds proposed by *April March* are not regressive; only the manner of writing their history is so: regressive and ramified, as I have already said. The work is made up of thirteen chapters. The first reports the ambiguous dialogue of certain strangers on a railway platform. The second narrates the events on the eve of the first act. The third, also retrograde, describes the events of *another* possible eve to the first day; the fourth, still another. Each one of these three eves (each of which rigorously excludes the others) is divided into three other eves each of a very different kind. The entire work, thus, constitutes nine novels; each novel contains three long chapters. (The first chapter, naturally, is common to all.) The temper of one of these novels is symbolic; that of another, psychological; of another, communist; of still another, anticommunist; and so on.

Surely no one needs to be told that "Herbert Quain" is Jorge Luis Borges.

I do not mean to say that Borges was a madman, forever wandering the forking paths of his own mind—far from it. It is quite true, of course, that geniuses sometimes go mad; it is even more true that people of sub-normal ability do. Madness is not the result of genius, but of stress, which is why rats can be driven mad in a laboratory. (What a pity it is that Lafferty and Borges never collaborated on that story.)

I was going to say that just as Borges himself was clearly a Borges character, Lafferty is a Lafferty character. When you read about such colossal absurdities as John Barkley Towntower and Solomon Izzersted, you must remember that it is no more absurd that they should exist in Hilary Ardri's world than that R.A. Lafferty should exist in yours. Atrox Fabulinus, the Roman Rabelais, once broke off the account of his hero Raphaelus in the act of opening a giant goose egg to fry it in an iron skillet of six yards' span. Fabulinus interrupted the action with these words: "Here it becomes necessary to recount to you the history of the world up to this point." Surely no one needs to be told that Atrox Fabulinus is really Raphael Aloysius Lafferty. (Although perhaps I should remind you that "goose egg" means zero, and that Helen of Troy was hatched from a swan's egg.)

Lafferty is—as you would certainly have guessed without me—one of the seven scribbling giants who write the world. That I know, sounds like one of the world's tallest tales; and it is, because plain truth, even when it is a homely and humble truth, always stands head-and-shoulders above a lie. Thanks to Nils Bohr, it has become a commonplace of physics that observation changes the thing observed—we merely pretend that it does not. Our objections to Lafferty (like our objections to Borges and Bohr) nearly always boil down to a protest that he will not play with us; and the truth is that he is too playful to play with us—our game is too dull for him. He would rather play in that most fantastical world in which some of the animals wear three-piece suits, the world called Terra, that is as wild and lonely as any other a star.

Thoreau said, "I do not know how to distinguish between our waking life and a dream. Are we not always living the life that we imagine we are?" Lafferty is one of those rare writers who has imagined waking.

Barrington, Illinois
January, 1988

This work © 1988, 1990, 2017 Gene Wolfe

Gene Wolfe is the author of numerous novels and short story collections, including The Fifth Head of Cerberus, Peace, The Island of Doctor Death and Other Stories and Other Stories, Free Live Free, Soldier of the Mist, Storeys from the Old Hotel, There Are Doors, The Sorcerer's House, *and most recently,* A Borrowed Man. *He is best known for* The Book of the New Sun *tetralogy, and its sequels,* The Book of the Long Sun *and* The Book of the Short Sun. *Wolfe is a winner of the World Fantasy Award for Life Achievement and many other awards. In 2007, he was inducted into the Science Fiction Hall of Fame. In 2013, he received the SFWA Grand Master award. He lives in Peoria, Illinois.*

Introduction to "The Configuration of the North Shore"

by Gardner Dozois

R. A. Lafferty started writing in 1960, at the relatively advanced age (for a new writer, anyway) of forty-six, and in the years before his retirement in 1987, he published some of the freshest and funniest short stories ever written, almost all of them dancing on the borderlines between fantasy, science fiction, and the tall tale in its most boisterous and quintessentially American forms.

Lafferty has published memorable novels that stand up quite well today—among the best of them are *Past Master*, *The Devil Is Dead*, *The Reefs of Earth*, the historical novel *Okla Hannali*, and the totally unclassifiable (a fantasy novel disguised as a non-fiction historical study, perhaps?) *The Fall of Rome*—but it was the prolific stream of short stories he began publishing in 1960 that would eventually establish his reputation. Stories like "Slow Tuesday Night," "Thus We Frustrate Charlemagne," "Hog-Belly Honey," "The Hole on the Corner," "All Pieces of a River Shore," "Among the Hairy Earthmen," "Seven Day Terror," "Continued on Next Rock," "All But the Words," and many others, are among the most original and pyrotechnic stories of our times.

Almost any of those stories would have served for this anthology, even those published ostensibly as science fiction—but I finally settled on the story that follows. It's one of Lafferty's least-known and least-reprinted, but a little gem regardless that demonstrates all of Lafferty's virtues: folksy exuberance, a singing lyricism of surprising depth and power, outlandish imagination, a store of offbeat erudition matched only by Avram Davidson, and a strong, shaggy sense of humor unrivalled by anyone.

His short work has been gathered in the landmark collection *Nine Hundred Grandmothers*, as well as in *Strange Doings, Does Anyone Else Have Something Further to Add?*,

Golden Gate and Other Stories, and *Ringing Changes*. Some of his work is available only in small press editions—like the very strange novel *Archipelago*, or *My Heart Leaps Up*, which was serialized as a sequence of chapbooks—but his other novels available in trade editions (although many of them are long out of print) include, *Fourth Mansions*, *Arrive at Easterwine*, *Space Chantey*, and *The Flame Is Green*. Lafferty won the Hugo Award in 1973 for his story "Eurema's Dam," and in 1990 received the World Fantasy Award, the prestigious Life Achievement Award. His most recent books are the collections *Lafferty in Orbit* and *Iron Star* [sic; the correct title is *Iron Tears*].

"The Configuration of the North Shore" in *Modern Classics of Fantasy* (1997), edited by Gardner Dozois

This work © 1997 Gardner Dozois. Originally published as an intro to "The Configuration of the North Shore" published in in Modern Classics of Fantasy *(1997), edited by Gardner Dozois*

Gardner Dozois is the past editor for Asimov's SF Magazine, The Year's Best SF *anthologies, and several other publications, winning 15 Hugo awards for his pains. He is also a downright amazing writer with two Nebula awards to his name. He currently lives and writes in Philadelphia.*

Arrive At Easterwine: Some Arrant Roadmapping
by Sheryl Smith

Sheryl Smith lives in Chicago, and is an ardent theatre goer and Wagner fan. She is also, in my opinion, one of the most intelligent and delightful critics of sf writing for fanzines. Now when this essay first appeared in the fanzine *Gorbett,* R.A. Lafferty wrote in response: "Writing things like *Arrive at Easterwine* is like throwing rocks over a hill. They don't hit in the pattern intended, and the sound that comes back from them is usually confused or too faint to be heard. That's the trouble with all communication. But your echoes were coherent enough to show that part of it is being received by part of the people; and it's an authentic feedback that adds a dimension to the work."

Cy Chauvin, Editor, *A Multitude of Visions* (1975)

Criticism is a form of literary dalliance. The *raison d'etre* of an art-work lies in its total experience, which can be had only from the work itself; all that criticism can contribute is academic data on this aesthetic organism, or perhaps a (figurative) dissection, so really, there isn't much excuse for it. . . Still, since I am writing the stuff, it behooves me to make one up.

How about, say, criticism can help art be noticed better? Of course, that's only true if the critic is a good noticer, which is in no way guaranteed. I have, for example, encountered literary analyses whose writers displayed an all-around proficiency in the use of dialectic criticese, while the English of the fiction under discussion, presuming they had read same, was apparently beyond their comprehensions. Critical credentials are not always based on artistic sensibilities; indeed, they do not have to be based on any qualifications whatsoever. (Check out the arts yourself—you have to.)

Eventually this rhetorical foray is going to trace through some of the structuring, and maybe even a little meaning, in *Arrive At Easterwine.* This is the third and perhaps most difficult of the three *great* end-the-world comedy(!) novels by one R.A. Lafferty, an unassuming old gentleman currently practicing tall-tale mythopoesis in the cultural wilds of Tulsa, Oklahoma. He is categorized a "science fiction writer" because his genre is no longer current. (These days a "mythopoeic" is a stylistically-Victorian fantasist who prettifies and emasculates old myth-symbols; surely these are called "myth-creators" only facetiously. Lafferty, however, is a *real* one.) In my experience, Lafferty is the only writer in sf— as there is only John Gardner in the contemporary mainstream—to whom the overused accolade "genius" might be rightly, if gingerly applied. (At least, only these have moved me to stick my neck out so far.)

First, though, I shall presume to explain fiction as an art-form—just a few brisk paragraphs. I have been annoyed lately by people whose idea of good fiction is one with a fast-moving plot: i.e., the reader is anxious to get to the end of same, quickly. To hold this quality as a primary literary standard, therefore, seems fraught with internal contradiction: what, praise a book you "couldn't put down" and now can't pick up again because you know the ending? Nonsense! Really excellent art is not so easily disposed of (as Charles Ives, or maybe Emerson said about nature); and it's about time someone (me, as it happens) superciliously points out elements of fiction that tend to get lost in the mad pursuit of plot-suspense. (We will get to Lafferty shortly; but he is definitely doing more in his work than can be contained by mere efficiency, and I do want you primed to pay attention).

Heretically then: until fairly recently, the science fiction genre has consisted of lazy writing for lazy readers—I'm not sure which came first. The idea was, take a short verbal sprint from here to there, go on a single line of fantastic/technological speculation, and touch a few gross emotional bases on the way. This is a great workout for the so-called "sense of wonder" (that is, for the sentimental response to an oversimplification which happens to be vast or exotic);

but since human beings, and the "human condition," are too emotionally complex to find expression in such facile wonderment, this lazy and limited formula eventually gets boring (at least it bores me—there are always some who are utterly unboreable.)

When a writer is merely shoving protagonists around from crisis to crisis, there is no leisure to explore anything but the convolutions of ingenuity. But read some of the more highly-regarded works of fiction outside the sf genre (the "classics," if you will), and you will find that they are not too rushed to be human. (*Moby Dick*, you will note, has a 100-page plot; but if Melville hadn't allowed himself the other 400 pages, it wouldn't have been a 100-year book.)

More tangible reasons for de-emphasizing plot-centricity are to be found, if we dig for the basics: what is fiction, what does it need, what does it do? (No, I haven't *really* forgotten this article is to be on Lafferty; it's just going to be on fiction first.) Well, fiction is an art-form, so you can expect it to make you feel something, to experience something—though this experience does not feel the same as it would if you lived through it. (Maxim No. 1: Artistic emotions are different from "real" emotions.) And now that we have fiction labeled, we should be able to get at its unique requirements and properties by comparing it with other art-forms.

So what does fiction need to convey its effects? Language, for a starter, since language is what it's made of. And even though reading is a visual activity, fiction, like other language arts, appeals to the sense of sound; for the aesthetics of a story are not absorbed by staring at the typography, but by comprehending the words in sequence. Words read to oneself are not so distinctly "heard" as words read aloud, but they are comprehended as sound nevertheless.

All right: sound, to have meaning, must take up—and move through—time (in contrast to the visual arts, which must take up space). And like all sound-arts, fiction takes its own time, for artistic experience is very condensed: years may pass in the book during your several hours' reading. But note: the experience of fiction, unlike that of drama, does not need to be absorbed all in one lump. A story, once begun, will not go on without you, whereas a play (in its intended medium, performance), will continue at its own pace until it is finished. Drama must maintain an illusion of present time: it is happening *now*. Fiction, however, deals in past time, and as its events are all over with at the time they are conveyed, there is no artistic loss if the experience is not completed in one sitting.

Unlike poetry, fiction and drama *must* deal in human occurrence. (But fiction, particularly, does not require poetry's metric/syllabic structures, nor its linguistic condensation; drama seems only to *require* these poetic elements in the case of tragedy.) In drama this human occurrence is present and ongoing; the characters are right there, they produce the event and demonstrate themselves directly. In fiction, however, the human occurrence is not ongoing; the characters are not there to demonstrate themselves—rather, they are conveyed, and the event recounted, by narration. Fiction, therefore, has a narrative viewpoint at all times (not necessarily the same one throughout), who may himself have had the experience he tells of, or may have witnessed it, or may have heard of it, or may be outside its "world" altogether, an external observer and perhaps an omniscient one (an "omniscient" narrator can give out what his characters are thinking). And for this reason fiction is particularly suited to express the understanding and illumination to be gleaned from reflecting on things past; it is a vehicle for contemplation and epiphany more than anything else.

That does it—I have only to assemble the definition. Fiction is a human occurrence (implying plot, character, setting) which is told (implying narrative viewpoint, which may also be the source of the organizing idea or theme) in (the uncondensed, unmetric language of) prose (implying style and all constituents thereof), (whew!) Therefore, the experience of fiction should arise from an interrelation between what (plot and etc.), who (narrator and etc.), and how (style): these are the three angles to be covered in reading, and in good fiction all three should merit appreciative scrutiny.

As they do in Lafferty's *Arrive at Easterwine*, at which this rappage-safari has finally arrived.

Having reduced the plot-character complex to merely one element of fiction among several, I now proceed to make a liar out of myself by discussing primarily that constituent of this novel. (Oh, there seems to be some babbling about symbolism in the back of my rough draft somewhere; true, the rewrite up to now has not left two sentences in their original abutment, but further up the line, how should *I* know what's going in? Symbols are part of the "what"-complex anyway— everything in art is symbolic, even the people: nothing breathes there, though in prime works the whole organism seems to. . . Anyway remember that, in case the subject does come up again.) Lafferty's style, after all, is too panoramic to start on now—and going into it would preclude rather than clarify any single work of his. (A separate article on Lafferty's style would be in order, if there is a critic around up to describing the ineffable.) The narrative of *Easterwine* is first-person participant, as the tale is told autobiographically by a whacky, weird, all-too-human and hence, eminently Lafferteian computer (or something), whose ingenious perception of the archetypal underneath-reality is what effects the Jungian vision/progression of the novel and I hope you don't think I'm going to flounder around trying to synopsize Epiktistes when I can do something *manageable*, like the plot! (Even when critics are dumb, they try not to sound dumb in public. . .) Besides, the consensus seems to be that *Easterwine*'s primary difficulty involves the plot; folk of my acquaintance, at least, have evinced to uncertainty as to the character of Epiktistes, but seem severally and variously puzzled about what, precisely, happens.

> Should these journals ever fall into the hands of human persons, they will encounter great difficulties in much of them. . .
> We believe that human persons have the right to know what has happened and is happening to human persons. . . (p. 60)[1]

---

[1] All page numbers refer to *Arrive at Easterwine*, the paperback edition published by Ballantine Books, March, 1973.

So: we are expected to be able to fathom what's going on—though if we are humans, we may have to try harder.

All right, a hint: Lafferty almost always forecasts his plot-progressions, particularly when he works at novel length. One tends to finish his fiction anyway (at least once)—which shows you right there how little a reader actually needs to be motivated by "finding out how it ends." So you know where you're going—perhaps have even been there before—but why should *that* stop you? The trip is the thing, after all; and in Lafferty your ride is all through substance and delight. This practice of forecasting removes the distraction of suspense, encouraging the reader to stay with the emotional pace of the novel, while according him as well an opportunity to explore the relationship of goal to journey.

In *Arrive at Easterwine*, the novel's entire structure is capsule-forecast very early on:

> ". . . this fine-honed machine . . . must now be set to three primary tasks. These may be the types of all tasks and problems there are. The three tasks (and I will outline them as briefly as possible, no more than an hour to each) will be to establish or create—"
> "A Leader," said Valery.
> "A Love," said Aloysius.
> "And a Liaison," said Cecil Corn." (p. 19)

It isn't until page 46 that we learn these tasks will be failures, but that's still in plenty of time to prefigure the conclusion of the first one.

This three-part premonition leads naturally into what is probably Lafferty's most tightly-balanced novel structure. Virtually everything in *Easterwine* falls into a prevailing pattern of three—plus one (yes, yes, it's Christian—that *too*). Each project takes up one-third of the book—four chapters out of thirteen, the "plus one" chapter being the final one (and if you're not sure what an incident is doing—as at first I was not about Valery's snowfall—merely placing it in the first, second, or third set of four chapters will indicate a tie-in with one or another of the three tasks. Which helps). Each project/failure is distinctly associated with a group of three symbolically-classed individuals of the Institute of Impure Science (did I mention that *Easterwine* is the apotheosis of Lafferty's Institute stories?); and these persons are each introduced and characterized in detail within the section on "their" group's project. Also, each of the failures generates a sort of personified residue within Epiktistes. Epikt, as a compendium of all nine primary Institute-persons, is the "plus one" of all three groups. But this is much easier to chart than to explain, viz.

1st	2nd	3rd
Leader	*Love*	*Liaison*
("Primordials")	("Fellahin")	("Elegants")
Gaetan Balbo	Aloysius Shiplap	Diogenes Pontifex
Gregory Smirnov	Charles Cogsworth	Audifax O'Hanlon
Valery Mok	Gerald Glasser	Cecil Corn

E P I K T I S T E S

generates	*generates*	*generates*
Snake	"Mary Sawdust"	"Easterwine"

There is a subsidiary character in the first episode, one Peter the Great of Ganymede, who is also labeled a Primordial, and does participate in the symbolic representation of that failure—illustrating the leader as amoral madman. I didn't put this in the chart as he is not one of the permanent Institute crowd, and anyway, he messes up the symmetry. Still, unlike George Bernard Shaw confronting *Gotterdammerung*, I can't discount him altogether just because he doesn't fit. Well, since when does fiction ever graph perfectly? What do you think this is, mathematics?)

It is safe to say that all tripartite symbology (yes, and three-plus-one stuff) "means" to this pattern—that is, whatever symbols come in threes (or sometimes fours) will correspond in some way with the major divisions I have charted. These symbol-groups, as they double the main pattern, augment it also by evoking much emotional variety. This ranges from the eerie solemnity of the Balbo family crest (chapter three), a Primordial device incorporating divisions into both four parts (a quartered escutcheon, whose four figures are representative of the three Primordials plus Epiktistes), and into three parts (the thrice-drawn center, which echoes the three tasks); to the whimsical mobile-extension caricature of the three person-groupings (chapter six); and even to Epiktistes' self-satisfied declaration that "the celestials, the machines and the demons are from ever. . ." (p. 171).

Symbols which are not so grouped help to illustrate each failure individually. Leadership, therefore, becomes a pompous giant, a mad king from Ganymede (who "by his gruesome inhuman humor . . . was human after all." [p. 66]), a Compassionate Tyrant who under-wrenches pattern through torture, a thriving snake, and tigers. Love is harmless bug-bites, millet-cakes, opulent clods and sawdust madonnas. And Liaison appears as a sky-city of impossible snow-crystals, a sign that is both obscenity and mystic travel-schedule, ceramic bulls, muddled apparitions, transcendent wine. (Those are just a few prominent examples, not a full compendium.)

And I will speak of symbols generally, to emphasize that, properly used, they are *emotional* representations, not purely intellectual ones. If symbols are doing their job—and in *Arrive at Easterwine* they are on voluntary overtime—their emotional ramifications are so compelling and so various that their associated concepts are expanded clear off the map; and intellect, though fascinated, cannot keep up with or classify all the subtle implications of this interplay. Double-stress that: the symbols of art must evoke a rather complex emotion; and only emotional responses can be immediate/ambivalent/ simultaneous enough to grasp the shifting viewpoints, the expressed distillations of cultures that is the "human condition," for the whole thing is just too much for plodding reason, alone, to perambulate. By these lights therefore, when an artistic representation calls up feeling too facile or too one-sided—as might be evoked by mother, the flag, a stereotyped Christ-figure, the phallus a la Mailer or Lawrence—then it is a symbol but not a very good one; and when an artistic representation does not move you at all, except perhaps to send you scurrying to *The Golden Bough* or Bulfinch to try to make some sense out of it, it is not symbol at all, it is a reference.

How far afield are we now? . . . Hmm, seems not so remote; a short transitionary ramble should get us back on the track. First, to get our bearings: I've covered the structure of *Arrive at Easterwine,* in large and in little; then got going on symbolism and stopped to define it. Since the novel has therefore been analyzed to pieces, it's time we reassemble it in our detail-ridden minds (it was never fragmented outside them), and clarify, at last, what goes on here.

At the beginning of this essay, I called *Arrive at Easterwine* an end-the-world comedy novel—which would've been a safe guess to make if I hadn't read the thing, since nearly all of Lafferty's novels are end-the-world comedies ("And now, live from Ragnarok—lotsa laughs!"). The difficulty then seems to be, not 'what is it' so much as 'where is it'—i.e., understanding the work is an angle-of-vision problem. For in this subtly-wrought novel the world is killed, then resurrected, purely through imagery and viewpoint.

Look, I'll show you. Recall the culmination of the third failure, the attempt to achieve linkage and communication by apprehending the basic shape of the universe. Epikt correlates data from vast, intuitive pattern-studies, labors mightily, and projects the universe itself (the idea of a cosmic panorama containing its projector, its screen and its viewers within it is a mindblower right there!). I quote from the initial response of the Institute members:

> The Universe, new seen, grew in power and clarity, and ghastliness. . .
>
> "It's still a rotten apple?" Glasser gasped with a passion unusual to him. ". . . Oh, God of the gutted glob! The holes in it, the holes in it, the unfathomable abysses, the searing absences.
>
> What thing cries out of its absences? How will it be fulfilled?"
>
> "It's a sponge," said Cogsworth through closed teeth. "How sponges must suffer!"
>
> "It's a cheese," Valery offered hysterically, "rotted cheese and full of holes. A whole cosmos of maggotty cheese, turned green in its taint and rot. And the eggshells! What hatched out of them? I dreamed of them before I was born, pieces of broken eggshell millions of parsecs long." Her shoulders were shaking. I couldn't tell if she was crying or laughing. . .
>
> "It's a weeping face," said Aloysius Shiplap. "It's the leprous face of a horrified and horrifying man, a face made out of livid and wormeaten parchment, horrid with elliptical gaps."
>
> "No, Aloysius . . . it's a laughing face," Charles Cogsworth said with bitter wonder. "But can I have liaison with that face? What has it to laugh about? It must surely be demented laughter."
>
> "But it isn't," Glasser cut back in. "I see it right now. It's clear and innocent. It's a boy, a child laughing—"
>
> "—with holes rotted clear through him, dying in blinding pain—" Aloysius gagged.
>
> "—living in caves of excrement—" Valery burst out.
>
> "—childish, triumphant, leprous, ghostly—" Cogsworth chanted, "—dead and eternally damned to shrieking torture—a nightmare child surging through

putrid flame—"

"—still laughing, though," said Aloysius. "A shaggy kid, that."

. . .

"Oh, it is spiritless," Valery cried out. . . "It's a graveyard, isn't it folks? . . . And we're all dead things in it. Look at that place—piled billions of kilometers deep with estrogen and ectoplasm. . ."

. . . And they spent most of the night bemoaning the shape of their fate and their universe. (p. 207-210)

Holes, worms, caves; the graveyard and the fires of infernality—that is the night of world-death (and I had not noticed myself before now, how close the passage, its pain and despair, veers to tragedy). Now watch resurrection morning:

"This is the *limbus furtivus*," Cogsworth said sadly. "It is the most lost of all the limbos of which the Fathers wrote. There is no more hope at all in anything."

"I knew a fellow who lived in one of those limbos," Aloysius remembered . . . He delivered some mighty odd lectures, but they weren't at all hopeless. He was very peculiar, for a fellow who hadn't been born yet. Folks, it's just possible that the glow is ahead of us and not behind."

"Oh, it's all dead," Valery sighed. "It's a dead graveyard. You can see the inner caul about us, shutting us in, not a dozen parsecs away. It's an empty matrix, it's a double-damned dead machine."

"Have a care, doll," I issued angrily. "You think machines don't have feelings, too?"

"And Valery," said Charles Cogsworth, her unoutstanding husband, "a matrix is the very opposite of a graveyard. And estrogen, which you see piled so deep, is a sign of life and not death. Even the ectoplasm that you perceive is a sign of survival, though in one of its senses of a phony sort. And you sure the graveyard is quite dead, Valery? Are you sure the matrix is quite empty?"

"But it is! It's a dead quarry, a monument yard. All

the gravestones have been sculpted out of it. That's what makes the holes."

"Aye, the worlds going out leave the holes, Valery," Charles said, "and the holes are their sculpted monuments right enough.

But you don't know how they go out of it and where they go to. And you misunderstand what you take for rot. That may be new growth. Hozza, hozza, I believe the glow is ahead of us after all. Turn on the worlds again, Epikt.". . .

In my Ktistec person I turned on the shape and the universe once more. It came back in all its staggering strength and cryptic promise.

"Yes, it's a quarry, Valery," Cogsworth said, "the biggest one around this sector at least. But it's the matrix and not the graveyard. Don't you know what has been quarried out of it, girl?". . .

"Spheres and batilla and saddles," said Aloysius Shiplap, "distorted spheres after Gregory's own heart, exploding spheres after yours, blessed unfinished globes, globs, new worlds for old: the billion billion forms which are mutually complementary to each other. This . . . is the *limbus lautumiae* of which the Sons will write when they understand it more. This is no lost or furtive limbo. It is the quarrying limbo in all its agony and estrus. This is the mother quarry itself. All the grand worlds—which we have never seen, which we can't imagine—have been sculpted out of it. They are the holes in it, they are what gives it its wild and riven shape. But look how much else new space is left. And look also that the holes do not remain holes. We have gazed at it all wrong: we've seen only the dark afterimages, not the bright fire itself. Here in limbo we already have intimation of these creating worlds. . . From this young quarry may not great worlds still be called?". . .

"What do you silly brains mean?" Valery demanded. "That our cosmos and ourselves are not dead?"

"Maybe so, maybe not," said Aloysius. "Maybe we haven't been born yet."

And after that, there was a pause of a billion years, or perhaps much less." (pp. 210-214)

See? Another death and rebirth of cycles, clearly in the Lafferteian manner, and the only reason you might've missed it is that it is approached obliquely. As cause and effect between the three great failures and the ending/beginning of the world is left implicit and tenuous, the event seems more observed than enacted. Because the view is tangential, though, it allows the novel to actually get into the transcendent-rebirth period for the wind-up, instead of leaving things in optimistic uncertainty, in the timeless pause between worlds:

> There is a rumor that Gaetan Balbo will come back, that he may arrive this very day. . . The report also says, that Gaetan is as bloodcurdling as ever, and still as urbane, though his *urbis* is now the transcendent city, the city beyond. This latter I can hardly believe.
>
> And my Ganymede informant tells me that Peter the Great will visit us again if the lines fall that way; that Peter is a completely changed monster; that once, on a portentous night, Peter, like Peter, went out and wept. Oh, brother, I will have to get me a new Ganymede informant! (pp. 216-217)

Well, he's oblique there too. But he sure has done it!

Oh, yes, one more thing: Lafferty's two other great end-the-world comedy novels are *Past Master* and *Fourth Mansions*. Read them too. In fact—logistics permitting—read them first.

***

A PUBLIC APOLOGY TO EPIKTISTES

Do forgive me, sir or machine, that I regrettably found it necessary to refer to your autobiog. as the work of Mr. Lafferty. Of course the similarity in your styles indicates only that there was some literary influence—perhaps mutual, who knows?—in your relationship; but I fear the science fiction community believes, despite all disclaimers, that Mr. Lafferty wrote *Arrive at Easterwine*. I decided that I had best fall in with this fib and not risk squeezing prejudices too gallingly; for literary talent in machines is still considered a threat to one's manhood in some circles, and I feared there must be damage to the reputation of your book, if unnecessary spleens should be vented.

This work © 1975, 2017 Sheryl Smith

Sheryl Smith was born in Illinois and attended the University of Chicago. Besides her love of literature and the theatre, Smith was a software tester by trade who owned her own company, and often referred to herself as a computer geek. In addition to essays on Science Fiction, Smith wrote novels, stories, plays, poetry and technical pieces. A devoted lover of music, early in life she admired classical music, especially the operas of Richard Wagner, and then later of early jazz, particularly the work of Bix Beiderbecke, and belonged to several jazz clubs. She also expressed her artistry in a line of unique custom jewelry.

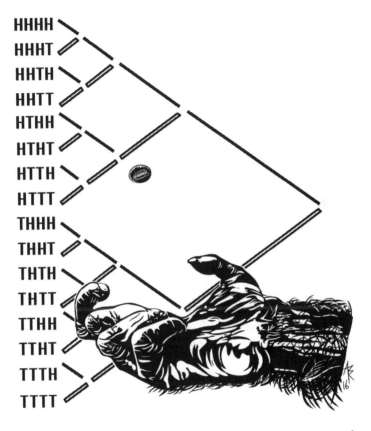

HHHH
HHHT
HHTH
HHTT
HTHH
HTHT
HTTH
HTTT
THHH
THHT
THTH
THTT
TTHH
TTHT
TTTH
TTTT

Flip O'Grady was a chimpanzee of mature years and unusual intelligence. He stood a full four feet tall. He was employed as a penny-flipper at the "Probability Division"; it was under the directorship of Doctor Vonk, and so was Flip.

R. A. Lafferty, "Jack Bangs Eyes"

Illustration © 2016 Anthony Ryan Rhodes

Varieties of Apocalypse in Science Fiction
by Andrew M. Greeley

The science fiction "little magazines" (*Analog, Galaxy,* etc.) have been distinctly ambivalent about *Star Wars* and *Close Encounters of the Third Kind.* On the one hand, they are delighted to see science fiction forms appeal to a broad range of consumers of popular culture. On the other hand, like all cultists, the SF purists who review for the science fiction journals are appalled at how disrespectful both of the films were of the solemn and sacred Forms which currently reign in "authentic" science fiction. Heroic sagas of the *Star Wars* sort, particularly those with reasonably happy endings (living happily ever after for Luke Skywalker and Princess Leia must mean at least several fights a week) were abandoned by the SF purists long ago and the thought that the wee folk on the flying saucers might be benign (even Cherubic) is enough to send the canonists of SF off to the local office of their Inquisition to demand that Orthodox Doctrine be enforced. For one knows that the saucer folk are either callously indifferent to us lesser mortals here on earth or ultimately impatient with our stupidity and bent upon either reforming us despite ourselves or simply eliminating us from the universe as a dangerous lower life form which does not deserve to exist. The smiling little fellows from *Close Encounters* are not apocalyptic visitors at all.

Apocalypse, ah, that's the word! Science fiction was born from an apocalyptic vision, and currently flourishes on another apocalyptic vision, but does not seem to understand what apocalypse really is.

In the Christian scriptures there is the Book of Revelation (once called by the papists such as the present writer, "Apocalypse") which is filled with falling stars, suns going out, moons disappearing from the heavens, blasting trumpets and the general dissolution of the world. The book represents in a sense an extended reflection on the descriptions of the final days of the world given by Jesus in the gospel stories.

The apocalyptic literary style, it turns out, was the most popular religious literary form in the Middle East, and particularly, in Palestine during the Second Temple era. If you wanted to communicate religiously with Jews and proselytes (fellow travelers of Jews who did not practice the full rigors of the Mosaic Law)—who may have been one-quarter of the citizens of the Roman Empire—the apocalyptic religious mode of expression was almost essential. Hence, its popularity with the writers of the Christian scriptures.

It is very difficult for those of us who live in a different era to penetrate back into the minds of the apocalyptic writers and preachers. Were they speaking "literally" or "poetically"? Did they really think the stars were going to fall from the heavens and that the world was going to be consumed by fire? Or were they rather describing in striking imagery the human condition and particularly the human religious condition? The best answer to that question seems to be that if we asked it of an apocalyptic preacher or writer he would not have the faintest notion of what we were talking about. If we could explain our terms he would probably say that his style was somewhere between poetry and literal description and would be baffled as to why anybody would be interested in a question such as ours. Later Christians' piety, however, became quite literal and rigid in its interpretation of apocalypse and identified the apocalyptic imagery with the "end of the world" or "Judgment Day," a specific event with which history was to terminate, and at which all the imagery described in the apocalyptic literature would *physically* occur. The medieval Latin hymn *Dies Irae* is the epitome of the extreme literalization of apocalyptic imagery as it has found its way into the Western imagination (think, for example, of the wild music of Verdi's *Dies Irae* in his *Requiem)*. The end of the world, and its possible renewal, then, is a major theme in the Western creative imagination although destruction of the cosmos has always seemed far more important to popular Christian piety and to elite artistic and literary imaginations than the renewal which may come afterwards. One need only think of the horrors of Michelangelo's Last Judgment in the Sistine Chapel (horrors which never seem to terrify the College of Cardinals all that much when it assembles to elect a new pope) to realize that what fascinated Michelangelo's genius was destruction, not reconstruction.

One of the curious anomalies of the development of the apocalyptic/eschatological imagery in the Western imagination is that those literary scholars who have very skillfully attempted to reconstruct the style and the imagination of Jesus himself are now pretty well persuaded that he personally avoided almost entirely the apocalyptic imagery and that apocalypse in the New Testament is an adaptation of the message of Jesus to a popular literary and oratorical style carried on by his followers. Jesus himself, it would seem, much preferred to shatter people's preconceptions with parables instead of with falling stars, exploding suns, vanishing moons and great conflagrations sweeping across the earth. But if we wish to understand the importance of the apocalypse in the Western imagination and in the science fiction segment of popular culture we must go back beyond the Christian scriptures to the origins of apocalypse in the post-exilic, pre-Second Temple era of Judaism. As good a place as any to start is the fourteenth chapter of the book of Zechariah.

> See, a day is coming for Yahweh when the spoils taken from you will be divided among you. Yahweh will gather all the nations to Jerusalem for battle. The city will be taken, the houses plundered, the women ravished. Half the city will go into captivity, but the remnant of the people will not be cut off from the city. Then Yahweh will take the field; he will fight against these nations as he fights in the day of battle. On that day, his feet will rest on the Mount of Olives, which faces Jerusalem from the east. The Mount of Olives will be split in half from east to west, forming a huge gorge; half the Mount will recede northwards, the other half southwards. And the Vale of Hinnom will be filled up from Goah to Jasol; it will be blocked as it was by the earthquake in the days of Uzziah king of

Judah. Yahweh your God will come, and all the holy ones with him. When that day comes, there will be no more cold, no more frost. It will be a day of wonder—Yahweh knows it—with no alternation of day and night; in the evening it will be light. When that day comes, running waters will issue from Jerusalem, half of them to the eastern sea, half of them to the western sea; they will flow summer and winter. And Yahweh will be king of the whole world. When that day comes, Yahweh will be unique and his name unique. The entire country will be transformed into plain, from Geba to Rimmon in the Negeb. And Jerusalem will be raised higher, though still in the same place; from the Gate of Benjamin to the site of the First Gate, that is to say to the Gate of the Comer and from the Tower Hananel to the king's winepress, people will make their homes. The ban will be lifted; Jerusalem will be safe to live in.

And this is the plague with which Yahweh will strike all the nations who have fought against Jerusalem; their flesh will molder while they are still standing on their feet; their eyes will rot in their sockets; their tongues will rot in their mouths. And such will be the plague on the horses and mules, camels and donkeys, and all the animals to be found in that camp. When that day comes, a great terror will fall on them from Yahweh; each man will grab his neighbor's hand and they will hit out at each other. Even Judah will fight against Jerusalem. The wealth of all the surrounding nations will be heaped together; gold, silver, clothing, in vast quantity.

All who survive of all the nations that have marched against Jerusalem will go up year by year to worship the King, Yahweh Sabaoth, and to keep the feast of Tabernacles. Should one of the races of the world fail to go up to Jerusalem to worship the King, Yahweh Sabaoth, there will be no rain for that one. Should the race of Egypt fail to go up and pay its visit, on it will fall the plague which Yahweh will inflict on each one of those nations that fail to go up to keep the feast of Tabernacles. When that day comes, the horse bells will be inscribed with the words, "Sacred to Yahweh," and in the Temple of Yahweh the very cooking pots will be as fine as the sprinkling bowls at the altar. And every cooking pot in Jerusalem and in Judah shall become sacred to Yahweh Sabaoth; all who want to offer sacrifice will come and help themselves from them for their cooking; there will be no more traders in the Temple of Yahweh Sabaoth, when that day comes. (from the *Jerusalem Bible*)

Leaving aside the references to Yahweh, and the bizarre Middle Eastern names, the images are not all that foreign to the addicted reader of science fiction. Indeed, Zechariah might be giving a brief synopsis of *Lucifer's Hammer* by Larry Niven and Jerry Pournelle (an account of a comet colliding with earth). What did Zechariah have in mind?

Contemporary research on the apocalyptic literature (see, for example, Paul D. Hansen, *The Dawn of Apocalyptic: The Historical and Sociological Roots of Jewish Apocalyptic Eschatology.* Fortress Press, 1975) are reasonably persuaded that apocalyptic literature is fundamentally Jewish in its origins and influenced only very slightly by the neighboring pagan literary styles. Jewish literature of the immediate pre-exile era was prophetic, heavily concerned with moral striving, humanist in obligation in Yahweh's name to create a just and moral society. It would remain free and powerful, not by force of arms, but because of its fidelity to him, and the moral excellence which characterized the lives of its people. The moral and religious visions of the prophets, of course, are the core of the Jewish and Christian religions and represent one of the major breakthroughs in religious consciousness of all human history. However, the prophetic vision of a just and religious messianic age was not achieved and later prophets such as Jeremiah wrestled with an explanation. Had Yahweh's promise been misunderstood or had the people been faithless? In any event, the kingdom was destroyed, the people carried off into captivity, and the messianic hopes dashed. Upon return from exile the Israelite elites, discouraged, disheartened and oppressed, fell back on the older creation symbols which their religious heritage shared with the rest of the Middle East—images of the struggle between cosmos and chaos, between good and evil, between light and darkness. Creation was the ordering of the universe by Yahweh (or by demigods in other Eastern religions). The fires were put out, the darkness was illuminated, disorder and conflict was held at bay, and life became possible in the world though sometimes only tenuously and barely possible. If the first creation had not inaugurated a process which led to fulfillment, so argued some of the post-exilic elite, most notably Zechariah and the author of the second part of Isaiah, then perhaps what was needed was a dissolution of the old world back into its primal chaos and a recreation of the cosmos by a new and decisive act of the Ordering Principle. The notion of a new beginning, of the destruction of the old and the creation of the new, was apparently widespread in ancient times-widespread in the era after the exile. The old kingdoms and empires were breaking up and new were being born. It was, for those who followed the stars, the end of Taurus the Bull and the beginning of the Age of the Fish. If the apocalyptic literary style was Jewish and even prophetic in its formation, it reached backwards into the creation images of the Middle Eastern nature religions and sideways into the conviction that a new era was beginning which was prevalent in Mediterranean Hellenism (when the Emperor Augustus closed the door to the Temple of Mars the event was hailed as the beginning of a new era of peace, not totally dissimilar to the messianic eras hailed in the Jewish scriptures-given the enormous influence of Judaism in the Roman Empire at the time of Augustus, of course, it is quite possible that most of the in-flow of imagery was from Judaism to Roman Hellenism instead of vice versa).

Note well that in its origins, as described in the passage from Zechariah, apocalypse is more reconstruction than destruction, more of a beginning of a new than an ending of the old, more of a vision of hope than a vision of dissolution. Even by the time of the Christian scriptures, however, the fascination of writers and preachers with dazzling accounts of destruction was already well under way the *Dies Irae* would take thirteen more centuries to write but the raw material was already there.

The apocalypse image, as such, is unique to those cultural environments where Yahwehism—in its Jewish and/or Christian forms—has had an impact. Both eschatological themes are muted, or nonexistent, in other religious traditions. We so take for granted the apocalyptic theme, it is so much part of the unconscious cultural environment, the literary air we breathe, that we hardly distinguish it and are hence quite unaware of its special impact, particularly on the Western imagination. Still, it is not unreasonable to assert that if it were not for apocalypse there would not be science fiction because there would not be a vision of a future that is better than the past nor of a decisive intervention of a saving force which leads to a recreation, a reconstruction, a renewal of the world.

In the nineteenth century, philosophy believed that science could eliminate human misery and suffering, and the literary imagination strove to construct scientific paradises in which the good life, guided by a benign (if mildly totalitarian) science, was possible. The work of the American Ignatius Donnelly and the Englishman H.G. Wells testified to that bright scientific vision. It was science as a reconstructing agent that was intervening in a more or less gentle apocalypse to renew the earth.

The vision has faded. We are now in post-exilic times and the Second Temple has yet to be constructed. It is an era of pessimism, not to say fatalism, which makes Zechariah seem like a naive optimist. The SF imagination no longer constructs scientific utopias but either partial or total apocalypses in which the bad we know is wiped out and replaced by something worse or, alternatively, something every bit as bad. The positive component, then, of the apocalyptic imagination has been lost and the science fiction writer of the day has more in common with Thomas of Celano (the author of the *Dies Irae*) than he does with Zechariah.

Much of the science fiction literature simply assumes that there has been a nuclear war. Even the benign *Star Trek* series operated on such an assumption, and so do the future histories of Isaac Asimov, Poul Anderson (in his Nicholas van Rijn series), and Robert Heinlein. The world which has evolved is almost invariably at least as bad as the one that antedated the catastrophe and oftentimes much worse—humankind sinking back into barbarism and savagery, made even worse by the presence of mutants produced by radioactive fallout.

Thus, in *Lucifer's Hammer,* life goes on after the collision with the comet but it is a life much like that of the Dark Ages with the ruthless war lords presiding over small territorial kingdoms locked in endless combat with their neighbors. Human nature is, the writers say, following the popularizers of primate research, basically evil, aggressive, destructive. All the apocalyptic events do is strip away the veneer of civilization and turn us back into savages.

(The serious scholarly research in comparative primatology doubts that there is any such thing as an aggressive instinct and suggests that our pre-hominid and proto-hominid ancestors had to develop abilities at both cooperation and love before we could evolve into human beings-far too benign a view of human nature for the currently fashionable pessimism.) In addition to the manmade holocausts, which usually end with the human race badly damaged but struggling on, and the extra-terrestrially induced holocausts in which human nature is sometimes renewed but other times virtually eliminated (in one science fiction series, recently serialized in a magazine, genetic experiments produce god-like creatures who oppress and virtually destroy the descendants of the original human species), there are also the cataclysmic apocalypses which sound in their descriptions much like those in the scriptures but which result (like the comet collision in *Lucifer's Hammer)* from the blind working of astronomical fate—not infrequently ending completely the world and the human race (though somehow or other, accounts manage to get written after the apocalypse, often in ways never explained by the author). For example, in Isaac Asimov's classic, "Nightfall," darkness descends. "This was the dark-the dark and the cold and the doom. The bright walls of the universe were shattered and their awful black fragments were falling down to crush and squeeze and obliterate him . . . on the horizon outside the window . . . a crimson glow began growing, strengthening in brightness that was not the glow of the sun...the long night had come again."

Thomas of Celano would really have liked that.

And in Arthur Clarke's "The Nine Billion Names of God," the Mark V computer, programmed by Tibetan monks, does indeed speak the nine billion names of God. The universe has had its purpose and "overhead, without any fuss, the stars were going out."

Sometimes, however, while destruction is induced by fates, the agent of the fate is human, as in L. Sprague de Camp's "Judgment Day," in which Wade Ormont, a "mad scientist," who has been persecuted by other human beings all his life, is pushed to the breaking point by "mischief night" (the night before Hallowe'en when the local kids raise hell). The kids had "soaped the windows and scattered the garbage and spread the toilet paper around . . . they had also burgled my garage and gone over my little British two-seater. The tires were punctured, the upholstery slashed, the paint scratched and the wiring ripped out of the engine . . . to make sure I knew what they thought, had lettered a lot of shirt cardboards and left them around, reading: 'Old lady Ormont is a nut; beware of the mad scientist!' That decided me. There is one way I can be happy during my remaining years and that is by the knowledge that all these bullies will get theirs. I hate them, I hate them, I hate everybody; I want to kill mankind; I'd kill them by slow torture if I could; if I can't blowing up the earth will do."

Why are the current science fiction apocalypses almost totally gloomy and destructive events, why is the pessimism even worse than at the time of Zechariah, and even more gloomy than that of the time of Thomas Celano, who managed in the last couple of stanzas of the *Dies Irae* to breathe a few words of hope?

The modernist approach in literature, of course, precludes the possibility of hopefulness or happiness in serious novels. Science fiction writers aspire to be serious novelists and therefore they have become more pessimistic, or as they strive to achieve something beyond what they consider merely pulp popularity (so as mystery writers come to be more "serious" they give up the mythological conflict between good and evil, in which good as represented by the detective tends to win, and either have the detective defeated or identify the detective ambiguously with the forces of evil—such are the requirements of literary modernism). Furthermore, in the years since the 1945 bombings of Hiroshima and Nagasaki, and in particular since the discovery of the apocalyptic possibilities of pollution, science has become another one of the gods that failed and is perceived now by many American intellectuals as a malign and destructive force. (One writer has observed that evolution made a mistake when it produced humankind and human reflective self-consciousness because it produced a force which would eventually terminate the evolutionary process—Manichaeism which would make St. Augustine look like a flaming Pelagian optimist!) As destructive apocalypse has become part of the mythology and the imagery of the wider national intelligentsia (Robert Heilbruner, in his *On the Human Prospect,* asks whether there is hope for humankind and responds vigorously in the negative), then that segment of the elite or would-be elite which produces science fiction is necessarily driven to apocalypse, but always, of course, the apocalypse of destruction, and rarely the apocalypse in which destruction is a prelude to reconstruction.

There is, however, one fascinating exception, a writer who continues to practice the apocalyptic tradition in a style that would please Zechariah and Deutero Isaias. His name is Raphael Aloysius Lafferty, and he was born in Neola, Iowa, in 1914, of Irish immigrant parents. A self-educated electrical engineer (for thirty-five years before he turned to writing full-time), Lafferty has a literary style which reminds one of Gilbert Keith Chesterton, and a creative imagination filled with light, fire and divine lunacy.

For Lafferty, apocalypses, even savage ones, are gracious and often comic.

In his novel *Past Master,* Thomas More is rescued from the headman's block by a people who are able to reach back into history and brought him into another era in which he is charged with saving a world that is coming apart at the seams. More does brilliantly and ends up on the headman's scaffold once again. After having been world president and king for nine days, he's doomed to die again. His allies, led by a marvelous young woman named Evita (and a boy named

Adam, who dies repeatedly only to be born again), storm the scaffold but are driven back. "The boy Adam, in particular, died magnificently, as he always did." Evita destroys More's enemy, but More himself is executed—*possibly*—though a stranger does appear on the platform and speaks with him. "Thomas seemed both excited and pleased."

"Will it work, do you think?" he cried loudly, with almost delight. "How droll. Can a man have more heads than two? I'll do it, I'll go with you."

But then there is apocalypse.

> But one thing *did* really happen at that moment. At the moment that life flickered out of the beheaded corpse, *the worlds came to an end.*
>
> All life and heat and pulse went out of the world. It died in every bird and rock and plant and person of it, in every mountain and sea and cloud. It died in its gravity and light and heat, in its germ-life and in its life-code. Everything ceased. And all the stars went out.
>
> Was it for a moment? Or a billion years? Or forever? There is no difference in them, when the world is ended, when there is no time to measure time by.[1] (Author's emphasis)

But all of this is not yet quite the end; in fact it might not be the end at all for, as Lafferty concludes the book:

> Remember it? Then it happened?
> *Be quiet. We wait.*
> The spirit came down once on water and clay. Could it not come down on gell-cells and fluxfix? The sterile wood, whether of human or programmed tree, shall it fruit after all? The Avid Nothingness, the diabolically empty Point-Big-o, is it cast away again? Is there then no room for life? Shall there be return to real life?

---

[1] Raphael A. Lafferty, *Past Master,* New York: Ace Books, 1968, p.246.

Well, does it happen? Does the reaction become the birthing? What does it look like? Will we see it now, in fact and rump, the new-born world?
Be quiet. We hope. (pp. 247-8; author's emphasis)

In the book *Apocalypses*[2] (oh, yes, Lafferty is well aware of what he's up to), there is a long novella called "The Three Armageddons of Enniscorthy Sweeny," in which a long chronology is presented of the life and times of the picaresque genius Enniscorthy Sweeny, 1894 to 1984—including the election of Robert Taft as president of the United States in 1948 and Douglas MacArthur in 1952, John XXIII as pope in 1958 and Richard Nixon as president in 1960. In 1984, Enniscorthy Sweeny himself dies (and the year is no accident) and his opera, *Armageddon Three,* is performed, apparently beginning the process that leads to the end of the world. The final entrance in the chronology is 1984, "the situation worsens." After the chronology, the world may or may not end, but one is not quite clear because, as one preacher, warning of the end of the world, says in the tale, "...when the world is finally destroyed will it *act* as though it is destroyed? Or will it be the most casual and nonbelieving cinder ever?" (p. 361)

It is quite clear that "just at the wind down of the years, the world and its people have gotten mighty mean. They were the meanest and the rottenest people that anyone ever saw." Enniscorthy Sweeny may not have been dead either; he may simply have been sitting in the tree like Mad Sweeny, the king in ancient Irish legend, and his wife Mary Margaret, who stood beneath the tree and crooned, "Aw, c'mon down, Sweeny." It would appear that some people set Sweeny's tree on fire to roast him to death and that began the final fire of the world.

So Final Armageddon was burning and raging out of control, and the World was ending.

---

[2] Raphael A. Lafferty, *Apocalypses,* Los Angeles: Pinnacle Books, 1977.

> That's funny. The people didn't *act* as if the world were ending. But they didn't act quite as if it were going to continue either.
>
> They behaved as though they didn't very much care whether it ended or not (p. 374).

Thus, the end of the world and the end of Enniscorthy Sweeny—maybe, and then, maybe not, because it would appear that Sweeny had been killed many times before and kept coming back.

But the wildest of Lafferty's apocalypses is in his brilliant story—perhaps his masterpiece—"And Walk Now Gently Through the Fire," a tale about the Ichthyans, or queer fish, a group of people who keep alive a strange version of Christianity after "The Great Copout."

> ...the Day of the Great Copout was worldwide. As though at a given signal (but there had been no signal) people in every city and town and village and countryside of earth dropped their tools and implements and swore that they would work no more. Officials and paper shufflers ceased to officiate and to shuffle paper. Retailers closed up and retailed no more. Distributors no longer distributed. Producers produced nothing. The clock of the people stopped although some had believed that the hour was still early.
>
> The Last Day had been, according to some.
>
> "The Last Day has not been," said a prophet. "They will know it when it has been." (pp. 45)

The leading characters of "And Walk Now Gently Through the Fire" are the Thatcher family—Judy, the young mother, and her two early teenage children, Trumpet and Gregory. The head of the family, one John Thatcher, had been one of the Twelve, a leader of the Ichthyans, but he had been killed. However, he rose from the dead for a brief period of time to pass on his leadership function to his wife, who casually jots off Epistles, such as the Epistle to the Church of Omaha in Dispersal.

Judy was a Queer Fish. She was also, according to the story, "a young and handsome woman of rowdy intellect." Her son Gregory, who clearly has an important role to play, is early in the novel tempted by a minor devil. "His name was Azazel. He wasn't the great one of that name but one of his numerous nephews. There is an economy of name among the devils." Azazel asks Gregory to "command that these stones be made bread." "Does it always have to start with those same words?" Gregory asks in response. He is then instructed to cast himself down from a height because, "if you are one of the elect you will not be dashed to pieces." Gregory dodges the temptation. "I'll not be dashed to pieces yet. It's high but not really steep, not a good selection." And finally Azazel offers him the "world and all that is in it." Greg Thatcher grins, "It really isn't much of a world you have to offer . . . Really, where is the temptation?" However, Gregory does not give the devil the traditional dismissal. "I'll not say, 'Get thee behind me, Satan,' for I wouldn't trust you behind me for one stride."

Trumpet and Judy, alas, are killed in a fierce battle and Gregory and a certain Levi Cain band together with a group of other young people named Simon Canon, Tom Culpa (his name meant Tom Twin), Joanna Cromova (daughter of Thunder), Andy Johnson, Matty Miracle, and Peter Johnson—who seems to be their leader.

Then, "events have gathered into constellations" and the big fire begins, though it is an acre of fire, fire through which the young Ichthyans must walk.

One may be offended by Lafferty's playful manipulation of the Christian symbols in this episode, offended because one believes that the symbols are too sacred to be manipulated, or alternately, offended because one believes the symbols are too false to be discussed. Still, one has to say that the apocalypses of R.A. Lafferty are the closest things in science fiction to Zechariah, who started the whole thing, because Lafferty's apocalypses are apocalypses of rebirth, renewal and beginnings again.

He may, in other words, be right or wrong about the nature of reality, but he certainly is right about the nature of apocalypse.

With one exception, Zechariah was not a humorist. R.A. Lafferty imagines wild, renewing, destructive, manic, recreating apocalypses just as Zechariah did, but R.A. Lafferty's apocalypses are also comic—a phenomenon which might well have offended Zechariah and certainly would have offended Thomas of Celano.

But then, neither of these two worthies was Irish.

Father Greeley, who passed away in 2013, was a priest, sociologist of religion, professor at the University of Chicago, theorist of the Catholic "analogical imagination," and novelist. What is less known is that he was a fan of SF and a very early advocate of Lafferty's genius within the academy.

Hooking the World on Lafferty
By Kevin Cheek

If I were involved in the republication of Lafferty's work, here are some thoughts I have about a mass-market collection of short stories to hook a wide readership on his work. I have no say in the matter, but I don't see why that should stop me from saying.

First, an analogy: There are two great collections of Cordwainer Smith's short stories that share the same name: *The Rediscovery of Man* published by Gollancz as part of their SF Masterworks series and *The Rediscovery of Man* published by NESFA Press. The Gollancz book is a greatest hits kind of collection. It contains 12 very strong stories in chronological order (by the order of events in the stories, not by writing date). The NESFA Press book contains the complete short fiction of Cordwainer Smith.

In my opinion, the Gollancz book is the much stronger book. It is the one I force into the hands of friends and co-workers when I want to get them hooked on Cordwainer Smith or at least to understand what I am talking about. The NESFA book is not as good an introduction to his work. It is far better for a new reader to start with "Scanners Live in Vain" than "No, No, Not Rogov!" or "War no. 81-Q." Not that those aren't good stories, they are, but they do not introduce readers to the power and strangeness of Smith's world of the Instrumentality of Mankind as forcefully. The NESFA book is a book for hardcore fans and Cordwainer Smith completists.

The same analogy could apply to republishing R. A. Lafferty. Not everything he wrote possesses the same power to grab you and make you look at the world in entirely new ways. To grab new readers—to introduce them to a deep appreciation of Lafferty's work, we need not to hit them with everything at once, but to dazzle them with those stories that simultaneously soar high and reach deep. This is how I developed my Lafferty habit and I assume this is how most of us discovered his writing—a great story here, an amazing story there—hey there's a pattern, time to start seeking him out—*Orbit* anthologies (those were almost all great stories, and showed them balanced with other well done, progressive work), *Nine Hundred Grandmothers*—jackpot and addiction.

So I think the first thing that needs to be published is a collection of the most masterful of his most approachable stories. For me, this list is similar to but not identical to my list of favorite stories. Several of the ones I love are pieces of virtuoso writing, but perhaps better for the second course rather than the appetizer. Here is my proposed first course of Lafferty:

1. "Narrow Valley" - The Great American Short Story. This has it all: homesteaders, a sheriff, Indians, eminent scientists complete with scientific babble, precocious children, and a joyous hopeful ending.
2. "Slow Tuesday Night" - Somehow more relevant today than when he wrote it.
3. "Eurema's Dam" - Perhaps the greatest example of Lafferty's madness and tight storytelling.
4. "Through Other Eyes" - His perfectly structured pure science fiction story—Lafferty style.
5. "Thus We Frustrate Charlemagne" - Pure tour-de-force SF. Pure fun.
6. "Ride a Tin Can" - Beautiful, sad, devastating, cautionary.
7. "Hog Belly Honey" - The most joyous of romps after the sadness of the previous story.
8. "Funnyfingers" - Beautiful, sad, devastating, and proof that Lafferty can write about love.
9. "In Our Block" - Provide a sense of how fantastical the everyday world can be.
10. "Snuffles" - About the right place in the collection for a novella. It's a hard one to read, but shows his immense power. This story is hard, not because of the prose, but because the characters grab you and their deaths devastate you—because they represent parts of you.
11. "Marsillia V." - Keeping up the sustained horror theme here.

12. "Days of Grass, Days of Straw" - Transmuting the horror into a sense of wonder.
13. "Frog on the Mountain" - Lafferty does Hemingway, much in the same way that Zelazny did with "The Doors of His Face, The Lamps of His Mouth."
14. "Hole on the Corner" - Essential Lafferty reading—pure madness and pure fun!
15. "Continued on Next Rock" - A great mix of personalities and science and myth.
16. "The Tongues of Matagorda" - Remind the reader that storytelling and mythmaking are essential elements of Lafferty's work.
17. "One at a Time" - The essential Laffertian Irish brawler and essential Laffertian wordplay.
18. "Encased in Ancient Rind" - Topical today! Climate Change with a different vengeance.
19. "Golden Gate" - Has the greatest opening paragraph in short fiction.
20. "Been a Long, Long Time" - Go out with a (big) bang.

There are about a dozen more I'd love to include—there are no stories here about Austro, the men who knew everything and Laf, I'd love to include both the Phosphor McCabe stories, and more of Epikt and the Institute. I'd love to add "The Ugly Sea," "Sky," "Land of the Great Horses," and many, many more! However this collection seemed intuitively right to me. It is what I'd put on the menu if I wanted to hook people with a sample, and make them crave to come back for more.

This work © 2013, 2017 Kevin Cheek.

Remembering Ray Lafferty
by Joseph L. Green

In the 60s through 70s I attended a lot of Cons. I've forgotten the specific one at which I met Ray Lafferty, but am fairly sure it happened somewhere in the Southlands. At the time I had read only a little of his work, but been impressed by the short story "Slow Tuesday Night"—impressed by how unbelievable I found it. My thought at the time was "this guy isn't going very far." Over 40 years later I still think it was bad science fiction. But I remember "Slow Tuesday Night", while thousands of "good" science fiction stories have faded away.

And that could serve as a metaphor for Ray's work in general. Bad science fiction (in my not-so-humble opinion, science fiction tropes worked into what was in reality fantasy) of such original and compelling character that it assaulted your mind, storming ashore like the U.S. marines, then taking up residence like the Vikings in England and France – there to stay.

At our first meeting Ray was kind enough to say he had read and enjoyed some of my work. We became casual friends, and afterward always found each other at the Cons we both attended. We had many conversations, more often on topics common to free-lancers—writing, markets, sales here and overseas, etc.—than on the wild nature of his fiction, or the more science-oriented background of mine. Ray largely saved his far-out ideas and skewed views of life for his writing. We both had several novels selling in the European markets in those years, and when we compared figures, it surprised me to learn my sales were better than his. The distinctive and highly idiosyncratic approach Ray Lafferty took to science fiction did not at first go over well with what were then somewhat conservative European tastes. (The rise of the New Wave, exemplified by Michael Moorcock, Ballard, and others, changed that, I think.)

In person Ray was an average height, middle-aged, balding man, with a mostly gray fringe of hair around prominent ears. He made casual dressing look like a bad idea, the image not helped by a large, protruding belly. But his most obvious physical attribute was bad teeth. He had lost most of them, but one long, yellow fang still hung from his upper jaw, becoming very obvious when he spoke. And he was usually half-drunk, or working hard to get that way. None of this changed the fact I very much enjoyed our chats. More often than not, when I knew he would be at a specific Con and went looking for him, I found him sitting alone in the bar. He clearly enjoyed conventions, and sought the company of fellow fans and writers; otherwise he wouldn't have attended so many. But at heart I think he was rather shy, happy to talk if someone sought him out, but reluctant to actively initiate social contacts.

In regard to his drinking . . . Ray had a reputation for being a drunk, and it's certainly true he drank heavily at Cons, the venue in which most fans saw him. But I'm reminded of something Gordy Dickson, who also had a reputation for heavy drinking, told me in person once while at the Greenhouse.

Gordy said that the first drop of alcohol he consumed went straight to his brain, and turned off the creative writing center.

So he didn't drink at all when at home; he couldn't afford to. A person who drinks only at parties or other social occasions is not a drunk, and that certainly applies to Gordy Dickson. I never visited Ray Lafferty at his home in Tulsa, but I seriously doubt he drank while working. From the time in his forties when he started selling regularly, through the next 20 years or more, he produced a very large body of work (see his bibliography on Wikipedia). Unless he was that very rare creature who could drink and still produce great writing, I think Ray, like Gordy, confined his drinking to social occasions.

I was a close friend of one of the founders of New Orleans fandom, Harry B. Moore, Chairman of the 1951 Worldcon (Nolacon I) long before the current stalwarts—John Guidry, Justin Winston, Dennis Dolbear, et al—arrived on the scene. Pre-Katrina New Orleans was my favorite city, certainly the most visited, and I consider myself an honorary member of the N.O. fan group. About 1970 someone (who, now forgotten) came up with idea of holding "rump" Nebula banquets in New Orleans, for those of us who didn't really want to travel to New York. I always served as MC, and Don Walsh, John Guidry, Rick Norwood (then living in N.O) and other local fans did all the real work of organizing the event. Whoever in SFWA had the winners' names provided them to me, and I made the announcement at roughly the same time the awards were being presented in New York. A fair number of writers chose to attend N.O. instead of New York, and I suspect had an easier trip, a better meal, and far more fun. But when Jerry Pournelle was elected SFWA president in 1973 (and I chaired the elections committee that year), he put a stop to them. Jerry wanted to hold the Nebula bash in Los Angeles on alternate years, with the intention of gaining financial support from the several large aerospace contractors in the area. (This never worked out, but he made a valiant effort.) Having an unofficial awards banquet in N.O. would work against this idea. I was informed I could no longer learn the winners in advance, which effectively killed the N.O. banquets.

I remember that at various times James Sallis, Joe Haldeman, various others—plus of course the local writers like Dan Galouye—chose N.O. over New York. But one of our most regular attendees, I think catching every one, was Ray Lafferty. At some point during those years he had his teeth fixed, replacing the single long yellow fang with a set of nice and quite real-looking choppers. I also think the N.O. group, most strong Lafferty fans, did a better job than most of making him feel welcome, and at home. He seemed to mellow under the attention, and became more outgoing and obviously happy than when sitting alone in the bar at conventions.

Ray was in the audience in 1971, when I had the heartbreaking duty of announcing that Sturgeon's "Slow Sculpture" had beaten out Ray's "Continued On Next Rock" for the best novelette Nebula. ("Slow Sculpture" also took the Hugo that year.) While I agree that "Slow" is first-class, I thought "Continued" a better story; one of Ray's best. And Sturgeon wasn't there to hear me announce the winners; Ray was. I did, though, have the pleasure of seeing Ray, at Torcon

II in 1973, slowly shuffling toward the stage to receive a Hugo for "Eurema's Dam"—a split award with Pohl and Kornbluth's "The Meeting." I think his footing seemed uncertain because his eyes were blurred by tears. Despite his shyness, he very much wanted the approbation of fans, and recognition by his peers.

That became his only Hugo or Nebula, despite numerous nominations.

On another occasion at one of the N.O. Nebula bashes, I threatened Ray's life. Our programmed guest speaker hadn't made it, and we urgently needed a substitute. One of the organizers urged me to take the spot, knowing I was a pretty good extemporaneous speaker, but I had what I thought a better idea. I found Ray, and asked him to give us a little talk. The dialog went something like this:

"Ray, our guest speaker didn't make it, and we need someone to fill in. It doesn't have to be anything major, just get up and tell us a little about your work."

"Joe, you know I'm not a public speaker. I couldn't get up there and give a talk if my life depended on it." Giving him my best steely glare, I said, "Ray, your life *does* depend on it, because if you don't get up there and speak, I'm going to kill you."

Ray Lafferty got up when I called on him, and gave a darn good extemporaneous talk, well received by an appreciative audience. If he ever gave another speech in public, I wasn't there.

Ray is still a presence in the Greenhouse. In *The Devil Is Dead* he had a group of hard-drinking characters name each bottle of Scotch they emptied in an evening, on the theory that a good soldier who had done his duty shouldn't go to his grave without a name. And they did it in alphabetical order; if you got down to G or H, that had been a pretty heavy evening. We adopted that custom in a modified form, wine instead of Scotch and the alphabetical numbering continuing over time. Also, the winning name has to be suitable to the particular occasion. Over the years we've gone through the alphabet several times.

Ray wrote very little after about 1980, and if he still went to Cons, he was not at the ones I attended. Until then I hadn't made a serious effort to collect his works, just buying his books when I saw them. I started specifically looking for Lafferty, and found a number of lesser-known short novels, often by semi-pro publishers. I also looked for his hard to find fact articles, eventually ending up with about 30 short special printings of essay and commentary (I haven't yet read them all; there will be no more, and I enjoy knowing there's still some original Lafferty waiting in my future). One of these, "At The Sleepy Sailor: A Tribute To R.A. Lafferty", was edited by one Guy H. Lillian III. It contained articles by Harlan Ellison, Poul Anderson, Fred Chappell and others, with a closing appreciation by yours truly. I said then that he was one of the most original talents ever to grace our field, and I can't think of any better short description now. "In both style and content, Ray Lafferty clears his own path through the forest of literature. And he walks it alone."

Ray the man, like Ray the writer, was a highly original creation. He spoke much more eloquently through his work than in person, and that remains with us. But I miss Ray the man.

This work © 2010 Joseph L Green.
Originally published in Challenger *32, Summer 2010 (GHLIII Press Publication #1073)*

Joseph Green worked for 37 years in the American space program, retiring from NASA as Deputy Chief of the Education Office at the Kennedy Space Center. He specialized in preparing NASA fact sheets, brochures and other semi-technical publications for the general public. As a part-time freelancer he published five novels and about 70 short works in print magazines and books. In 2015 he and three associates established Greenhouse Scribes, an independent e-publisher, and new material now appears at the "Joseph Green" page on Amazon.

HUMAN
by Dan Knight

Upon reading a scholarly essay Ray once quipped to me, "This Lafferty guy is a pretty sharp character. I'd like to meet him one day." As those who knew him will attest, he wrote as he thought and (thankfully) thought as he wrote. The unique voice that so many celebrate was not an affectation. Neither was it a carefully crafted persona fashioned to cunningly go over the wall during that literary jailbreak that was SF in the mid-sixties. The man was just being himself

If you, gentle reader, have something unique to express you will probably be the last one to know it. Ray was the last one to know it. I'm not saying he couldn't tell his good from his bad. He was an astute writer and sharp enough to know which of his novels, or more often short stories, were cream and which were just good old wholesome milk. What I am saying is that the ghost who mussed my hair, slapped me on the back and ended up living in my pocket like a talisman— the essential and personal anima of Ray's stories—was not known to him. It *was* him. There are folks who spend years plotting out story arcs, experimenting with Voice to achieve just that particular shade of nuance. Ray wrote. Ray wrote Ray. He might have been capable of artificially recreating the style of somebody else but I doubt it. Take a look at the stories in The *Early Lafferty* chapbook (our first publishing adventure). He thought he was doing a *Saturday Evening Post* pastiche on one of them. Don't bother trying to guess which. They're all Lafferty stories. Even in 1960 they could be mistaken for nothing else.

Genius, someone said, isn't about being the smartest buffalo in the herd, but in seeing the world from a different perspective. To—in the lingo of the last decade—see outside of the box. Ray came from outside the box. We (and you know who you are) got him because we embraced him as one of our own.

It wasn't a sure thing. His first and still unpublished novel *Manta* was a murder mystery. Read *Okla Hannali* (a

223

novel my buddy Terry Bisson believes is the Great and as yet Uncelebrated American book—kin to Melville's *Moby Dick*) or *The Fall of Rome* (reprinted under its original title *Alaric* recently). These and the very good unpublished *Esteban* are historical fiction at its most entertaining. All of you aging hippies who tripped out on *Arrive at Easterwine* and *Past Master* give yourselves a pat on the back. Thank you, SF and not those other guys got the lion's share of his work.

Here's another good quote. "Effectual people live life. Ineffectual people write about it." There's a revealing statement. I don't care if you believe it or not. Ray did. These are not the words of a man with high thoughts of himself. This is a very human person with feelings of inadequacy like most of us. Some of you may recall one of his stories— "Eurema's Dam", Ray's Hugo winner—in which a little boy is forced to invent the most amazing devices not because he was so intelligent but because he believed himself dumber than dirt. He even created a mechanical simulacrum to deal with girls because he was too tongue-tied to do his own courting. There was a lot of Ray in there.

There will be, I expect, quite a bit of memorializing over the next little while. People will say many grand and beautiful things (you can almost see Ray's ears go red in embarrassment). It's proper to celebrate a good man's life. It is proper to overcome loss with fond remembrance or to acknowledge professional or personal debts. Beware though. It would be easy to recreate him in retrospect a Giant and therefore untouchable and ultimately unknowable. That would be tragic because who he was, in truth, was a funny, intelligent, self-critical, kind, opinionated, God-fearing, loving and sometimes-cranky guy, just like the best and the rest of us. Or, in a word, human. Not distant like some piece of classical Greek statuary but close. He was the Old Man who threw your ball back over the fence with a smile. Who collected comic books and baseball cards, bad jokes and new friends. Remember him. Remember him fondly with a grin and a wink. And, in the phrase he most often closed his letters with —

"Have fun!"

Dan Knight is the creator of United Mythologies Press *and an important publisher of Lafferty's work. His* Boomer Flats Gazette *periodical was a seminal outlet for Lafferty scholarship and appreciation.*

"Come all you little Singing-Pig-Shelni," a bell man shouts. "Come get your free rides in the tin cans all the way to Earth! Hey, Ben, what other animal jumps onto the slaughter wagon when you only ring a bell?"

R. A. Lafferty, "Ride a Tin Can"

Illustration © 2016 Anthony Ryan Rhodes

R. A. Lafferty—Aurelia (1982)
by David Langford

Aurelia is a fourteen-year-old girl from Shining World, where her class did Marriage and Reproduction at thirteen: the final stage of her schooling is World Government. Each in his or her own home-made spacecraft, Aurelia and classmates scatter to rule and single-handedly reform those backward planets judged to be in need of governance. But our heroine is herself backward; her cack-handed journeying leads to a specially weird world which is probably though not assuredly Earth; her rule, which should be accepted by all, generates cultism and controversy; a mysterious Dark Counterpart appears to (perhaps) oppose her; three final days of processions, meals, intrigue and speechifying end with the predicted deaths of Aurelia and dark "Cousin Clootie," the initial hilarity having steadily dimmed.

Naturally the phantasmagoric Lafferty offers more than these bare bones. One could compile long lists of black humor, clever phrases, glittering chips of outrageousness. "The worst that could happen to her was that she might fail the assignment. The commonest way of failing such an assignment was getting killed or vaporized in flight or in governorship. That caused one automatically to fail the course." There is the appalling Instrumental Knot into which Aurelia by a secret technique ties the, ah, instrument of a man who harasses her. ("Certainly the whole Universe has to be pulled through the loop to untie it, but that's easier than it sounds.") On some worlds there is an extra prime number between five and seven. ("A variant version says that the rogue number is inserted between Eight and Nine.") By a certain private device a character talks to the "fluvial and oceanic components of himself" while believing himself to be talking to fish ("Then how did other people hear the fish talking to Rex if it was done by private device? Oh, other people possess private devices also").

By such tidbits and by his inimitable style, Lafferty holds the attention: but no really satisfying shape emerges from the text. What is actually going on in his *Fourth Mansions*, in *The Devil is Dead*, in *The Three Armageddons of Enniscorthy Sweeney*, gains power through never being too clearly articulated but growing out of oblique touches seen from the corner of the eye. In *Aurelia* it seems either that the surface distractions have proliferated to the extent of obscuring the deeps, or that—a reluctant hypothesis—there is nothing much happening beneath that clever surface at all.

The final third of the book is dominated by Aurelia's flatulent speeches to the multitudes, which use moderately simple language but achieve considerable opacity, not to mention forgettability, "There is a unified theory covering all sorts of laws, for all true laws are interlinked. We should never ask of a law of any sort whether it is good or bad. We should ask whether it is true or false..." And Aurelia and her dark cousin, at first glance opposites representing bungling good and better-organized evil, prove to be well-meaning complements.

Meanwhile, the nastiest characters of all have for their symbol the balanced yin-yang, concretized as a murderous double-bladed yo-yo; the emblem of complementarity is finally used to polish off nice Aurelia and her complement. Presumably Lafferty is implying that one should be absolute for black or white, and never embrace a compromise (a similar theme emerges early in G. K. Chesterton's *The Ball and the Cross*, and Lafferty is a Chesterton fan). Even this much is rather difficult to extract from a welter of symbology concerning horned and antlered men, mysteriously appearing primitive creatures, at least one orthodox Christian miracle, etc.

Despite confusions and disappointments, *Aurelia* does remain worth reading. Even when using familiar material (Aurelia's education recalls the Camiroi stories; the horned men recall *Fourth Mansions*; so many prior works feature a bloody Eucharist and conclude on or near the moment of death), even while losing control of his inventiveness and his plot, Lafferty still writes engagingly well.

David Langford

David Langford is a writer, critic, editor, publisher and SF fan based in the UK. Langford began to publish sf professionally with "Heatwave" for New Writings in SF 27 (1975) and has written a number of novels, among them The Space Eater *(1982) and* The Leaky Establishment *(1984). His numerous magazine columns have appeared in* Interzone, Ansible, *and* SFX. *Langford was nonfiction editor of the short-lived* Extro, *and also edited* Starlight SF. *He has been SF reviewer for the UK newspapers* The Guardian *as well as* The Sunday Telegraph. *Langford now devotes most of his time to nonfiction and editorial work including the Encyclopedia of Science, which he co-edits along with John Clute, Peter Nicholls, and Graham Sleight. Langford has won an unprecedented 29 Hugo Awards for his fan journalism and editorial efforts.*

Does Anyone Else Have Something Further to Add?
by Stephen R. Case

Gene Wolfe has said of writing short stories that it is not enough to simply show people your ideas. He uses the analogy of a lion-tamer. A writer can't just say to people, "Hey, look at this lion" and expect them to be impressed with her skills at showing them a lion. A writer has to do something with the lion, preferably something daring and unexpected. Wolfe says that the writer has to put her head in the idea's mouth.

For me, that is the most difficult part of writing. Often I simply want to show people my ideas—an interesting imaginary place, for instance, or a character or device or image—but finding that narrative twist and plunge that makes the idea spark and come alive as a leaping, writhing story is something very different.

As important as Wolfe's advice is though, I don't feel like his requirement applies to R. A. Lafferty. There are in his stories—and specifically in the stories of this volume—rarely those unexpected twists that make you feel as though the bottom has fallen out of the narrative. In many of the stories that make up this collection, a reader can feel the end coming, can get a sense for the ultimate trajectory of the story, within the first few paragraphs. Part of this is because Lafferty does not craft those literary artifacts called short stories. Instead, he tells fables, and most fables have been told in some form before. But I think there's also something deeper going on here with Lafferty and Wolfe's lion-tamer analogy.

To return to Wolfe's image, Lafferty does not need to stick his head in the idea's mouth. Lafferty is the lion-tamer, but he's a lion-tamer saying, "My God, it's a *lion*. No, you haven't ever really looked at a lion before. And you haven't seen a lion like this. *Look at it*. This is the lionest lion that ever lived; this is the Ur-lion." And then the lion—which, you realize, is indeed wilder and more savage and yet more merry

230

than any lion you've seen before—rips out the lion-tamer's throat and eats it with a wet chuckle, and both lion and lion-tamer have a good laugh together because that's what lions *are* and that's what lions *do*.

The story "Golden Trabant" in this volume is a good example of this approach. Narratively, the story is incredibly simple and has indeed been told many times before: a man discovers the El Dorado of asteroids, a rock not far from Earth formed completely of gold. What happens next? Exactly what you would expect. Pirates lay claim to it and become fabulously rich. Earth's economy becomes unbalanced by the sudden influx of off-planet gold. The pirates build a kingdom with their new gold, sail the high skies hauling back their treasure in ship-loads, and ultimately turn on each other. The asteroid becomes an irradiated waste haunted by a ghost. It's every lost treasure story you've heard before with only the (now-blasé) element of being set in space. Maybe that was a new wrinkle when Lafferty wrote it, but beyond that there's no unexpected twist that makes the story leap up out of the page like a living thing.

And yet it's a fantastic story. Like so many of Lafferty's, it simply *works*. The whole thing is alive. This is the case with many of the stories here. In some, it's unclear what exactly is happening or has happened, plot-wise. "About a Secret Crocodile," "Nor Limestone Islands," and "Boomer Flats" are examples of this. "Boomer Flats" and "Maybe Jones and the City" in particular I found a bit frustrating, but the richness and jollity of Lafferty's tone always wins me over eventually, even when they seem spun around nothing. If the bones of the story are a bit hollow, you still get Lafferty telling them. And that's what you want. I'm convinced that had Lafferty taken it upon himself to re-write a phone book, it would be fun to read.

To be fair, there are stories with twists. There's one at the end of "In the Garden" and "This Grand Carcass Yet" and "The Ultimate Creature." "The Weirdest World" is all twist, and it may be one of the funniest Lafferty stories I've read yet. But the twist is secondary; the story is not built around it. And you probably saw it coming anyway. Moreover, the twist is usually twisted: this is a volume that highlights Lafferty's

231

brutal, grotesque humor, which is especially ripe in "This Grand Carcass Yet," "Pig in a Pokey," and "The Ultimate Creature."

An annoying and puzzling (though easily ignored) feature of this volume is the needless division of the stories into those related to "Secret Places" and those about "Mean Men." The stories in this work alternate back and forth between these two headings. In my edition of the book, this is even reflected by stories under each division having a differentiating font. Lafferty (not surprisingly) offers no explanation for this division, but it's unlike Lafferty to offer much explanation for anything.

The reason the division doesn't work though– or at least seems unnecessary and arbitrary– is that all of Lafferty's stories are in some sense about secret places, and they're all in some sense about mean men. They're stories about the hidden, real world lurking just below the skin of this one and about the god or the devil lurking just below our own skins. That's why their twists aren't wholly unexpected: we feel them in our bones. We catch hints of them when we we're not asleep.

If you're new to Lafferty, this is as good a place to start with him as any. It's hard to know what angle to approach his writings, but wading out into his short stories and learning how they rise and fall is easier than diving into one of his novels. Because, to be fair, you might not like his bright and bloody world. You might not want to get too close to that lionest of lions and hear its throaty chuckle. With his short stories, it's easier to run away.

This work © 2014 Stephen R. Case

"I have incurred a lot of ill will in my day, and sometimes it boils over. There was one time when a whole shipful of men had had enough of me."

R. A. Lafferty, "One at a Time"

Illustration © 2016 Anthony Ryan Rhodes

Cranky Old Man From Tulsa
An Interview With R.A. Lafferty
by Darrell Schweitzer

This interview was conducted at the World Science Fiction Convention, Chicago, 1982.

Darrell Schweitzer: What were you doing before you became a writer?

R. A. Lafferty: I worked for an electric wholesaler from the time I was out of high school, with time out for the Army, and after that for about thirty-five years. So it's mostly electrical jobbing. All sorts of electrical material I bought. About ten thousand items I kept stock on, and I got to like the business.

DS: What made you take up writing?

RAL: Well, it was just one of those days in the middle of life when I thought I might want to try something else, so I tried it. After a while it started to work.

DS: Didn't you mention somewhere that you were writing poetry before you were writing stories?

RAL: I was, but I didn't consider that commercial. Of course I have used a lot of those since then as chapter heads, and little verses I have scattered in. In fact I have used up all the good ones.

DS: How much of your past life comes out in works like *Archipelago*, which has an autobiographical feel to it?

RAL: Well, the background is authentic, in the war years and in the cities and so forth. Possibly the five characters are composites of people I met along the way. In fact I was at an Army reunion with my old outfit just a month ago, and I recognized several of the guys in the book that I didn't know I had put in quite so definitely. I thought that I was writing fiction, but I found that there was more of the real people in several of those characters than I realized when I was writing it.

DS: Did you put yourself in it?

RAL: Oh, just fragments of me through all the Dirty Five and a couple other characters there.

DS: When you started writing, why did you start in science fiction?

RAL: Well, I started writing everything. I wrote a *Saturday Evening Post* story and an *American Magazine* story and a *Collier's* story, and some sort of a western story, and science fiction and mystery stories. I sent them around. The science fiction story sold and the others didn't, so after several repetitions then, I just wrote science fiction. It took me about a year before I was selling.

DS: You have been quoted as saying that there are periods in science fiction in which all the stories are rotten, with exceptions, and periods when all the stories are rotten and there are no exceptions, and that we are in a type 2 period at the moment. Why do you think this is so?

RAL: I was probably just in a type 2 day when I wrote that. Some days it seems pretty good, and some days it does seem rotten, but so does everything else. It was kind of a subjective judgment. Sometimes there are glimmers of hope for it.

DS: What do you see wrong most of the time?

RAL: Most of the time it's just gone down with most of the other fiction. It's not too interesting, and that's the cardinal sin of fiction, of course.

DS: You're somewhat unusual in being one of the few

science fiction writers to use religious material. A few touch on it, and there are a lot of fake church stories like *Gather, Darkness!*, but most writers seem to shy away from the actual substance. Why do you think this is?

RAL: Actually, religion is becoming more interesting, more important I believe. I think there's a lag. Most of them just haven't gone to that yet. There's the idea that religion is a drag, and so forth, but that idea is probably several decades out of date.

DS: It seems to me that science fiction often covers all the ground of religion, but does so in a non-religious manner. *Childhood's End*, for example.

RAL: Well, I think *Childhood's End* was religious, but that's more the case with fantasy than with science fiction. In fact almost all the high fantasy is really based on the Low Middle Ages of Europe, which was a very religious period. But all the religion is taken out of it, and the background of the Low Middle Ages, the Dark Ages, is used for sword and sorcery. They've taken the motive power out and used the furniture and costuming. I don't know why they did that. They're leaving out the main part.

DS: My experience is that often if a story even touches on such things, the editor will freeze up and think he's being preached at. You can write about, say, Hindu gods with no problem, but if you touch on Christianity, even if all the characters are doubters, the editor freezes. Have you ever found this to be so?

RAL: Yes, that's very much so. But you've got it backwards. The preachers are really those of a religion that is not called a religion, which is secular liberalism. That's really the established religion of our country, and of our world. It doesn't allow too much opposition. Now people who go down the secular liberal line don't want anything that challenges it. Hinduism doesn't challenge it because it is too distant. Christianity does, even Born-Again Christianity and the emotional ones. They have something that the secular liberal world is lacking.

DS: In *Archipelago* you talk about this sort of thing infiltrating real religion. What sort of a response did you get from that book on this point?

RAL: Well, actually the only response to the book I ever got was from people I knew pretty well, who bought the book early. Now those people were already familiar with my thinking, and they went along with it, but lately I'm getting it from people I don't know, and some of it is kind of strong opposition. And I get some friendly pieces too. I don't know what the result is going to be there.

DS: You've stated that you think this is your best novel. Why do you consider it to be your best?

RAL: Well, I don't know. I just caught a lot of things in there. It's not science fiction, although the other parts of the trilogy are. It's really a valid piece of recent history, starting about 1943 and carrying on for ten years, and implying to carry on for quite a bit later than that, to the present. But it's really, I think, valid, almost modern history.

DS: It does have fantasy tie-ins, at least on a metaphorical level. You're dealing with great mythic archetypes who go out drinking a lot together.

RAL: That's a valid part of near-modern history. There's a lot more of those now than there used to be. [Laughs.] Boozy philosophy and so forth. That's become one of the new motive powers, of trying to talk things out anyhow. For better or worse it has.

DS: Have you ever seen any of those drinking stunts done, like the guy who broke the record before the contest, just to get in shape?

RAL: No, but I saw the contest itself. That happened.

DS: On a more serious level, what about the idea that science fiction is a form of mythology?

RAL: For that matter, science is a form of mythology. Myth isn't something false ordinarily. It's just a way of handling or coming on to a truth. When it can't be direct, there are lots of mythical things in science. They were in there quite a while before science was finally formulated. This is taking us quite far afield.

DS: Is this the reason for science fiction's popularity? It seems to me that if a literature works like mythology, it will push a lot of the reader's subconscious buttons, and it will appeal to him even if he doesn't know why.

RAL: Yes, but science is activated by a lot of those subconscious buttons. I was reading Newton himself on his optics last week. He was yawning all the way there. He believed in the corpuscular theory rather than the wave theory. He was actually writing mythology. Yet all his optic diagrams were valid, but his idea of how it worked, the corpuscular theory with little things bouncing around, instead of the wave theory, was wrong. Both are pretty much mythologies, really, because they can't be seen, can't be anything but implied. Radio waves—there's no way you can see them. You just get results from them. There were sort of myths for a long time, with laboratory people trying to find explanations for the. Corpuscular theory, with all these things knocking against each other, coming out with intricate results, is a myth It'll give you the right answers, but is still wrong.

DS: Whenever you mention myths, the term "archetype" always comes up before too long. Jung's idea, as far as I understand it, was that these images or whatever are shared by all of us in the universal unconscious, and therefore anything which appeals to these will move us, because they're there, whether we understand it or not. Do you think this is the case in fiction involving myth elements?

RAL: In fiction, you're hitting it right there when the reader thinks he's the only one who had that thought and hasn't been able to say it. If you have a good one, every reader will have that idea: "That's what I was thinking and never could say." That is how the universal subconscious works. You may have dredged up something that hits everybody. Then you might miss completely. You might really be the only one who thought that, and leave everybody else blind.

DS: **One is tempted to fake it, and make it up so persuasively they all think they did.**

RAL: Of course you can never know whether they really did or they just think they did. If it rings a bell in there somewhere, there's some resonance that's on the subconscious level or some level.

DS: **Speaking of making it all up, what is the relationship between your stories and the traditional tall tale?**

RAL: I think I got the tall tales from my father, who was a great tall tale teller. He first came to Oklahoma as a boy, and he homesteaded with these other young fellows. One of them was my mother's brother and one was her cousin, although she was still a girl up in Iowa. They'd each homestead a hundred and sixty acres, and they'd build a shack on the four corners together there. About all they had for entertainment was tall stories. That was repeated so many times on so many frontiers. You get the tall stories of the mountain men and the campers and the trackers and so forth. Well, there's just the basic American stories, and they keep getting handed down. I think I got mine from three master story-tellers I happened to be related to.

DS: **How much of the traditional material turns up in your fiction, or do you simply borrow the method?**

RAL: More method, because the tall story has to be spontaneous. You just start raveling one out and pretty soon things start to happen in it. Just like exaggeration, it has to be spontaneous. The method is still there, the attitude to it.

DS: Do you write your short stories the way you would tell a tall tale?

RAL: I try to, yeah, but the handwriting gets in the way of it, if you want to put it that way. I think the oral tales are more authentic than the written ones that came later, and I think the oral ones are better. But you can't get them here anymore.

DS: Have you ever tried to tell the story into a tape recorder, then transcribe it?

RAL: No, I never tried that, but that's one idea. I told about an oral story teller in one of my stories, "The Cliffs That Laughed." This was a Malayan. Now that's the only time I've touched that culture, but I guess there's a lot of them in the world yet. The Malays have a professional class of verbal story teller. Now this particular one was a translator around the Army base there. But he could tell them, and that was the way he made his living ordinarily.

DS: There are some Americans who do this on stage. I've encountered a little of it. Have you seen any of it?

RAL: Yes, but they're mostly anecdotes rather than stories, aren't they? I don't know. There seems to be a little difference there, or else I haven't heard the good ones. There's skits and there's anecdotes but I've never heard longer tall tales on stage, although there might well be now. Now that's not the same thing as reading, though, because reading gets a little bit artificial. The tall tale is being put together and told at the same time. It isn't just recited, or something already put together.

DS: Can you use any of this method when writing a longer work, like a novel?

RAL: I can try it, and I do it for short periods, but I can't sustain it, which is the main reason my novels are choppy, I guess. They're really just short stories strung together. I never learned the sustained novel very well, and what I do write in it isn't very good. So I was meant to write choppy novels or none at all.

DS: What are your writing methods like?

RAL: I'll do it several ways. I'll start a story going till it busts. Then I'll set it aside for maybe six months, and I'll write stuff that's come to my mind about that story in the meantime. Then I may start it at the first again, do some, and it may bust again, and I'll set it aside for another six months to a year. But I've done around two hundred stories and not more than a dozen have I ever gone through without busting for a while.

DS: Can you take the stories that have busted and never recovered and reuse their material?

RAL: Most of my best stories have been busted once or twice. Sometimes they're made out of fragments of several of them. They get the conflicts and contrasts in there that they weren't having when I first tried to write them.

DS: How do you tell when it's going right, when it hasn't busted?

RAL: When a story busts, I know it, because I get tired of it myself. I say, "This has gone wrong," and I stop before it goes further wrong. Sometimes I'll tear up the last two or three pages and set it aside, till I go back to where it started to go wrong. When the thing goes sour you can tell it. Especially when it's your own.

DS: Then you have to drop it, because there's nothing you can do?

RAL: Let time work on it, which may be the subconscious correcting it to make it back to what you meant to say there.

241

With me it's usually about six months till that happens, though some are longer than that, and I try to forget them but they're still working there. Then I have better luck when I come back.

DS: Do you find that the writing of stories is a spontaneous thing that you have to do, and if you don't do it for a while you get uneasy?

RAL: Sometimes the start is spontaneous. I get up very early in the morning and start writing like mad for an hour or two, but it's like I've got the thing started then, and I don't worry if it doesn't come the rest of the way. I'll either set it aside or go through slowly on it, or sometimes I'll work on two or three things at a time. I might write a day or two on something, and change to a different type of thing. But I really haven't ever written two stories quite the same way.

DS: Are you at all influenced by what is being published now in science fiction, either positively or by reacting against it?

RAL: No, I don't think I am too much. For a while I was, but it doesn't seem to influence me too much now. I don't know why. It seems like I'm more on my own then I ever was. I guess I get a little bit stubborn about writing my own stuff and not going along with those guys.

DS: Did any editor early in your career shape what you wrote?

RAL: No, unless Horace Gold did a little bit. But I actually had less trouble with him than anybody else did. A lot of those old *Galaxy* writers said he gave them fits. He made them change everything, and he'd seldom do that with mine. He did give me some pretty good advice on a couple of them and he was the first one who did. But none of them have changed me very much. The way I write seems to be too stubborn in me to make any real changes in it.

DS: To me this looks like a good thing. Otherwise everybody would write alike.

RAL: They say the style is the person, and if he doesn't write his own way, he has an awkward style, which might be, or he has a tedious style if he doesn't, but then if the style is the person there will be bad styles and good styles still coming out. There'll be bad writers and good writers.

DS: Given ideal circumstances, say, that someone has promised to buy the results and not interfere, have you got any projects you would really like to do?

RAL: No. I've got a couple things that I'm going to do, but they're not pressing. I'd like to write the last two novels of *The Flame Is Green* series, which I'm going to do someday. The first one is sold and the other two are not sold, so the other two aren't written yet. That's still one of the series I want to finish. There are quite a few things I'm going to finish up someday, but none of them seem really pressing right now.

DS: In a case like *The Flame Is Green*, where the first book is sold and the second isn't, what do you do in the third to make up for the fact that the reader hasn't seen the second? Or do you hope that this will generate interest and get the second published?

RAL: Well, that is a difficulty. I hope they'll be bought in series. Now this other series of mine, which consists of *The Devil Is Dead*, *Archipelago*, and *More Than Melchisedech*— they're not really a series of novels. They're what I call simultaneous novels. Some of the years are duplicated, but from different viewpoints, and with different characters emphasized. This series was published backwards because *The Devil Is Dead* was published ten years before *Archipelago*. But that doesn't make too much conflict. They're not really tied together closely, although the unsold novel *More Than Melchisedech* does tie them together considerably.

DS: I have encountered people who don't understand your work. What do you have to say to them?

RAL: I don't know. Maybe it doesn't matter if they do or not. I was talking to Barry Malzberg today. We both write a page in a little Italian science fiction magazine, and I told him that his column in that was the first thing of his I ever understood. (Laughs.) He said that I'm as obscure as he is and he's not going to change and I'm not going to change. Yeah, I'm a little bit confusing at times, but I say things as clearly as I can, but sometimes the things themselves are kind of intricate, and maybe it's better off to not quite come off with something like that than to come off with easier things.

DS: Do you sometimes get editors insisting that you dilute complex material so that the book will be more saleable?

RAL: No, the only editors I've ever had that interfered with me were Fred Pohl and Damon Knight, and that was mostly on short stories, although Damon Knight was the editor on *Reefs Of Earth*. He was working at Berkley then. No, I haven't had a whole lot of trouble but they don't influence me as much as I think they do. I could put it that way. Sometimes I'll make a few verbal changes and still not change anything.

DS: You mean make a couple of small changes and make them think you've changed something larger?

RAL: Yeah. You see, Damon always had this thing about ending. The ending of the story is the most important thing. Well, maybe it is, but I think that sometimes I wonder. The writer best known for ending was O. Henry, and I was reading through his stories just a little while ago as an experiment, and thinking, "Well, if he'd stopped that story just before the trick ending." And they're improved. You can come up with about three possible endings in your mind. Some of them are better than his. This cute ending can be overworked. Leave out a little bit there.

DS: In one of his collections there is a story that gets you by surprise in this context because *it doesn't have a trick ending*.

RAL: Ring Lardner did that years ago. A couple of them.

DS: It strikes me as a potentially interesting device. You start the story as if it is to be vast and complicated, and then — you get them.

RAL: I don't know if it makes much difference how you end it exactly. In *Archipelago* I ended it up in the air, of course, with everybody shooting at everybody. I'd rather stop right there.

DS: On the subject of endings, I think we're at the end of the tape. Thank you, Mr. Lafferty.

This work © 1983, 1990, 2016 Darrell Schweitzer
This interview was published in Amazing Science Fiction, September 1983, in The Cranky Old Man from Tulsa, *1990, and in the* LaffCon 1 Booklet, *2016.*

Darrell Schweitzer is the author of 3 novels and about 300 published stories, a former editor of Weird Tales, *and a prolific essayist, critic, and interviewer. His work appears in* The New York Review of SF *regularly.*

Maybe They Needed Killing & the Importance Of Happiness: An Interview with R. A. Lafferty

by Robert Whitaker Sirignano

This interview was assembled from five years correspondence with R.A. Lafferty. Where he thought it necessary, the interviewer included the date of certain statements in parenthesis. Portions of the interview appeared in various publications, most notably in The Hunting of the Snark No. 10 (September, 1976), pp. 11-20, and in At The Sleepy Sailor: A Tribute to R.A. Lafferty, pp. 6-17, the souvenir chapbook for DeepSouthCon 17, held in New Orleans, July 20-22, 1979. This version was published in Cranky Old Man from Tulsa: Interviews with R.A. Lafferty (United Mythologies Press, Weston, Ont.: 1990), pp. 8-25.

Robert Whitaker Sirignano: Could you give a little biography and why you started writing and when?

R. A. Lafferty: John Lafferty, my grandfather, and Anna Kelly, my grandmother, were born in 1828; my grandfather in County Donegal, Ireland, and my grandmother in County Kilkenny. They both died in 1889. They met and married in 1848 as a couple of young immigrants. My father was the eleventh of thirteen children and he was past fifty when I was born, so there was quite a span of years in the three generations.

Grandfather Lafferty was both a tailor and a farmer, and as soon as he got a farm in Iowa, near Council Bluffs which was still named Kanesville then, he had a commercial sewing machine sent up the river from New Orleans. He is supposed to have been a well-read man. But his wife (Anna Kelly) could read and write Irish only and always refused to learn to read and write English. The only ones she wrote to were her sisters, and all they could read was Irish too. I originally had more than forty first cousins on my father's side, all of them from five years to thirty years older than me. Now I believe there are only seven of them still living.

My mother's family goes back a little bit longer in this country. It was my great-grandparents who came from Ireland on the Burke side of the family. My mother's grandfather was born on Christmas day 1800, in Tuam, Ireland and he became a saddle maker. He landed in Boston in 1832 and then came to Dubuque. His wife was Mary McCarthy. My mother's father was Edward Burke born in 1855 near Dubuque, Iowa. My mother's mother was named Catherine Delahunt.

In our family the oldest child was Edward who was born in 1906 and died before he was two years old. Then Joseph (born 1908), Frank (born 1910), Anna (born 1912), and myself, Raphael (born 1914). None of us four ever married. My parents married in Anadarko, Oklahoma Territory, went back to Iowa twice (I was born the second time they went back there), and then came to Oklahoma for good in 1919. My father was a carpenter, farmer, homesteader, store-keeper, and oil lease broker.

I was always closer to my cousins on my mother's side of the family than those on my father's, as they all lived in Oklahoma when we were young. With the four of us Laffertys there were thirteen of us, which circle was not broken till last July when my older brother died, and December 27 when a cousin in Dallas died (1985). I probably base a lot of my characters on my kindred. Whenever I want an intricate and pleasant character I borrow traits from one or several. There's quite a few nuns and priests in the kinship, but a lot of them have died off.

As for me: I was born November 7, 1914 in Neola, Iowa, moved to Ferry, Oklahoma when I was four years old. With summertime visits back North again and with many relatives in both states, I have enjoyed what have been called the two most educative experiences: to be a small Northern boy in a small Southern town, and to be a small Southern boy in a small

Northern town. Later we moved to Tulsa, Oklahoma, which qualifies as a city. Having traveled in forty-five of the fifty states and a few foreign countries, I still find Tulsa to be the favorite city in the world.

No particular events in the life. I went through school, and then only a few college courses taken at night. I worked one year on a civil service job in Washington, D.C., then to Tulsa again. I worked most of my life in the electrical wholesale business. Took an ICS Electrical Engineering course and a few other technical courses. In the spring of 1942 I went into the Army. I was twenty-seven years old, about ten years older than a man should first go to sea, go to war, go to the enchanted islands, have his adventures. I did have quite a few modified adventures in Australia, New Guinea, Morotai (then in the Dutch East Indies, now in Indonesia) and the Philippines, and a few smaller islands. Some of the islands really were enchanted; some of the people we lived with were still in the stone-age: both of these conditions have been partially corrected since then. Our combat encounters were pretty sporadic and not very important. Or so I thought. But at a group reunion of the old outfit in Fort Worth, Texas last year, I found that these things loomed much larger in retrospect than they had at the time of their happening. Hell, we were a bunch of heroes. Anyway, I have seen a lot of the world.

After about five years of it I was out of the Army and back home and working for electrical firms again, and there were no particular events. In 1959 I began to write. I had tried it a little bit twenty-five years before, evening writing slipped in between correspondence courses, but nothing had come of it that first time. In '59 I took it up again to try to find a hobby that would make a little money instead of costing a lot, and also to fill a gap caused by my cutting down on drinking and fooling around. I sold my first stories later in that year, and sold my first novels in 1967. Then in 1971, after developing a wobbly heart and a disinclination to work any more, I retired from regular work to try to get by on my writing. *Okla Hannali*, coming a little bit after this, helped. It didn't put me on easy street but it put me on easy alley, which is probably better for a person of my predilections.

At the World Convention in Toronto in 1973 I won a Hugo (the highest award that the world can give, according to s.f. people). So that is the end of the biography. I've always believed that people should have the grace to die quietly after touching the top. I've put it off for one reason or another, but I know that's a shoddy thing to do. There are even some who repeat the award, but that is in very bad taste. Things are going pretty well at the moment though. What I don't have, I don't need. If I were fictionalizing this biography, I would put more events in it; but there really aren't any.

RWS: I saw you in Toronto in 1973 when you won your Hugo. When you received it you looked both pleased and embarrassed. Was this a reaction to winning the award or are you just shy?

RAL: Pleased and slightly embarrassed? Reactive or shy? Yes, I'm always a little bit shy when confronting large groups of people, for which reason I booze too much at conventions to counteract it. I was probably a mixture of emotions at Toronto: pleasure surely at winning something, pleasure at the mellow table companionship I had been enjoying, disappointment for Joe Haldeman, one of those table companions, missing the Hugo with the best story in the category with the award going to the worst story in its group. Then there was considerable exasperation at the two worst stories in the short story group tying for the award, and one of them being mine. This isn't a put on. I had come in second the year before with the best short story in the group and didn't think I would ever be able to beat it. And in the fateful year I had five stories published that were much better than "Eurema's Dam." Slightly embarrassed, yes. I excuse myself by saying that there was some sort of compensation at work there.

RWS: What sort of childhood did you have? Was it odd or unusual? Was it mean?

RAL: So far I have had a mostly happy childhood, and it continues to be so. I'm one of the persons who never grew up, but we may be a slight majority in the world. I had two older brothers and an older sister, and I've been told by several older cousins in later years that I was a rotten spoiled kid who had things all my own way. I had several impediments but they didn't impede me very much. I couldn't talk plain until I was nine or ten years old, and I was very clumsy, as I still am. One of the Sisters who taught me told my mother, when I was in perhaps the third grade, that I might be very intelligent but she couldn't be sure as she couldn't understand anything I said or read anything I wrote. I still write a very bad hand; the only thing I still write is my name; I mostly print everything else.

We didn't have any conflict in our house in my early childhood. My father was sixteen years older than my mother and was a peaceful and humorous man. We had plenty of money, during the 1920's at least, when I was age five to fifteen. We went touring a lot in the summertimes (the 1920's was the first great age of automobile touring), back to Iowa and to St. Louis and Chicago and Colorado and California (I first met the ocean at Ocean Park, California when I was about ten years old, and we struck up a good friendship), and to the Grand Canyon and Yosemite and Yellowstone Park and the Black Hills of South Dakota and such places.

I don't think there was anything odd or unusual about my childhood. I was odd only in such trivial things as being left-handed ("He's left-handed in the head too," I remember someone saying about me in the early days) and in my turning to reading very early. I was never a recluse, but I often found the people in books more interesting than the people around me. And no, my childhood was not mean. It was always happy, in the context of the Family and the Church and the Country, and it still is.

There were a few latter complications, the realization that I was an alcoholic, the realization that I must always be at odds with the devious people who took over the country in 1933 and took over most of the world before and after that (I'm referring to the secular-liberal imposture, of course): but all these things can be lived with. Most fiction writers describe themselves as having unhappy and unusual childhoods, but I believe that that is mostly fictionalized posturing.

RWS: What did you do during the war? Were you a member of a group like the "Dirty Five?"

RAL: During the war I was mostly with the 229th Anti-Aircraft Battalion. We had three field batteries of twelve sections each and we were usually scattered over a pretty wide area. Each of our sections, with an old 268 radar and AA searchlight, would be attached to an AA gun battalion, 45 or 90 mm, so we would have some thirty six sections of approximately 18 men each attached to a gun battery of approximately 250 men. So our 900 or so men would be mixed with approximately 10,000 gun men, with some sections fifty or so miles from others. This gave us pretty wide freedom and it gave me pretty wide acquaintanceship. I was a staff sergeant classed as an electrical specialist and was the trouble-shooter on the searchlights along with a couple of corporals. Anyhow I was familiar by night with a lot of jeep jungle trails and a lot of rough square miles of area. I could pretty well go wherever I wanted and stay with any of our sections as long as I wished.

After stations in Oklahoma, Texas, North Carolina, Florida, and California in the states, and some pleasant weeks in Australia, we were in Milne Bay, Finschhafen, Hollandia, Maffin Bay, Wadke Island, Sansapor in New Guinea; on Morotai Island in the Moluccas for eighteen months; and then in the Philippines, Batangas, Bauan, Manila. Nearly four years overseas in all. They were all the same places where the boys of the Dirty Five were, but that is merely coincidence. Yes, all the outfits and combinations of outfits were full of jokers and circles of jokers, but the "Dirty Five" were not taken directly from any one group. I've been going to reunions of the 229th Battalion the last several years, in Fort Worth this year (1978) and San Diego next year, and I am amazed at the smell of success on all those joker fellows. Of course, the hundred or so who attend the reunions, out of the thousands or so who were in the battalion at one time or another, are likely to be the most successful ones or among them. About two-thirds of the people in the battalion can't even be located.

One of the best things about all the Army days was the plain travel and scenery. "Incidents of Travel in The South Pacific" is a sort of color portfolio now.

RWS: What are your religious beliefs? Do you feel that your stories echo your beliefs soundly? Or do you try to keep these views from entering into your stories?

RAL: I am a Roman Catholic of what is considered an old-fashioned sort, as there are a number of modernities flickering over the Church now, none of them very deep. I do not attempt specifically to put my beliefs into my stories, nor to keep them out either. An exception is *Past Master*, because religion was the subject of that novel. But the belief is part of the person who writes the stories and it will be there naturally.

There's a double standard in this area though. There is considerable preaching against preaching, and an amazing amount of decrying religion by the people of the most intolerant religions. Belief is religion. The most rampantly righteous religions in the world are the religions of secularism, humanism, liberalism, nihilism, scientism, inhumanism, and diabolism. We have those with hatred as the central commodity, those with perversions as central, those with disorder as central, those with worthlessness as central. We have cheap-shotting as a crusading religion. And it is out of these that militant preachers come. Certainly three-quarters of SF is given over to the relentless preaching of those of the anti-religious religions. They are the ones who carry on the biggest feuds and the covert as well as open attacks and who recommend the boycotts. The longest work by an SF practitioner in recent years is a preachment for worthlessness for the sake of worthlessness, and it will not accept anything but total worthlessness for everyone.

Ah well, if I can't preach about preaching what can I preach about?

RWS: Do you believe in the devil, a devil?

RAL: ...could be a long one, but I'll try not to let it be. Sure, I consider the Devil-Satan as a real person or presence of species. I don't know to what extent individuality is a quality of that species.

Leaving aside all testimony of religion or revelation, I believe that a competent interdisciplinary biologist, working without prejudice, would come onto substantial evidence for unbodied beings or mentalities, from the effect they have on human persons: just as a competent interdisciplinary astronomer would arrive at the necessity of there being a moon of such a size and gravity and location and distance, even though the moon lacked the quality for visibility. And the physicist-astronomer would realize the necessity for such a moon from its influence on the earth. The biologist-psychologist should arrive at the necessity of the Devil-Satan, of such a power and location and activation-pattern, because of his influence on human beings.

Well there is something rampant in the collective unconscious, and if we ask "What is it?" we're naming one of its names. As God several times in Scripture gives Himself the name of the "I Am" or the "I Am Who Am", so the Devil-Satan species is given the name in many languages of something like the "What is it?" or the "Who is it?." An African tale begins "The Who-Is-It came and killed a man and cut him open." This particular Who-Is-It tale seemed to kill and cut open a man every morning to read him as if reading a morning paper. As to whether the diabolical species has individuality, that's a problem. Before being cast into the Gadarene Swine, one devil or multiplicity of devils told Christ either "My name is Legion" or "Our name is Legion", seeming to mean a multiplicity of guises for an individual or a multiplicity of individuals in the species.

Well, this diabolical species-person cannot read human minds and cannot invade the human individual, except in a few doubtful cases. But he can invade the human species, which he does by invading the group unconscious. There is the devil in the cellar of the mind. He-They-It does have influence on persons, on all persons.

Yeah, I did let the answer to that be a long one, and didn't say anything I wanted to say either.

RWS: What is *your* definition of the meaning of life?

RAL: Using your "meaning" in the only legitimate sense as "purpose" or "aim", the meaning or purpose of life is happiness. This was once clear to everybody in the world, and I don't know why so plain a thing should escape people now. Happiness often coincides with pleasure and enjoyment, but it isn't the same thing. There are many paradoxes about it, so there probably can't be any such thing as selfish happiness. The secular scriptures are correct in their understanding of this. "Oh happiness! Our being's end and aim," Alexander Pope writes. "It is the business of a wise man to be happy," old Doctor Johnson wrote. "There is no duty so much underrated as the duty of being happy," R.L. Stevenson said, and he was sounder than was T. Jefferson in the Declaration of Independence when he wrote of it as a right rather than a duty. But being happy is a duty we owe the world and every companion of ours in it, and that is the meaning and purpose of life.

Thomas Aquinas wrote that sin was an offense against happiness. Aurelia the space girl also taught that sin was an offense against happiness. People who don't believe in God, or the natural order, or form, or due process, who confuse pleasure with happiness, and who aren't at all sure of being, do not accept that there are such things as sins. They are presently the majority in the world.

RWS: Why do you write, other than for money?

RAL: Money isn't very important in it, since there's not any big money involved. I suppose I'm like the kid with the Crayolas: I want to make my mark on the world. The impulse would never admit that it was vanity, and yet it's the impulse to leave some kind of memento on the way through this vale of tears — and snuffles and snickers. And then it turns out to be enjoyable on its own.

RWS: What would you do if you could not write?

RAL: What would I do if I could not write? I would learn to write. Or I would try something else somewhat expressive. I tried some years to play the violin when I was young, and was no good at it. I have tried several times to draw and paint, and I sure cannot make any mark with pencil or brush. Maybe I would try to pluck chickens if everything else failed. I would attempt to be the most imaginative and innovative chicken-plucker in the world. Some expressiveness, for a hobby at least, seems to be necessary.

RWS: How do you compose a story? Do you do first draft writings or do you revise?

RAL: How do I compose a story? The only honest answer is that I prowl back through a bunch of busted or unfinished satires and salvage pieces out of several of them and put them together for a story that might go. It seems that time in discard is necessary for most of them, and the tension and juxtaposition that a story has to have can be made by a combination of old things. I usually make an outline of the new story then, though often only in my head and not written down. I usually do about two-thirds of the first draft writing. Then I start what I hope will be the final version and go right through without slowing down at the old stopping place. About half the time, this proves to be the final version, and I rewrite completely after letting it set aside for a month or so. In other cases, I will rewrite only two or three pages of it. Likewise after letting it set for a while.

RWS: Do you use slang in your stories?

RAL: No, I use colloquialisms, but not slang. The difference, I suppose, is that a colloquialism is also a localism of one region for a long time, and slang is wide-spread for a short time. But I don't want the here and now approach. I want always a perennial effect, whether I can get it or not.

RWS: When you first started writing back in 1959, how long did it take for you to get your first story published?

What was your reaction to a story finally being accepted for publication?

RAL: First story accepted and published, time and reaction. They weren't the same story. The first story accepted was "The Wagons" by the *New Mexico Quarterly*. This was after I had been sending stories around for four or five months. I was pleased but not overwhelmed, because this was a college-affiliated magazine (even though it paid $25.00, I believe) and seemed only semi-pro. But the story wasn't published until the spring of 1960. The first published story was "Day of the Glacier" in the December 1959 *Science Fiction Stories*, and my reaction was anger since I hadn't been paid for it and hadn't been informed of its acceptance, and they hadn't answered any of my letters asking about it. This was the old Columbia Publications that was just going out of business then. I did get paid a year or so later, but it took a lot of pursuit. But the real reaction was delight that the stories should appear under any circumstances, and that delight hasn't lessened a bit for any of a hundred and fifty subsequent sales.

RWS: In the writing you did 25 years prior to 1959, was there any difference in subject matter? Style? Is this where you salvage the "busted and unfinished" frames from which you manufacture and create new stories?

RAL: Of the writings of the twenty five years prior to 1959 there is nothing surviving except some verse. I plunder some of the verses now and then and adapt them for chapter headings, but there is nothing to rework. I believe that the early stories were partly imitations of sea stories of Stevenson and Conrad and Melville, but I had never been to sea then and I didn't know anything about it. The busted and unfinished material that I salvage from now is 1959 or later.

RWS: What writers influenced you? Stylistically and in the contents of your work, your stories bring to mind the American Tall Tale — are there folklore studies in your background?

RAL: What did I read that influenced me in my work? R.L. Stevenson, Twain, Bret Harte, Melville, Lafcadio Hearn, Hilaire Belloc, G.K. Chesterton, Dickens, Balzac, J.B. Cabell. They all seem pretty old. Then there was Miles Murdoch, the first writer I ever knew, a mystery story writer of the 1920's now forgotten, who was also our Bishop Kelly that served 6:30 mass for every morning one winter; this was when I was about ten: he was from French Canada and was more French than Irish. Then there was Donn Byrne and Graham Greene and Maugham. None of the SF writers. Not that I don't like them, but I didn't come to them early enough. I believe that literary influence on a person's style is set by the time he is come of age, even if he hasn't written anything by then. The twig has already received its bent.

Sure there's a lot of the American Tall Tale in my background. And I have a theory that the American Tall Tale had its shaggiest growth right here in Oklahoma, for the reason that this was a mixing bowl in the decade that the Tall Tale was the most flourishing. From the first land opening here, the "Run" in 1889, for the ten years through the other openings, this was the last block of free land left anywhere and people came from all the other states and territories to file on it. And this brought on a cross-fertilization of all the regional tall tales from all the frontiers as well as from all the settled regions. The three best tall tale tellers I ever knew, Hugh Lafferty my father, Ed Burke the brother of my mother-to-be, and Frank Burke her cousin, homesteaded near Snyder, Oklahoma in the 1890's along with another Irishman named McGuire. They built a shack in the middle of a section of land, so it covered the corners of each of their 160 acre claims, and lived there to prove up on them. There was nothing to do but to try to scrape out a living and tell tall stories. This McGuire started the first store around there and it was tall tale headquarters. Everybody, even the Texans and the Indians added to the mixture. From the uncle Ed Burke I picked up quite a bit of Indian lore much later, as he had gone to work as a stenographer (he was the only one for a long ways around) at the Wichita Indian Agency at Anadarko, Oklahoma nearby. But the tall tale element was from verbal rather than written sources with me.

RWS: Exactly when did you discover science fiction? How did you react to it? What do you prefer to read in it? Who do you like reading?

RAL: I don't know when I discovered science fiction. I had read most of the wonder stories and wonder novels of H.G. Wells without knowing they were SF. And I had read the Healy and McComas anthology *Adventures in Time and Space* when it came out (1946), and it did bear the alternate title *Famous Science Fiction Stories*; my reaction to that was that it was wonderful. My reaction when I began to look for other good science-fiction stories was that there weren't any other good ones; and there weren't. I then discovered the cycle in SF: periods when almost all the stories are rotten but there are a few good ones to be found; and periods when all the stories are rotten and there are not any good ones to be found. We are presently in a type 2 period (Nov. 1975). Maybe there will be a couple of good stories appearing in the next several years and then we will be in a type 1 period again. Oh, Niven, Poul Anderson, Brunner, Arthur Clarke, Pournelle, Malzberg do pretty well now and then. Sturgeon and Van Vogt could probably still do it if they wanted to. Joe Haldeman and Panshin and Harrison and Silverberg could do it if they would get off those shaggy horses they're riding. Of the younger ones, Michael Bishop and Stephen Utley and Jack Dann and Tom Reamy might start writing good ones any time now.

RWS: What do you look for in books?

RAL: I read books to hear what people are up to. This is the only approved and organized form of eavesdropping. I listen for whatever interests me. If I don't find it, I put the book away and go to another book. Eavesdropping is about as close as we can get to the quintessence of people. They fumble it when you encounter them directly, but they reveal a lot when you hear them in this or any other way. People, that is what I read for; to get the marrow out of their bones and to enjoy it.

RWS: Is there any one book that you have enjoyed to the point where you would not hesitate to recommend it to anyone?

RAL: How about Plutarch's *Lives* for the one book. No, it isn't affectation to reach that far back. It is my belief that Plutarch invented the Novel as well as the biography in this. There were fifty short or medium-length novels here (the degree of fiction in them can't be determined now) and they are good. He invented narration as distinguished from rhetoric and a few other things. He was the world's best novelist (Balzac comes in second) and nineteen hundred years haven't done him any harm at all. Part of him may be slipping away: he invented the concept of the Great Man, the Hero, and that erodes a little bit now. But nothing takes its place but a vacancy.

RWS: What sort of dreams do you experience?

RAL: The dreams. They just don't make them like they used to. Maybe a good one a month. There's one peculiarity about them that I notice in late years: after I've made use of one sort, they don't come around any more. I don't have the vivid ocean dreams since I wrote "Configuration of the North Shore." I don't have as many metamorphic dreams since I wrote "Continued On Next Rock." I don't have so many alien sublimation dreams since I wrote "Ride A Tin Can." But I can't identify them well until I have got them down and made them stop hollering. So I suppose that a dream cycle is clamoring for expression in some medium or other. I don't have as many smothering dreams since I tamed them with "Encased In Ancient Rind." There seems to be less frustration and more sense of free motion in my dreams now. Maybe that means I'm about to go over the edge. And the only way I can save myself is with a "Don't Go Over the Falls! Turn the River Off!" story.

RWS: What do you consider dystopic materialism?

RAL: Dystopic materialism? Can't I hate the stuff without being able to define it? I do not regard Utopias and Dystopias as opposites: they are the same thing, and they are always disastrous. And they are completely materialistic. They are highly organized error. "They want so thoroughly to organize freedom that they turn it into slavery," the Hungarian Thomas Molnar says in his *Utopia, The Perennial Heresy*. And he also says "pessimism about the individual, optimism about the collectivity, and enforced enthusiasm — these are not the only contradictions of the Utopian mind." In *Past Master*, I tried to show materialism at its best as being inadequate. The trouble is that most people will choose materialism again and again, and then wonder why they hurt. One point to note: Utopias are never establishment. They are always that much more tyrannical thing, the anti-establishment.

RWS: Why do you consider *Past Master* to be a failure?

RAL: *Past Master* was a failure because hardly anyone got what I was talking about: that Golden Astrobe was a rotten place. Many readers thought that it was a fine and desirable place. There is the same difficulty about the *Utopia* that its hero wrote. Most people who read it (and I don't believe there are too many who really read it) believe that it is a sort of ideal or heavenly vision; but it is a hellish vision, and intended to be. Golden Astrobe, which is present day Earth, has a lot of things wrong with it; but they are vested and defended, and it is only the things that are right with it that are howled down and hooted.

Maybe I'll write something someday to say the things I didn't know how to say in *Past Master*. There is still a very big gap in it. Somebody could fall into that thing and get killed.

RWS: In reading Past Master, I have gathered the feeling that you dislike cities and consider them the start of Armageddon. I may be misreading it here, but the feeling is that you like the countryside much more than something as conglomerate as New York City.

RAL: Wrong, wrong, wrong. I don't dislike cities. Some of my favorite places are cities, Tulsa here, Dallas, Denver, Santa Fe, Oklahoma City, San Antonio, Galveston, New Orleans, St. Louis, Omaha, Sioux City, San Francisco, Washington, New York, Sydney, Manila, Laredo, Toronto, Boston, Orlando, Chicago, Baltimore. There aren't any cities I don't like, but there's lots of them I don't know very well. I've walked lots of thousands of miles exploring cities on foot just because I like them. No, it was the dystopic materialism and not the cities I dislike in *Past Master*.

RWS: Was "Rangle-Dang Kaloof" written as a result of your experiences with heart problems?

RAL: Yes, "Rangle-Dang Kaloof" is autobiographical. I still have a wobbly heart that grabs me five or six times a day to show me just how easy it would be to turn me off completely. This makes for a bad feeling between my heart and me. It makes the whole world an uneasy place for me. What do you do when your Damocles Sword is on the inside?

RWS: Is it true that "Funnyfingers" was written for a member of your family?

RAL: A niece of mine, a nun in California, says that she is the nun in "Funnyfingers." I'm not sure that I even thought of her when I wrote it, but she says I had to. "Did you forget that I'm a funnyfingers?" she asks. She does have funny fingers. She can bend them back and touch her forearm behind them, and can bend the end joints of all of them without bending the other joints. But she's not the main character.

RWS: Do you know any children like those in *Reefs of Earth*?

RAL: Sure, I've probably known a dozen bunches of children like those in *Reefs of Earth*. Some of them I lose track of later (I think they go back to where they came from), and some of them merge in with the mass of humans (they are a gang of black-hearted fakers when they do this), and none of them grow up as visibly Puca. There's a lot about the Puca phenomena that I don't understand.

RWS: Were you a Puca-ish child when you were younger? Did you attempt to conquer the world?

RAL: Nah, I wasn't a Puca-ish child, never plotted to kill my parents or wanted them dead. And I never plotted to conquer the world, except figuratively. Those mean kids are fun to watch but tricky to be.

RWS: I have been informed that you wrote yourself into *Fourth Mansions*. Which character are you?

RAL: Yes, I've been accused of writing myself into *Fourth Mansions*, and I always say it's a lie. I've been accused of being Bertigrew Bagley, the Patrick of Tulsa. Well, maybe I looked like him about then, but I've since taken off fifty pounds to a skinny two hundred; I've got a good looking set of artificial teeth; I've sweetened up my disposition; and we're just not as much alike as we used to be. And we never were really the same person.

RWS: Do you often alter stories to please an editor?

RAL: As to altering a section or two in a story to please an editor, if the editor is right, I respond favorably. If he is wrong, I respond unfavorably. Damon Knight used to be right at least a third of the time, but no other editor was right nearly so often. Frederick Pohl, when he was *Galaxy*'s editor, was never right, but sometimes he was pretty insistent. I usually made the changes, or went through the motions of changing things to something not quite as bad as suggested.

RWS: Have you ever had any troubles with cuts in your novels and stories?

RAL: The only trouble I've had with novels being cut was with *The Devil Is Dead*, and I suppose that was my fault. Several changes and additions I made didn't get into it, but that's always the risk when something is changed after a work is sold and in the process.

RWS: What is this story I've heard about an editor who wanted to change the name of "Nine Hundred Grandmothers" and give its title to another story?

RAL: No, there was never any wanting to change the name of "Nine Hundred Grandmothers." There was something of it with the story "And Walk Now Gently Through the Fire." This was a Roger Elwood story, he didn't like the story much, but he did like the title. He was only half-kidding once when he asked if I would write another story with the title. But he finally bought it and made it the name story of the book. With Ace and 900GM the only anomaly was that they liked the title and made it the title story although it was one of the weakest stories in the book.

RWS: How closely does *Fall of Rome* follow history?

RAL: I followed history where the history could be found, and I invented where there were gaps in it. I don't know how Alaric got out of the Peloponnesian trap and neither does anyone else (probably by sharing booty with some of Stilcho's forces that were a little bit shaky), but maybe the Gulf of Corinth did freeze over. I could never even find out the Gothic name of Alaric's wife, only that her Christian name was Stella. I hung the Stairnon on her, since both of them mean "star," but it's probably wrong. The lack of dialog was just a notion of mine, since dialogue wasn't used by any of the ancient people except in dramas. Quotation markers hadn't been invented yet, and the dialog in fiction or biography hadn't taken hold. You will find them sometimes in writers like Petronius, or even in the Socratic dialogues, but the quotation marks are never found in the originals, and the Socratic dialogues are really drama sequences.

RWS: In reference to the unpublished novel *When All the World Was Young*, I note that in *Fourth Mansions*, there is a reference to a plague with end results similar to those

described in *WATWWY*.[1] It is described as having happened years and years earlier — are your stories a future history? I've encountered the characters of *Arrive at Easterwine* in several places. Are all your stories interconnected, or do you have several series which no one has pointed out before?

RAL: The plague, in fact, in *Fourth Mansions*, has the same tendency to kill adults and to leave children. The Black Death itself killed half the adults in Europe and bothered the children hardly at all.

My stories are slightly future history, set just far enough into the future as not to get stepped on by the present. Yes, I hope the bits and pieces will fall into it. I am always out in the rain with a bucket and trying to catch something.

Yes, sometimes I use the old trick of having stories connected by a common minor character or otherwise. Balzac was one of the inventors of this device a hundred and forty or so years ago. In his Human Comedy, he ran quite a few of his characters in and out of the hundred novels and novellas that made it up. Quite a few other writers have used the device since, and before (there is nothing wrong with imitating a thing in advance). Several sets of my people will know each other, even if they may not be on quite the same fictional or reality level.

RWS: How accurate is the historical background to *Okla Hannali*?

RAL: I maintain that the historical background of *Okla Hannali* is absolutely accurate. Hannali himself and his family are fictitious, but they are composites of real types. And most

---

[1] *When All the World Was Young* is an unpublished Lafferty novel completed in 1975. It is a contemporary narrative recounting the return of the bubonic plague as a world-wide pandemic that exterminates all of Earth's inhabitants over the age of ten. The original manuscript is located in the Department of Special Collections and University Archives, McFarlin Library, University of Tulsa.

of the characters in the book are historical persons and I know the descendants of many of them. There was more than thirty years of observation and reading on the general subject before I began to write. I had Indian classmates in every class I was ever in, and Indian co-workers on every job I have ever held, and there is more evidence to be gathered here in Tulsa than anywhere. Of course there are different versions of some of the events, but in selecting the most convincing ones I have tried to be as accurate as possible. The different versions still reflect the different sides of the Indian civil wars of more than a hundred years ago, and they are not going to be reconciled. Historical opinion is always partly subjective, however, and all historical evidence can be interpreted in several ways.

RWS: Do you think the American government has been fair in its treatment of the American Indian?

RAL: Sure, the American government has been fair in its treatment of the American Indians in most cases, thousands of times against the hundreds of times when it hasn't been. The all-fair instances do not produce the violence which is the stuff of novels though. The "Everything was lovely for a hundred years there" just doesn't make exciting reading unfortunately. I've got a pretty good reaction on *Okla Hannali*, especially from the Indians around here. Now they call me up sometimes to settle arguments on their own history. I'm going to get hurt someday, getting in the middle of an argument between Indians.

RWS: Did you ever write a story that disagreed with your philosophy?

RAL: No, I never write a story that disagreed with my philosophy, but I've written a few in areas where my philosophy wasn't settled, several of them, in an effort to settle my philosophy.

RWS: Do you think that drinking has affected your writing? If you did not drink would you have been a writer?

RAL: The only thing that drinking ever did for me was give me excuses. Yeah, if it hadn't been for drinking, I might have amounted to something, and such as that. Yes, I believe that if I didn't drink I would have been a writer, since I always was a book-worm. I'd probably have started to write earlier, and written much more and much better. Yes, there's the excuse working. Stay off that stuff though, if you're the two guys out of three who can't handle it. And I sure can't.

RWS: A question from a friend of mine in England (who likes your work) asks: "Why is he so preoccupied with killing? There's more casual slaughter in any of his novels than in Mickey Spillane, but you hardly notice it; people die as if it's not going to be permanent, as often it isn't." Well?

RAL: Why do I kill so many people? Oh, it's partly to help out their survivors and next of kin. These get double indemnity when the characters are killed. It helps the poor people out, and it doesn't cost me anything.

Or, if that answer isn't satisfactory, maybe I kill them because they need killing. A lot of people need it.

Beyond that, I don't know why I kill so many. That's just the way the stories are.

RWS: When you write about groups of people you seem to have a consistent element lurking and appearing within: a ghost, a machine (or machine priest) and a kaleidoscopic woman . . . what are these symbols? Are you attempting to mean something when you use these archetypes?

RAL: No, I'm not attempting to mean anything profound by my use of Archetypes. The essence of Archetypes is that everyone is supposed to have the same ones, individually felt. According to Jung, there should be four of them, the Quaternity. I suspect that the kaleidoscopic woman is the Anima, the machine is the Animus, and the ghost is the Shadow. I don't know what the Syzygy is, or whether it is my fourth archetype. In any case, there's a lot of flexibility to archetypes and I don't take them very seriously. I suspect that they will vary from story to story, archetypes being called up to support a theme.

RWS: Your narrator (or narrative viewpoint) seems to be always the superior of the people you write about, but takes a humorous viewpoint towards them objectively. This seems to be a description of your pose as a narrator. Do you feel this way towards the world in general?

RAL: Nah, that's not a description of my pose as a narrator. And it's not the way I feel towards the world in general. If a narrator seems superior to his characters then he's busting up his characterizations. The wig (world in general) is a cantankerous animal and pretty smelly, but it leads its opponents about seven rounds to two going into the tenth, and feeling superior to it is just not an answer to such a situation.

RWS: What do you think of the tendency of writers to allow evil to win out in a story, ending it with a depressing note, in spite of all the struggles the hero has gone through, that the whole effort was useless?

RAL: A story with evil winning out can be powerful and effective through the depressing irony of it, I suppose. One isn't supposed to like such a story, but only be impelled to take some action against the evil. I've never done a piece like that though. The stories that I do dislike are those that assume that the evil way is the only way and that nothing else can be considered even as a possibility, that are built on an evil premise and worked out to show no more than a dismal choice between two evils as conflict. Almost all SF stories of the last decade are of this sort, but I don't like them. SF has always been the most narrow-minded of writings, but it becomes more and more so. A breath of fresh air would be welcome in it, but it would be hated instead; even a breath of stale air would be welcome, but there wouldn't be much breath of anything. There's another mini-lecture.

RWS: Do you believe in the perfectibility of man, or is he a constant fool at odds with the gods of the universe to be forever rebuffed at his attempt to rise above the madness which surrounds him?

RAL: The perfectibility of "man"? I believe in the perfectibility of people — some people, possibly most people. I do not believe in the perfectibility of society, or of the world, or of "man" in the abstract. Maybe it is a madness that surrounds and rebuffs abstract man. But each person can select his own ambient, because it is subjective to such a large degree. The madness is optional, both for one's self and for the surroundings. You can send it back to be cooked right. But you don't have to accept the raw madness. Sure the individual is perfectible (though there's probably a less pompous word for it somewhere). Perfection (the real meaning of the word is "completion," not "faultlessness") is always there for the taking. A person will finally come to it unless he refuses it. You're making me sound pompous the way you put these questions "...constant fool at odds with the gods of the universe..." that's not a real phrase; that's one of the consensus impositions that somebody stuck in your pocket when you weren't looking. Throw it away.

RWS: With all your love and admiration of poetry, and your own poetic abilities, why is it that you never spent as much time with it as you do your fictional writing?

RAL: There's a technical difficulty that prevents me from doing more with poetry. I only compose poetry or verse when I'm walking, and I only write things down when I'm sitting down. Well, I walk a lot and I sit down a lot, but I hardly ever do both of them at the same time. I never learned to whistle (what's the matter with a grown man who never learned to whistle?) and people strolling along cut a sad figure when they're not whistling; unless, that is, they are manufacturing interior verse. I get about a mile to a poem. On the walk I just took before sitting down to answer letters, there was this:

The lorries jostle cheek to jowl
With crashing sound and horning
And rolling hunks of metal roll
How beautiful the morning!

The people rush to rendezvous
Anent their daily earning
At selling soap or making glue
How beautiful the morning!

The birds are barking up a storm
The beaming sun is boining
It's even getting kind of warm
How beautiful the moining!

Well, there were really five stanzas to that, but two of them are lost already. It's a shaggy venture where you lose forty percent of your product before you ever get it packaged, and probably the best forty percent. I suppose I never did anything with the versifying because I was told that there was no money in it. I hear now that very few of the modern poets make big money, as much as New York garbage collectors; but it's too late for me to take it seriously. I know a couple of early morning whistlers though whose product should be packaged and sold. Do you know anybody who publishes whistling?

RWS: What is your background in languages? How many do you know?

RAL: Background in languages? I haven't any. But I like to fool around with them and always have. Latin and Spanish were all that I took in high school, and a college course in German. I bought a lot of record courses. I can count them for thirteen languages from here in my chair, and there should be more in the backroom. But all that is languages as a pleasant game, and I have never gone deeply into any of them. Six of them I can read fluently enough for most purposes, and a dozen more I can make out slowly and torturously. But I haven't fooled with them much lately.

RWS: How are the translations of your work?

RAL: Quite a few of my books have been translated, into French, Dutch, Italian, Spanish. French and Dutch are tied now with four books each (Jan. 1976) but Dutch will move ahead with *Okla Hannali*. (It's fun to be in Dutch.) And there is a Swedish *Okla Hannali* coming out. Short stories but not complete books yet have been translated into Polish, Russian, and Japanese. Most of the translations seem to be all right, except for the verse translations. Demut, who does some of my books into French, has sent me several lists of inquiries on just what I meant. I remember he wanted me to explain the mythological implications of a phrase I used: "Nutty as a peach tree orchard boar" and I couldn't do it: I had to tell him it was just an old country phrase.

RWS: Has anyone considered making a film out of one of your stories?

RAL: There have been a couple of feelers on a couple of my books for films, and I wish that there were a lot more of them and that they would result in something. There was an Englishman who paid four hundred dollars a year for several years as an option on one of them, but I guess he let it run out.

RWS: What sort of artist would you like to illustrate your work? What do you think of Bodē's drawings for *Space Chantey*?

RAL: I haven't had many artists illustrate my work. Yes, liked Bodē's drawings for *Space Chantey*, but Bodē is dead now and he doesn't do much new illustrating. Guy Lillian in New Orleans remembers a drawing Bode made for me at the St. Louis Worldcon in 1969, and he wants to reproduce it in his fanzine for the DeepSouthcon (1979). Now all I have to do is find it. It's somewhere in the house, but I have a big house.[2]

---

[2] Vaughn Bodē's illustration was published in *At The Sleepy Sailor: A Tribute to R.A. Lafferty*, ed. G. H. Lillian, III (The Sons of the Sand: New Orleans, 1979), p.5.

A presumably French artist, J. P. Lamerand, did some Doré-like illustrations for the French version of *Space Chantey* (*Chants de L'Espace*, Galaxie/Bis n° 119, Éditions OPTA: Paris, 1974) which I rather like. They have a wood-cutting look like Bewick's illustrations of Aesop's fables, and they fit *Space Chantey* pretty well, it being a fable.

Danny Frolich illustrated two chapbooks of mine that Pendragon Press did, and the illustrations fit the tales rather well.[3] I liked the old Avon paperback copy of *The Devil Is Dead*, but I don't know who painted it.[4] I hate quite a few covers of my books. I really haven't had enough of my books illustrated to know who I would like for an illustrator.

RWS: Is there a difference between you-who-writes-the-stories and the you-who-lives-in-the-world?

RAL: No, not much difference between the me-who-writes-the-stories and the me-that-lives-in-the-world. One of us is on top of the rock and the other one on the under-side of the same rock, but I'm not sure which is which.

You seem to posit a real world, but that is doubtful. There isn't any reality except the various consensus realities. And no two persons belong to the same consensus. So the world that a person lives in is largely a world that he has fictionalized, whether he is a fictioner or not. Whatever frustration we find in the cantankerous combo-world is partly from our own inability to shape things just the way we want to.

RWS: Do you feel that the media has done harm to spiritual harmony? The past few stories you have written (June, 1978), you seem to be sniping about the ability of the media to create the wrong sort of hero, and destroy the

---

[3] *Horns on Their Heads* and *Funnyfingers & Cabrito* (Pendragon Press: Portland, OR, 1976).

[4] The cover for *The Devil Is Dead* (Avon Books: New York, 1971) was painted by Robert LoGrippo, perhaps most noted for the striking covers he produced in the early 70s for the Ballantine Adult Fantasy series.

right one. **Do you have anything against reporters in general, or are you finding fault with the media's obsession with the destruction of figureheads?**

RAL: I feel that the media make up a boggling deformity, whether there is malevolence in that deformity or not. They are a form of distorting crazy-house distortions. I don't know whether the earlier forms (recitation, oratory, manuscript, polemic, and history, then movable type printing and telegraphic communication) were and are such deformities or not; probably they are. But the newer media, instant journalism, cinema, advocacy photography and amplified sloganeering, radio, TV, computerized profiling are definite deformities. I don't know if they've done harm to spiritual harmony or not. But the media are only instruments available for everyone to use. It's a question whether it's right to regulate any instruments. I notice that the people most strongly for gun control are most strongly against media control; which is to say that it's all right to shoot people if you use big enough guns. If we are looking at everything, old as well as new, through many layers of deformity, well we had better work on the problem.

RWS: **Several science fiction writers of note (Ellison, Malzberg, Silverberg) have time and again denounced science fiction's label and have gone so far as to say that they would not bother with the field again. Do you think the label "SF" on your books hinders you to be acknowledged as a serious writer, or is the audience that welcomes you good enough for you?**

RAL: Ellison, Malzberg, and Silverberg threaten to break out of the science fiction ghetto. Do I also think it's a ghetto?

Now the fact is that Ellison, Malzberg, and Silverberg are all the same person who happens to maintain bodies in Sherman Oaks, California, Oakland, California, and Teaneck, New Jersey. Lots of persons maintain several bodies in several different places. But this person has a touch of posturing in his threats to leave, since the door isn't locked, and he already comes and goes from and to several different writing worlds

(Ellison's essays into the underground new journalism, Silverberg's writings on archaeological subjects, etc.). But farewell announcements are fun.

No, a label of SF on some books shouldn't be an impediment to acceptance by a larger audience, for the reason that the larger audience has never heard of SF or any SF writers. But the labels should be kept to keep from gulling the people.

Even with my own limited experience in several limited fields, I get protests that it "isn't SF" from persons who bought *The Fall of Rome* or *Okla Hannali*, or "it isn't historical" from persons who bought one of my SF books by mistake.

The only thing wrong with the SF audience is that it isn't larger, but how is it to be criticized for that? I can't tell a Tom Collins or a Robert Whitaker "How come there's only one of you? Clone dammit! Be a hundred each of you, and all buy books!" All the roads are open and all the maps pretty good, and painting out the name of the town called SF isn't going to improve the geography.

RWS: What do you think of the works of R. A. Lafferty?

RAL: I like the old Lafferty works, with five or more years on them, or the newer works, last year or so. But there is a place between where I am embarrassed to read them at all. The old ones are as if written by someone else and I can enjoy them sometimes as a reader. But it's those in the process of slipping away and turning into someone else's that make me uneasy. I suppose that the favorite short stories are "Continued on Next Rock," "One at a Time," "Ride a Tin Can," "Slow Tuesday Night," and "Snuffles." The favorite novels are *Past Master*, *Space Chantey*, and *Okla Hannali*.

Pax, paz, peace, irini, salaam, shalom, heiwa, amani, perdamaian, sulh, rusha, pokoj, fred, vrede, frieden, síocháin, mirno.

Robert says: A Postal Service worker for 46 years, I am half blind, half deaf, and dyslexic. I draw and write in my spare time. What I need is a gimmick. I reside on an 18 acre farm in Delaware, own goats, chickens, geese, cats and dogs. The house has lots of mice. Married with children and a mortgage.

by Yakov Varganov

Once a little Crocodile
Read a book about reptiles
He was so surprised to know
millions of years ago
Crocodiles could fly like snow!

Fly like snow! What a thought!
Crocodile devised a plot:

275

He will join a fitness class
And will learn to fly at once.

"Nonsense!" Coach boomed at him
"Crocodile's designed to swim!

With such tail and flippers on
you could be a champion!"

"Swimming's fun" was Croc's reply
"But I truly want to fly!"
Running, jumping, lifting weights
Crocodile was gaining pace
"My, oh my!" the coach sighed
"I can tell he wants to fly!"

Days went by, and weeks and months
Crocodile became advanced

"What a sight!" his coach screamed
Looking up in disbelief
Over roofs in sunny sky
Crocodile flew up like fly,
Giggling silly, chasing cars
Horror causing in the hearts
He was flying like a snow
Like the crocs of long ago!

Yakov Varganov is a research biologist and an aspiring writer-illustrator. His interest in Lafferty's writing was initiated by "Slow Tuesday Night" published in Esli. *Following his immigration to the US in 1997 he started collecting and reading all Lafferty's works he could find. Currently he resides in Scotch Plains, NJ.*

Three Mountain Works
by Bill Rogers

Come to the Mountain

At the tail end of winter, after Hannali had been in the Territory for onto four years, he awoke one morning from a charismatic dream. It was the dream of the mountain Nanih Waiya, not that of the great mound that was built by hands in the Mississippi country, but of the older mountain of which the mound was the memorial. The last of the Choctaw magic men called to Hannali in the dream — "Come to the mountain."
~Okla Hannali, R.A. Lafferty

"Come to the Mountain" © *2017 Bill Rogers*

Only a Magic Mountain

Nanih Waiya was the leaning mountain. It would not be a particularly high mountain, nor grand for its sheerness and a suddenness of aspect. It was only a magic mountain.

~Okla Hannali, R.A. Lafferty

"Only a Magic Mountain" © 2017 Bill Rogers

Come to the Mountain

dream mountain
old mountain
mound memorial mountain
leaning mountain
small mountain
treasure mountain
mountain full-of-water
homeland mountain
rattlesnake mountain
bending-down mountain
contrived mountain
manifold dream mountain
panther mountain
upshot mountain
mountain of the haruspex
nation-reconstituting mountain
folk memory mountain
turning point mountain
low mountain
splitting mountain
snake mountain
mountain of five bears
secret-preserving mountain
sheep mountain
suicide mountain
pinnacled mountain
ghost-tower mountain
river mountain
original mountain
white morning mountain
mule whiskey mountain
friendly mountain
death mountain
heaped-up mountain
luck-making mountain
coup-counting mountain
transfiguring mountain
mountain of abominations
bear mountain

mountain of rest
condor mountain
spire mountain
electric mountain
iron mountain
mountain full-of-sparks
tall-trap mountain
killer mountain
melchisedech mountain
soul-lifting mountain
transfixing mountain
hallucinating mountain
charged-air mountain
copperhead mountain
talking horse mountain
blood-drawing mountain
shale mountain
not a particularly high mountain
only a magic mountain

These works © 2017 Bill Rogers

The Carrion King
by Logan Giannini

Lo, the distant warning bell,
Pealing in the night,
Carrying over branch and dell,
Spurring feet to flight,
Hark! the final guard that fell,
For silence fills the dark,
Portent of the hordes of hell,
And their heartless monarch,

Gold and silver have no place,
As hasty bags are packed,
Provisions, needs must, fill the case,
For riches but detract,
As home and hearth are fled apace,
The dawn placed at your fore,
Feet now nervous for the chase,
From regent out of lore,

How quickly faces are forgot,
In flight across the heath,
The future's now the only plot,
Else to the grave bequeathed,
Through the ruin of Camelot,
Stones all that here remain,
Of brave and handsome Lancelot,
Naught left but chiseled name,

Hoofbeats score the passing time,
As months bleed into years,
Survival, Sisyphean, a climb,
Hounded by grim fears,
Endurance now your paradigm,
Potential cruelly frozen,
Riding hard, bedecked by grime,
Life paralyzed in motion,

Upon a hill without a name,
All strength is finally spent,
Clothes in tatters, feet gone lame,
No will for the descent,
From sticks you coax a warming flame,
Sit soft upon the loam,
Thusly marked you stake your claim,
Hill becomes a home,

Lo, the distant warning bell,
Drawing ever nearer,
Echoing a funeral knell,
Dark tidings and their bearer,
Final shreds of dread dispel,
Upon the plangent ring,
With open arms you say farewell,
And greet the Carrion King.

Logan Giannini lives and works out of Minnesota. He writes novels, short stories, poems, and comics (or "graphic novels" if he's wearing a suit). You can find more about him at counterfeitnickels.com.

Eccentrexity
by J Simon

There was not a single growing thing, yet the land was no less beautiful. A vast metal spider paused, the mind within transfixed with wonderment, to caress the softly glowing bubblegum crystals that blossomed profusely from a nearby crag. The land—one of twisted spires, waxen and flowing, a muted yet vibrant impressionist painting—began slowly to melt and reform. And the spider gave thanks for what it had seen.

#

For thousands of years, a humanity bent on expansion had railed against the cruel god Einstein whose limits defied their dreams of stars; against the cruel reality of cold hard worlds which, through failures each more spectacular than the last, proved terraforming nothing more than an impossible fiction; and against the harshest reality of all: Only one earth allotted the species—how unfair!—and none more ever to come. It was a warmer earth, now. An earth of storms and poisons, biotoxins and radiation leaks. The green was dying. The voice of the people became a scream.

Their children, unconcerned, played their virtual games, accepting cybernetic implants whose stimulation was hardly distinguishable from that of their own eyes and skin. The body became less important as their games grew increasingly real, and to their children's children even less so, until the day that the first volunteer accepted a total transplant from a crippled body to one of plastic and steel. The form was set: A metallic bush bristling with sensory apparatus, braincase slung between four main legs in vague resemblance of arachnid form. Over any terrain, through any habitat, the metal bush might ramble, enjoying absolute saturation of sensory stimuli. The indomitable human will, once bound by bodily constraints, had been sprung free.

#

They called it Factory Equus—massive, monolithic, inhabited solely by machines—more mausoleum than birthing-site, and the largest structure on the entire planetoid. In place of wombs were slender habitat cylinders, and within one, a young man: Twenty years old, but only four feet tall, weighing less than thirty-five pounds; paste-white eyelids, never opened; tissue-thin muscle, never used. Sensory grafts imposed virtual dreams upon his mind in a pattern lovingly crafted by his biological parents—a quasi-random program of simulated experiences, controlled partially by his own mental feedback, that would generate the personality and character of his adult self—a self soon to come to realization. It was time.

Several sensors ticked over, worried. Measurements did not match. Aberrant case detected. Harvest of the young man's brain was put on hold, the standard chassis of metallic-spider form returned to storage; an order was put in, requesting construction of a chassis custom-built to meet his particular requirements. That such an unusual order might attract unwanted attention was not something the machines had been programmed to consider.

#

The picketers waited; silent, watching. The fountain atop Factory Equus rumbled, remotely threatening but deactivated for the purpose of the birthling's release. Within the swirling smoke and haze that yet remained, a many-legged form was just visible, stepping with near-comic deliberateness as it struggled not to fall. Its extremities at first glance appeared misplaced or at least improperly connected, for this chassis had been built not with four legs, but with five.

"Lesson five hundred and sixty-eight, word seventy, Prattle," came an uncertain voice, gentle and distracted. "Seventy-one, Prawn. Seventy-two..." The newborn dipped and weaved, righted itself. "...Praxis. I believe my name will be Praxis," it said decisively.

At the head of the cordon of protestors, a trio of cybernetic spiders stood slightly before the others. One was swathed in vividly died scarves; another encased in a clear gel whose refractive properties were not unlike those of a funhouse mirror; and the last, metal limbs black and twisted, ripped and fused as by the fires of hell, stood unadorned. Pastor Glenn had never sought repair from any of his seven self-immolations nor from his three self-crucifixions: His faith was his pride, and he wore it with honor.

"I am Praxis," the newcomer repeated with increasing confidence. "And these large, many-legged objects are either very interesting sculptures cast in my approximate image; or, perhaps, there may conceivably exist sentient beings— 'people', as it were—other than myself. An intriguing concept. If I... hello, what's this?" Startled, Praxis refocused his optic gains downward, but succeeded only in confusing himself. His legs shook and began to walk steadily backward.

"...cast in *his* image!" the gel-clad lieutenant spat, trembling. "That *thing* can hardly walk without tripping over its own deformities and it dares cast aspersions on us!"

"It can't know any better," Glenn calmly replied. "Not without being told. But it may be taught; and, we should hope, repaired. Let us find out. My friend!" he called. "Praxis!"

"Well then, there do exist other sentiences!" Praxis replied, excited, "or else the sculptures possess oddly compelling skills of mimicry. Let us assume the former. Hello?"

"Hello, and welcome to the world," Glenn replied warmly, moving forward. "I am Pastor Glenn; and we, the Emissaries of Mental Purity. We greet you in a spirit of camaraderie and love."

"Hence the lines of people marching back and forth to protest the fact of my birth?" Praxis inquired ingenuously. "I fancy the sort of pink-paper-heart love described in chapter seventeen, myself."

Glenn chuckled. "We love *you*, Praxis, yet we may still protest if we feel something terribly wrong has been done *to* you. Do you understand the distinction? Please, allow me to explain. This is very important, and I think you'll find it very interesting."

"Explanations are welcome; for I have many questions," Praxis replied.

At Glenn's signal, mechanical figures swarmed around them, quietly and efficiently assembling a colorful privacy screen around them. Numerous broadcast ROMs were placed with equal care throughout the makeshift cubicle—the soothing warmth of a kitten's breath, the satiety of a meal well-earned, the liquid closeness of the womb. Praxis flexed several hundred delicately branched appendages, startled to find himself so suddenly enclosed within a gently humming cocoon of sensory projections.

"How snug!" he said appreciatively, "and how lovely—one would hardly notice the subtle narcotic effect! Yes, by all means make your arguments—but quickly, if you please. I estimate the present atmosphere will substantially impair my judgment within five minutes."

"Then let me offer an experiment," Glenn said, activating one of his optic units. "I will project an image for you to see. Look at it, and notice how your sensors focus on individual items within the picture. A face, a shape, a detail. Human beings are discrete thinkers, meant to focus on one thing at a time. Some claim they can absorb far more information, that they see all the world simultaneously as clearly as we see the details. This is a lie."

"I can see the image," Praxis said modestly, "and the entire room; and everything in it."

"To some degree," Glenn allowed. "It's called peripheral vision, and everyone has it—some more than others. Unfortunately, certain misguided factions have taken this variance to mean that there are actually two types of human mind! Discrete thinkers, and synthetic thinkers, who—according to this ludicrous theory—are completely immersed in their environment and perceive all of it at once."

"I am ludicrous?" Praxis asked, puzzled.

"What has been done to you is ludicrous!" Glenn cried, cilia rippling with agitation. "You are clumsier than most, and have stronger peripheral vision than most; and for that they have forced you into a braincase and chassis wired for synthetic perception!"

"It suits me well," Praxis said mildly.

"You are too young, and know no alternatives."

"My perceptions are clear."

"You are a discrete thinker," Glenn stated, "who is being forcibly subjected to stimuli no human brain was meant to comprehend. It will lead inevitably to unhappiness, discomfort, and sickness of the mind. Please tell me that you will accept our help!"

"Your arguments are compelling," Praxis confessed. "I can't imagine you'd resort to vaguely reasoned emotional appeals unsupported by evidence unless your concern for me was so great that you were freely willing to sacrifice all credibility in pursuit of your cause. Such devotion is indeed touching."

"Then you will come to our compound, where we may discuss such ideas at greater length?"

Praxis stirred uncomfortably. There was a moment's silence. ROMs murmured and hummed their sensory threnodies, weaved their comforting truths. Glenn leaned slowly forward; Praxis rippled a shrug. "I have many questions..."

"I am ready to hear them."

"Sadly, I have no time for such," Praxis said. "The narcotics are beginning to take effect. I must leave."

Pastor Glenn hissed a pneumatic sigh. "If that is your wish."

"It is. I may choose to visit your group; certainly, reasoned discourse would be welcome. But first, I must go abroad in the world and experience what else life has to offer. I expect this odyssey to take at least an afternoon. Will your offer remain open until then?"

"An afternoon? I think we can manage." Glenn graciously parted the wall-screen for Praxis with one char-blackened leg. "Go, then. But remember, you always have family to return to. We love you, Praxis, and we are more than eager to rescue you from this travesty to which you've been born."

"I believe I understand." Dipping its body in an abbreviated bow, the newborn brushed past gaily colored veils and was gone.

#

Hers was a small dreamshop but orderly, constructed of interlocking intricacies half spiderweb, half snowflake—purple or iridescent, crystalline or metallic. She stocked every ROM, legal or illegal, genius or insane—shortly, every sensory entertainment demanded by the people of a world devoid of organic life's comforting randomness. The landscape-machines fulfilled some of that need by constantly pushing the surface into soothingly fractal interpretations of almost-life—shards of trees, fracture toads, prismatic moss—but hers was a service oft in demand.

And it had been shaping up to be a slow day right up until the five-sider walked in. Rozy brightened her gains, immediately interested.

"Well, what have we here?" she transmitted, her maybe-whisper warm and kittenish and satisfied, teasing his sensory inputs. She watched him tremble as the first word plucked a chord of shimmering purple across his vision, the second beguiled a tongue he didn't have with tantalizing promise of tartness and sweet, the third touched him in intimate caress of parts, perhaps, that no living creature had ever possessed.

"My dreams did not prepare me for this," he said, greatly impressed.

"Cute," she said coyly, tones of burnt ginger. "And a five-sider, no less. Fresh out of the tank, aren't you?"

"I am," he said, and a moment later—"What is a five-sider? And why do I feel wary of the images you are projecting at me?"

"Because the young are born naive," she purred. "Can you imagine; people once thought there could be no such thing as 'perversity' once the body was forsaken and all things permitted." She shimmied playfully. "They should have known better."

"I have a feeling you are much more real that my lessons," he mused. "Alarming and exhilarating all at once. How odd that life should prove so contradictory. Is there an appendix of the rules not included in my lessons?"

"Cute," she said drolly, pulling a rack of sensory ROMs from behind the counter. "Very cute. Can I offer you a sniff?

A glow? A hum? No charge for a newbie."

"I'm not certain," Praxis said. "Sensory difficulties haunt me yet: For example—when I move my legs like *so*, I seem to suffer an eerily convincing illusion that the entire world is moving backward."

"It's called walking," she said drily, a teasing hue of cerulean laughter. "It's best to imagine that the universe is stationary, and *you* moving forward."

"Intriguing," he breathed, "how novel," and proceeded to practice. Rozy watched, amusement mingling with impatience, and took a drag on the illusion of a condor. Thinking better of it, she jacked herself into a fixed sensory shunt, waiting for the magnetic grips to seize the edge of her chassis, waiting for the projections to tease her mind with frothing intimations of darkness, lurid surrealities, sweeping angelic truths; fragments of meaning, or oily dark iniquities swilled like a beggar's beer—

"Take any ROM you want, and keep it," she said, sly as a jackal's glance. "The scent of orange blossoms, perhaps. Your word—a simple contract, a promissory statement—and it will be yours."

"Simple as that?" he asked, rocking back and forth on newborn legs.

"Take two," she said persuasively, a velvet cat creeping through the night. "Consider it a double value for the price of one; an entertaining product, and an important lesson on the risks of impulse buying and consumer debt."

"Such generosity!" he replied, impressed. "But—"

"Yes?"

"I find you quite fascinating," he confessed, "and charitable and giving and intriguing. But—for now—I seek satisfaction of the soul over that of the senses—"

"Apparently you've never tasted an angel," she countered archly.

"—which is why I must speak to my friend the pastor, who was courageous enough to picket my birthing, while a lesser friend might have valued my happiness over my safety. I'm sure he has many fine thoughts to share."

Rozy froze, cilia locking in place. She focused all of her gains on the birthling, the flavor of wry humor dropping from her sensory projectors.

"Praxis," she said carefully, "do you understand the words 'self-righteousness', 'dogma', or 'crusade'?"

"While further vocabulary is desirable," he said, moving toward the door, "the Emissaries have promised many answers..."

"There are things I need to talk to you about!" she said, alarmed to discover that she was unable to unjack herself from her sensory shunt. "Why don't you spend the evening? I'm sure I can satisfy your, ah, deeper curiosities." Her voice fuzzed a hopeful orangey peach, gradually darkening through sunset to molten lead. "...and I won't even charge for it!"

"There are certain questions of life in which I take a profound interest," he said apologetically. "I must go. But I hope to see you again soon, nonetheless." Bowing awkwardly, he turned a shaky circle and began to scramble from the shop.

"Wait!" Rozy cried. "You don't understand! There are people who think you are evil, who—"

The doors closed behind him. Pneumatic valves hissing in a mechanical sigh, Rozy tugged once again at her sensory shunt. Sensory stimuli washed over her, beat against her mind, inevitable and unrelenting. She gave in, finally, letting her thoughts go— capricious as tumbleweeds, fragments colliding and connecting, mingling and parting. Her mind touched, brooding, upon the five- siders she had known, no more than two or three in a lifetime, and upon those who hated them for what they were. And her troubled envisionings smelt of worry.

#

The intimate closeness of Rozy's shop still fresh in his mind, Praxis gazed, bewildered, at the bustling activity before him. It was an anthill run through a kaleidoscope, a bustling scene of more activity than he would have believed possible. Metal spiders scurried everywhere, and Praxis stood just within the polymer sheet that defined the edge of the Emissary's compound and considered.

"Perhaps they use mirrors," he mused, "or puppets. Or else my estimate of the world's population is hazardously low; 'Fifty' may be closer to true."

Praxis examined the vista before him. The compound was a hodgepodge of buildings assembled at different times and in different styles, the grounds themselves a malleably soft carpet of black-green ceramic whose pleasingly complex ripple-topology was constantly being rearranged by tiny mechanical caterpillars. Fountains, free-standing ROMs and other decorative touches were prevalent.

He descended a slope into the courtyard, crossing a series of embedded ROMs whose flickering sense-impressions, when taken in rapid sequence—darknessLIGHT!dirtmudsquirrel—animated an artist's rendition of Creation. Reaching the bottom, he spotted a familiar blackened form and began to wave.

"Praxis! I see you've joined us after all!" Pastor Glenn crossed the courtyard, scabrous flakes of charred metal falling in his wake. "Everything happens at once," he murmured ruefully; "Nonetheless, we welcome you with joy!"

"Is this level of activity usual, then?" Praxis inquired, swaying slightly. "I find it dizzying."

"I find it dizzying myself, at times," Glenn chuckled warmly. "Our members are just returning from picketing the funeral of a five-sider who fell off a bridge due to the unnatural profanity of his chassis; returning from spreading awareness, and warning, that those who do not choose salvation are punished by God. Only a fraction of those you see actually live here, but we do have a rectory for permanent residents. If you will follow me to your room—"

"My apologies," Praxis interrupted, having stumbled into a wading pool, "but the laws of physics seems to have abruptly changed, particularly as apply to air viscosity, light refraction, and propagation of sound. Are you aware of any rogue pocket universes infesting the grounds?"

"Not the last I'd heard," Glenn replied, amused. "But as I was saying; once you're settled, I'll take you to meet your family."

"Indeed?" Praxis rotated, surprised. "I didn't spontaneously generate?"

"What I meant," Glenn patiently explained, "is that—in our love for you, and in our desire to see you live healthy and free— we will welcome you to our family. God's family."

"Fancy that!" he murmured, pleased. "The 'discrete thinker' / 'synthetic thinker' question has been much on my mind as I examine my beliefs, seeking to better come to grips with how I feel about this crucial decision. It will be good to discuss it with family—"

"And we *are* your family, though we abhor what has been done to you."

"—and I am happy," Praxis continued, "that I will have caring, teaching companions to help me explore the issue's logical complexities—"

"We will do all we can," Glenn promised, "but only you can accept the truth; only you can choose salvation over perdition. We can do no more than set your feet upon the proper path."

"—knowing that their gentle support will assist me in making my decision, whatever it may be—"

"We can only encourage you to turn from the perversion which has been forced upon you," Glenn said, "by asking you—begging you- -to choose the path of righteousness and be saved; for only those who cleave to their shameful heritage shall be damned."

"—and that my new family, knowing that I have made my own decision according to my beliefs and to the best of my ability, will respect and support my—" Praxis refocused his optics, confused. "Beg pardon?"

Glenn sighed. "Perhaps you should meet your family *now*. Come with me, Praxis."

#

Rozy came down gradually from her fractured sensory high. Thoughts swam and blurred; twisted and connected. Praxis had seen through all her cunning with the serendipitous clarity of the young... yet he still liked her.

He liked her. Rozy remembered in sudden flashback the last Emissary of Mental Purity she'd met—the polished metal, the cloying sweetness of the lubricant-masker which suppressed his own personal scent. Rozy had been unimpressed. She dosed her own circulatory system with a delectably enticing combination of polymer synthetics uniquely hers—whisper of pomegranate, hint of myrrh, promise of passions yet to be fulfilled. Scent being one of the strongest keys to memory, she wanted to ensure that all her affairs were unforgettable. Those who wished to mask their personal scent, she found, generally had something to hide. Still, he'd seemed pleasant enough, and she'd accepted his offers of narcotics and copulation, distrust hardly being reason to be impolite. And then there was Praxis—

He liked her. So many others had tired of her sardonic hedonism. She surrounded herself with pleasures and still none stayed... except the last five-sider she had known. She still received transmissions from five-sider city every 7/27 of a year, though she could never bring herself to read them. And now there was Praxis.

That innocence. That naive cleverness. That affection, so readily granted but no less real. Rozy thrashed unsteadily, working her way free of her dreams. She had to find Praxis. But how? With no crime to report she couldn't rely on the authorities, yet he hadn't given a destination, hadn't left any trace—

The last fragments of her dreams snapped into place, and Rozy knew. The Emissaries used lubricant-maskers just as she employed her own special mix, but Praxis had to be the only person on the entire planetoid with uncut, factory-standard virgin oil. He'd been in her shop long enough to leave a scent trail; possibly, she could trace him herself.

Gathering herself, trembling slightly, Rozy caught the scent and began to follow it, refusing to think what might happen if she arrived too late.

#

The compound's commons were a comfortably intimate suite of rooms which—for the amusement of their occupants—were flooded with varying liquid substances.

Glenn kept to the elevated causeways, but Praxis enthusiastically thrashed through foamed cream and synthesized pudding, perfumed oils and carbonated effervescence.

"Through there," Glenn instructed him, pointing to a dimly lit tunnel. "We'll need a minute to set ourselves up, but I'm sure you'll find sufficient distractions until we're ready."

Praxis went, eager to see what he might find. The tunnel was wholly flooded with tepid water in which hung suspended millions of colorful waxy globules—dense and slippery as rainbow caviar, but parting without resistance as Praxis passed—and in each tiny globule was embedded a tiny rice-grain of a ROM. Whispered almost-sensations prickled at the edge of his consciousness—the flutter of wings, half-seen teasings of his peripheral vision, a touch familiar yet fleeting. Scent and aftertaste, echo and aura enveloped him and conveyed him safe to the tunnel's end. A light, shimmering gently, drew closer...

Praxis gasped. Emerging into air—into the utter absence of imposed sensation—was a chill and unwelcome shock. He found himself standing in the center of a shallow pool of plain water. Pastor Glenn stood on the elevated ledge that encircled the pool, as did sixteen others—a silent, foreboding ring of humanity. They looked down upon him, waiting.

"You have arrived," Glenn said somberly, his charred wreck of a body softly rattling, "but your journey has only just begun. Will you join us? Will you forsake your past and join your family?"

"I am certain you wouldn't mean to pressure an uninformed decision," Praxis mused, "so I must conclude that you are expressing a form of humor I've yet to learn. I decline your generous offer."

"As is your right," Glenn said somberly. "I only wish you could understand the deep and abiding sadness I feel as I look at you—a brother, a sibling, a child—standing alone, cold, and forsaken, shivering in the dark. Your family and friends surround you, but by your own choice you stand apart. I ask only that you consider, carefully, whether the path on which you stand will bring you fulfillment."

Praxis shifted unhappily, cilia tasting the sensory barrenness of the plain, tepid water. "I am uncertain," he said at last. "Apart from your own personal wishes, can you give me a reason I *should* join you?"

"Several," Glenn replied, a touch of humor returning to his voice. "We've gathered here precisely to demonstrate what you've been missing; to show you the wholesome, virtuous diversions of the four-legged norm. You may find these a bit mundane, but when shared by a family, even simple things bring joy." Walking around the encircling ledge, he paused in turn before each of his sixteen companions. "Kechik, as you can see, is enjoying the wholesome pureness of sensory impulses shunted to the sexual. What discrete thinker hasn't 'had' strawberries and chocolate on many an occasion? And here's Mikel, enjoying the holy bliss of psychedelics, hallucinogens, and anti-depressants—only the legal ones, of course, but then, Mikel has always been a man of values. Then we see faithful Keyli, whose inebriation-ROM never runs dry, and Jumara's erotic interjunct with her own hindbrain, and Hamari's joy-shunt, and this impassioned couple engaging in the wholesome, natural love of God's creation!" He paused, looking over the pair of ecstatically writhing, intertangled mechanical bodies. "Not sure which is which," he coughed, "but you can see they're having a good time. Surely such ecstasy must be in service to God. Surely you will join us?"

Praxis swayed, catching a tantalizing shadow-impression of each ROM in turn; the teasing red plumpness of strawberry, a great vastness of euphoric well-being, a brazen invincibility borne of intoxication. He stumbled, and again all was empty, all was barren.

"It is your choice," Pastor Glenn gently told him. "It always has been. And so—simply—I ask of you: Leave behind the five-sided profanity of your birth and come to us; to the natural, healthy mainstream of society. This is our deepest desire; and we wait, hopeful, of your decision."

A rippling pseudo-shrug made the circuit of Praxis' body, making small waves in the tepid waters. "Then you will be pleased to hear my answer," he replied, "for I have decided to join you."

#

Rozy sampled the air, seeking the elusive trace she'd been following for nearly an hour. She'd nearly lost his scent at a compound of buildings apparently controlled by the Emissaries, but by circling the enclosure she'd picked the trail up again—his, and hundreds of others. It had taken her another half hour to trace the procession this far, and she was beginning to worry. Recently, the scent of Praxis' virgin oil had become tainted by something else—

Ashes. Something was burning. Hastening her step, Rozy crested a shallow rise, slipped, righted herself. Before her stretched the Caldera; a broad bowl-shaped valley in every conceivable color of glass, a sea of marbles melted and reformed. Scrambling across the variegated glass-floe and its sub-surface corkscrew spirallings, she rounded a silicate outcropping and came upon the Emissaries of Mental Purity.

Gathered as for mass, the assembled host was resplendent in their full regalia. Elaborately embroidered tetrahedrons adorned each arachnoid figure. Censors burned, bluish haze lazily flowing from their bowls; a chant reverberated, felt more than heard, marking the occasion. At the four cardinal points of the gathering, five-sided polygons burned in effigy.

"Hello?" Rozy called, hurrying forward. Their leader—a fire-blackened old warhorse—came to meet her, his bearing one of unconcerned inquiry.

"I am Pastor Glenn," the charred figure said pleasantly. "May I help you?"

"Yes. I need to see Praxis."

He chuckled kindly. "To congratulate him, or to pry him from our wicked grasp? No matter; the ceremony is already complete. Of course you may see the newest member of our family."

He led her into the crowd and through it; past a trio of tetrahedron-decorated figures triumphantly parading a jointed shaft of metal back and forth, past others waving soldering guns and screaming victory. A mechanoid scurried aside, and the way was clear to see.

Her foremost cilia snapped, her projectors trembling crazily. Praxis. The same metallic form. But. Spilled oil and

299

coolant spreading beneath him. Torn metal glinting severed wires broken trembling—

Praxis turned, the lone tetrahedron strapped to his chassis wobbling with the unsteadiness of his own limping gait. The solder-smeared stump of his missing fifth leg rotated fitfully, struggling to help him. He slipped, fell, stood again, turned to face her.

"Praxis!" Rozy cried, hopeful smudges of raspberry and gingerale coloring her fear. "Praxis—my god—"

"She may tell you dangerous and wicked things," Glenn began.

"I will speak with her."

Pastor Glenn hesitated, then bowed and marched away. Praxis stumbled closer; Rozy twined her foreleg around his, to hold him up as much as to transmit simple human warmth.

"Praxis, Praxis. You didn't need to do this. The Emissaries may speak with kindness..."

"...but also with astonishing logical inconsistencies," he replied. "I know. They are very earnest in their works, but this does little to excuse the irresponsibility of their tactics."

Rozy looked Praxis over from foot-pad to cilia-crest, examining his every surface, her projectors threatening to lose focus as they passed over his wounds.

"If you know that the Emissaries are... inconsistent... in their logic," she finally asked, "why did you go with them?"

Praxis hesitated. "It's true that their behaviour is peculiar. At times quaint, even amusing; at others, inexplicable and frustrating. But this is why I must stay with them, no more and no less: They need my help."

"They need..." Rozy's cilia rippled, startled. "You stayed with them... to teach them?"

"They are good people. In many ways, loving people," he explained, shyly extending one of his remaining legs to fleetingly caress one of hers. "I will not leave them as long as there is a chance I might help them to accept myself—and all five-siders—as we are."

"They may be beyond help."

Praxis chuckled. "I am not convinced of that."

"Don't try to change them. Not yet. You need to learn, to mature, to know more about your world and yourself..."

"You may be right," he admitted, "and I appreciate your concern. Nevertheless, I must try."

Rozy sighed ruefully. "You are one weird cooky, you know that?"

"Ah. You perceive me as a baked good," he mused. "And what sort of ROM is responsible for that?"

Rozy lapsed into thoughtful silence. She looked at Praxis; at the broad glassy bowl of the Caldera; at the Emissaries with their tetrahedral garb and their polygons burning in effigy.

"Lord help me but you're too innocent," she breathed. "Too trusting. But I can't kill that part of you. I can't fight that part of you. If you have to go with them..." She sent an image of a rose; crisp, red, until it suddenly grew fangs and vomited forth a mocking cheshire grin. "...then go."

His reply was wordless; a glance, a rippling wave of fondness, of appreciation. One more fleeting caress; and then he began to amble awkwardly back toward the Emissaries.

"You don't have to be a martyr," she called, cilia flexing.

"I know."

"They'll crucify you," she said. "Innocence always dies."

"Perhaps," he called back. "But afterward, when I've done all I can—then, I'll come back to you. Until then!"

She stood, watching, until her optic gains lost focus, turning the land into a muted yet vibrant impressionist painting which flowed, and melted. Dusk gave way to night, leaving her alone. And the machine, which could not cry, watched, and waited. Until the landscape did.

This work © 1998 J Simon

J Simon is an author and programmer based in Wisconsin. His most recently published novel, Fossilized Gods, is available at majra.org. Some years ago, he read Lafferty's "Eurema's Dam" in the Robert Silverberg edited anthology The Best of New Dimensions, and has never been quite the same since (or before really).

I See Through All of Me, I See For Parsecs
by Daniel Otto Jack Petersen

The bird and the bear and the debater convened. The bear was made of stars and when it hurtled down to earth for the convening, it destroyed one third of the planet. The bird was a kaleidoscopic composite of all birds, and its form constantly shifted. The debater was an old man who pretended to be an ancient king of exceptional majesty. He was known to possess wisdom. They met at a grand tree in full foliage. The bird lit branchwise upon this tree and the bear and the man came and stood beneath it. It was a tree of knowledge and it augmented their sight as they looked to the East, their gaze reaching round the curve of the earth to the distant regions and ecosystems where the bear had touched down. A vast growth of smoke billowed across the horizon like some gargantuan black fungus.

Considering these geographies of sudden ruin, the man pronounced: "All is bubble-pop."

The bird contested this pronouncement. "Seeds!" it chirped. Its tone was either strident or exuberant, it was hard to tell which.

"Yea, brother bird, I planted them," growled the star-bear.

"It's a great wound in a great head," said the man. "Meaningless."

The bear rose to its full standing height and towered over the man and glowered down at him. The bear's glower might have been a look of deep thought or of ire, it was hard to tell which. Starwise, the bear filled parsecs in its towering. Earthside, it stood some four feet above the man's head and was three times his width, its fur luminescent with starshine even in this terrestrial iteration of itself. The every-bird flitted down to the bear's shoulder and pointed its ever-changing beak down at the man and cawed: "Seeds die!"

302

"Aye," concurred the bear, "and give birth to something greater."

The man turned away from the burning oceans and continents in the East. He stared at the ground and watched crumbs of bread move antwise toward a little mound of sand, the crumbs borne aloft by a procession of the tiny insects. "So mighty for the lifting of morsels many times your size, yet so fragile in the face of a man's whim," mumbled the man as he squatted. He put the tip of his gnarled index finger down in the middle of the line of ants and watched them diverted from their path. The bear dropped to all fours for a closer look, the bird flapping upward in a cascade of changing wings. The ground shook at the impact of the bear's forepaws, but the ants were not toppled. When the bear exhaled from the descent of its own weight, however, the ants were scattered, crumbs dislodged, their work undone in a hot carrion gust.

"Bubble-pop," pronounced the man, and stood up again.

"And yet a world containing so much capacity for production," said the bear, which was shoulder high to the man even on all fours. He smelled the animal reek of its fur mixed with the sharp odor of stellar ionization, and heard a faint electric crackling.

"Fecund!" concurred the bird.

"Neo-nil sub-solar," countered the man.

"Fecund! Fecund! Fecund!" the bird twittered on.

The man looked along the curve of the earth to the smoke-blooming horizon once more. The immense heat, half a world away, was beginning to reach them now in warm waves. "Eat the wind, both of you," he said.

"Ruach! Ruach!" exclaimed the bird with ecstasy in its calls.

"Spirit, wind, breath," said the man. "Vapor!"

"Hebel? Hebel?" asked the bird.

"A vain vapor," the man confirmed. "Bubble-pop."

The bear stood erect again at the man's left side, facing the East like him, following his gaze. The bird flew to his right shoulder and he felt its constantly varying weights as it shifted through its myriad forms.

"She's gone," said the man. "No one can find her. No one ever has."

303

"Can you see every possible tinge, search every quadrant, every quantum crumb?" the bear asked him, nodding its great shaggy head at the bird as it flew from the man's shoulder to a limb of the tree again. It was shifting rapidly through every color of the ornithological spectrum. He looked at the bird and witnessed pulsing reds, soft blues, screaming greens, inky blacks, fiery oranges, and on and on without repetition of a single hue.

"Neo-nil sub-solar," he insisted. "And I've learned to live without her."

"Just because your grasshopper droops and drags and hops no more," said the bear, "doesn't mean all its previous hopping was for naught."

"Bubble-pop of bubble-pops!" sneered the man with palpable bitterness. "Suds of multiverses bursting to infinity!"

"Progeny!" retorted the bird.

The man stared at the bird with tired but smoldering eyes. Then he moistened his lips and formed a bubble of saliva between them, opening his mouth until the bubble grew large and then popped. "Vanity," he pronounced, wet-lipped. "Hebel."

"You may find her yet," said the bear gently. The bird perched now on the bear's wide head and preened its shifting pinions.

The man's face softened. "I was sure I saw her several times, once in a crowded street of a vast city, another time on the coast of an island I was sailing towards, and elsewhere. But every time she eluded me. Or else my mind deluded me. Once I supervised a mining crew working a bejeweled tract of land and the tunneling brought us to a wall, an inexplicable wall in that freshly turned depth of earth. I stilled the miners because I thought I heard a sound, beyond the wall, or within it. I leaned my ear to it and heard a faint moaning, a woman's weeping! Some of the others heard it too. I called out to her and thought I heard her call for help in reply. Indeed, I was sure I heard her calling out to me "Qoheleth! Qoheleth!" It was her pet name for me, for she always laughed at my searchings and kindly teased me, calling me Qoheleth, Collector of sayings, Convener of debates. At my command the crew laid into the wall with picks, calling for her to stand back, and when it seemed we were nearly upon her, I alone broke carefully through. And a serpent leapt out and bit my hand! The venom fevered me for weeks, but did not kill me. The miners testified that no other creature than the serpent lay beyond that inexplicable underground wall. We were rich with precious stones from that dig, but I was ever after impoverished in wisdom, for she had evaded me yet again."

He rubbed two white dots on the back of his right hand with the index and middle fingers of his left. The sun was dying in the West now, oozing bloodlight over everything. The interlocutors beneath the tree stood between bleeding red in the West and smoking black in the East. "We come from it and go to it," said Qoheleth in a small voice.

"Mystery!" the bird trilled once, and then struck up a simple song: "Mystery! Mastery! Mystery! Mastery!"

"Meaningless!" cut in Qoheleth. "Death! For everyone and everything."

The birdsong changed to a taunt: "Misery! Miserly! Misery! Miserly!"

Qoheleth ignored this. "Our firstborn was stillborn," he said. The sky overhead was purpling like a bruise. "In my grief and inexperience, I dug a very shallow grave in the winter-hard ground for the tiny corpse. The jackals were at it by spring and I came upon them one dawn cracking the tiny bones in their mouths with pops and snaps like the munching of nuts or tart berries."

Silence between them a moment. "She began to leave me then," he said.

Then the bird let fly the long, wordless wail of some jungle species.

"Yes, oh yes, and oh, I am so sorry," said the bear in a kindly growl. Huge tears welled in her large eyes. Only now did Qoheleth somehow notice it was a she-bear. "But remember," said the bear, "Zeke saw skin climbing bones."

"Ah, Zeke the Dreamer!" snapped Qoheleth. "His dreams too will burst like thought bubbles and snap like newborn bones. Zeke's dreams are jackal snacks!"

The warm wind from the East was becoming a hot blast. It ruffled the bird's sequences of feathers and riffled the bear's starspun pelt and lifted Qoheleth's grey hair.

"No. What is warped cannot be righted," Qoheleth resumed. Dusk had settled over the land and his voice spoke from out of the night. "Those baby bones are not laying about getting dusty, awaiting prophecy. They were chewed, digested, and excreted. And the billions of bones from the exploded earth yonder are burned to dust and less than dust. No. What is lacking cannot be counted." He tasted something gritty blowing into his mouth that didn't seem like sand. He worried it was ashes, human and otherwise, and spat. "There's nothing to do but grease our mortality bonewise with food and drink and happy work and family while they last, if they last. That's all we're given. The stillborn are the truly fortunate."

"Ah, but the less-than-dust can climb the dust and then the dust can climb itself back into bones and then the flesh and blood can climb the bones," insisted the bear, "if Zeke prophesies to them as he was commanded."

"Seeds die!" sang the bird.

"To bear fruit," the bear concurred.

The fluctuating shadow-shapes of the every-bird were obscured in the darkened tree. The bear illumined only her own starry outline.

"Can this bonedust live?" said Qoheleth. "Neo-nil sub-solar."

"Neo-nephesh supra-solar," challenged the bear. "Indeed, neo-kosmos meta-kosmic."

"Old worlds! New Worlds!" sang the bird in its alternating bird cries.

And then the sky shifted.

"My cubs are coming down now," announced the bear, and Qoheleth saw from the North and South horizons a cluster of mighty starcubs detach themselves from the starscape and come roaring toward the Earth from each direction. The bear's fur now coruscated with gathering lights and Qoheleth wanted to hate her for the pride and joy he saw in her eyes gazing heavenward at her cubs. But he found he couldn't. He also found his gaze couldn't take in the cubs as they grew nearer, larger.

"My eyes can't see this," said Qoheleth. "My eyes."

"You are no wise king," said the bear. Her judgment was

stark, but not without pity.

"Wise King! Wise King!" cried the bird in mockery or invocation, it was hard to tell which.

"My eyes aren't strong enough to see this," Qoheleth confessed. "I accept the augmentation of my sight that enables me to look round the curve of the earth, but I cannot see what's from beyond it. No tree can give that, can it?"

The bird and the bear exchanged a glance.

"Here," said the bear. "Take mine."

The bird swooped down swiftly and pecked the eyes from the bear and brought them beakwise to the man.

"What about the bear? How will she see her cubs?" cried Qoheleth in horror.

"I see through all of me," the eyeless bear said. "I see for parsecs."

Qoheleth hesitated a moment more, but then opened and raised his hands, receiving into each palm a large eye, the trailing stems of which slid into open wounds the man found he now had at each wrist. And instantly he saw. His skin gazed from the astro-ursine eyes into the heavens and he saw.

"I see through all of me," Qoheleth whispered. "I see for parsecs."

Every loosed star-coordinate shooting at the earth was egg and estrus, commingling with star pips, laden matrices descending and exploding into new orders of life and careening structure. The cosmic cubs were mauling the earth, tilling it, sowing it.

"Seeds!" called the bird and flew in a million directions as a million different birds, momentarily blotting out the stars with billows of murmuration and migration.

"Seeds!" roared the bear and resumed her astronomical shape, her roar now galactic.

The starcubs tore away again from the scored and scorched earth and resumed their celestial coordinates, the planet now wholly blasted, fully seeded.

The borrowed eyeballs turned to dust in Qoheleth's hands and he began his long journey home, singing a lullaby to baby bones. He thought of bubbles popping.

His wrists were already healing, but the old snakebite on his hand throbbed.

His own eyes were all he had now in this howling wasteland. Yet he sensed something incredibly vast rising up behind him.

It might be the world.

Daniel Otto Jack Petersen is a PhD candidate at the University of Glasgow. His doctoral thesis is an "ecomonstrous" reading of the fiction of Cormac McCarthy and R. A. Lafferty.

Driving East
by Stephen R. Case

The world had not always ended at the eastern border of Illinois. I was fairly certain of that, and I think had you been with me you would have agreed. There was a road-closed sign and a detour arrow pointing left along a narrow dirt road. I knew that I was not running late, and as far as I knew campus and the life it entailed still waited over the border in Indiana. I turned onto the dirt track.

For a long time the road ran beside a tall hedge of dark trees. The sun was about two fists' height in the sky. It stayed that way for what seemed like hours, and finally I stopped in front of a small farmhouse with a thatched roof (which seemed odd) to ask directions.

The woman at the door shook her head.

"Interstate sixty-five?"

Blank stare.

"Where does this road go?"

She pointed in the direction I had been driving, and I assumed she simply did not know. There were voices coming from the rear of the house, so I left her at the front door (which was split in the middle so just the top half could open, like the old back door at the farm) and walked around.

"Good morning."

It was a young man of perhaps sixteen or seventeen with sandy hair and overalls. Beside him stood what I first took to be a dog.

"Who were you talking to?"

He looked around. "No one. Myself, I guess."

"I heard two voices."

He looked up at the line of trees. The dog beside him followed his gaze. The sun was where it had been all morning, hanging in a tangle of branches. The hedge of trees I had followed along the road seemed thicker here.

"I'm trying to get around the detour," I explained. "How long until this road meets up with another one going east?"

"There aren't any roads east," he said, smiling as though I had told a joke. When it became clear he was not going to say anything else, I walked back to my truck. His dog followed me to the corner of the house.

Perhaps another half-hour of driving and I began to get nervous. The line of trees continued unbroken on my right, and to my left there were only fields that held no houses, telephone poles, or roads leading west. When I was down to less than a quarter of a tank I turned around.

"Do you have a phone?"

He was standing in the same place I had left him, the dog beside him, staring up at the sun. It had not moved, even though it had to be eleven o'clock by now. The haze made it seem like it was still early morning, and through it the sun could be viewed straight on without blinking.

The boy shook his head.

"I don't think I have enough gas to get back to seventeen," I told him.

"I don't have a big enough ax," he said, as though we had been commiserating together regarding our problems for a while. "Those trees are too big. They don't look it from here, but I don't think anyone

but father could cut through them."

The dog beside him nodded.

"The sun is stuck," he said, turning to me. I was thinking about the ax. If I screamed, would the woman in the house do anything? He pointed. "I guess we've let the hedge get too thick, because it's finally gotten caught in the branches."

He meant the sun, and I explained about perception, anxious to turn the conversation away from axes. "It just looks like the sun is in the trees."

His face brightened.

"Walk this way." I led him about a dozen paces to the right. "Now it looks like it's in a different . . ."

I trailed off, and he squinted at the trees, waiting.

The sun did not seem to be in a different place.

"The trees must be larger," I told him. "We must be farther away from them than I thought."

The line of trees stood maybe a hundred yards away over a lawn of high grass. I glanced backward at the house and then started walking toward them. The dog followed, and in a minute so did the boy.

The sun rose. It rose ahead of me as I walked closer to the base of the hedge. The branches rose as well and seemed to carry the sun with them. After perhaps three minutes of walking the trees did not seem appreciably closer, though the branches towered above us. The sun was still stubbornly lodged among them.

"What the hell is this?" I looked at the boy. "Where are we?"

He stared at me.

"What kind of trees are those?"

"They're hedge apples," he said. "We let them get too big."

I walked back toward the house, which was now some distance behind us. The trees receded to a reasonable size, and the sun sank until it was barely two fists' height above the horizon, still among the branches. I started my truck and drove it around the house and onto the lawn, setting off bouncing slightly across the field. The trees grew more quickly this time. I opened the passenger-side door when I reached the boy and the dog.

"Is it really still morning?"

The boy's face was anguished as he nodded.

"Get in."

The dog jumped in first and sat between us. It was small with pointed ears and a white-tipped tail. It really didn't look much like a dog, but it acted like one.

Another five minutes or so of driving and we were at the base of the trees. They were far larger than I had thought, with trunks each easily fifty feet in diameter. The branches bent back over us like arches in a cathedral. The sun rested in them now nearly overhead.

I stepped out of the truck.

"It's a hot air balloon or something, right? This is a set for some kind of movie that was filmed years ago that no one's ever heard of, and you and your crazy mother live here and murder people like me who get lost."

The boy stared, and the dog cocked its head and asked if that was a hot air balloon then where was the sun.

My truck was solid. I felt of it to be sure. I leaned back and placed my hand on the cold red sweep of the fender. Inside the window half a dozen CDs were scattered on the floor, and my satchel was wedged behind my seat. It bulged with books for the new semester.

I ordered my thoughts slowly. There was a real possibility, I admitted, that I was lying in a ditch somewhere, staring up at the actual sun through a cracked windshield. My neurons were stitching this together in some last, uncoordinated gasp as they winked out one by one. I banged on the side of the truck, reaffirming its solidity. I blinked deliberately. My neurons felt fine. The trees and unmoved sun remained.

The fox voiced his question again and pointed upward with his muzzle.

"You're right," I said.

The sun seemed as solid as the truck, solid enough to touch. The branches that crisscrossed its face stood out clearly.

"If it is the sun, why doesn't it burn the trees?"

The boy shrugged. "The wood is wet. Lots of rain lately."

The sound of cursing came from above.

"It is a balloon. I can hear someone in it."

There were stairs at the base of each tree that spiraled up the trunks. I started up the one that looked closest to where the sun was caught, and the boy and fox followed wordlessly. We climbed, and the sun grew larger until it was a smooth yellow curve hanging above our heads. Higher, out onto a branch that seemed as wide as a road, and I looked down over its side.

"It's a boat," I shouted.

The bottom was perfectly hemispherical, but from above I could see masts, a golden rudder, and a swarm of sailors with orange and yellow skin. A lined face with red beard pushed forward as the boy joined me.

"Gregory!" it bellowed. "Where the hell is your father?"

The boy gaped and stammered that his father had left.

"I've warned him about these god-damned trees!" the man in the sun roared. "How does he expect me to keep this thing on course if he's growing a thrice-damned Charybdis in his backyard?"

"Scylla," I said without thinking. "Charybdis was the whirlpool."

"They were both pains in my ass, is what they bloody well —" He glanced at me and choked back whatever he was going to say. "Who is this?"

The sailors around him (women as well as men, with yellow eyes and hair like fire) were trying to push the branches back with long oars. A few of the branches bore the marks of blades, and there were broken swords on the ship's deck.

When the boy just looked at me and shrugged, the man asked him again about his father.

"He went west," Gregory muttered. "I don't know when he'll be back."

"Don't know when he'll be back!" Several of his crew had abandoned their efforts and were gathering to observe the exchange. "Damned lazy, is what it is. Damned negligent."

The fox growled low in his throat.

I asked Gregory who his father was.

"Lord of the Eastern March!" the captain of the sun barked. "Supposed to be keeping things over here in line, not letting rows of crabbing trees climb into the damned sky."

I looked around as though I could determine the borders of this March and see clearly where I had passed into it. The truck was so far below that the sun glinting off its roof made it look like a piece of glass resting in the dirt, like maybe this was a normal tree after all and some.one had only shattered an old beer bottle against its trunk. Beyond the hedge I could see nothing but clouds and another boat sailing up out of them.

"The moon is rising," the fox said.

"God damn," the captain groaned, passing his hand over his eyes.

"Maybe they can help."

"Oh, great idea, boy." The man rolled his eyes. "They're plotted for a course far astern on this pass, and I don't think that boat would stop if the stars themselves fell."

The boy apparently disagreed, because he was already moving away from the side of sun, following the second boat with his eyes. It had torn sails and was rising through clouds that sat on the horizon like steam boiling out of a crack in the earth. The fox darted past Gregory and out along a branch that stretched near where the moon would pass.

"Are you coming?" I asked the captain. "Maybe they can help."

"They're cold, those are," he said.

"He can't get off the ship," the fox explained.

The captain grinned and shrugged. "Our oars and sails are gold, but we cannot leave them."

The sailors watched me as I followed the boy and the fox. From here, farther from the immense trunks, the branch we were on stretched like a bridge across the world from east to west. There was nothing east though, just the clouds. Behind us I could see everything: the road I had followed running like a thread from the pucker of cement on the horizon that was my town. Beyond that there were plains and then the mountains.

The moon rose before us, and Gregory lifted an arm. Torn sails hung limp from a splintered mast. We were high enough to see the deck, and the slope of the ship's hull was mottled with grey, rotting wood and warped planks.

"I have tow-cables in my truck," I told Gregory, and when he stared at me I said, "Ropes. Maybe they can pull the other ship out."

He nodded, and I ran back along the branch, down the stairs that spiraled around the trunk. When I was at the bottom and stood again beside the truck, I looked upward. I could see no sailors, no sails, no boy, no fox. The sun was where it had been all morning, lodged in the tangle of branches. The moon was a sliver rising beside it.

I pulled the cables from the toolbox Dad had insisted I carry in the truck's bed. They were ridiculously long, longer than I had ever thought would be needed. They fell around me like snakes, and I had to wind them a dozen times from palm to elbow before walking back to the trees.

I stared upward before climbing. It was just the moon and the sun. There were no stairs into the trees, and the trees were no larger than normal. I could climb into my truck and drive back toward the road, and were I to do so the sun would keep pace with me, slip from the hedge, and hang over the road as I drove east. I would go back to the highway and ignore the arrows. Classes would start in a few days. I'd write papers and emails home.

Then I heard Gregory calling from above, and I climbed.

The moon was beside the branch where I had left them. It rocked slightly in the breeze, and aboard veiled figures were working thin oars to hold it steady. There was a woman standing beside the swan-shaped prow.

"She says she will help," the fox growled in a half-whisper, "if someone will come with her."

I could feel her eyes on me through the veil.

Gregory looked terrified. He stared at the silver ship and then back to where the sun was beached against the branches below.

"Okay," he whispered. "All right."

The fox growled again.

They moved the ship away and through the sky to come even with the sun. We kept pace along black branches. The sailors on the sun seemed to have abandoned their efforts with the oars and were staring suspiciously as the moon pulled alongside.

"They'll help," Gregory said, and the captain nodded slowly.

The boy climbed aboard the sun and looped one end of the tow-rope around the mast. The metal hook at its end looked like burnished bronze against the gold of the ship's planks. I tossed the other end of the cable over the edge of the moon, but the figures there drew back.

"They can't touch it," the fox whispered.

"Because it's iron?"

He shrugged.

I hesitated a moment and jumped aboard.

Figures crowded around me, but I pushed through them and looped my end around the mast. The deck planks were the color of bone and groaned under my weight.

Gregory had scrambled back onto a branch and pulled me up next to him.

"Now pull," he told the woman in the moon.

The veiled figures had moved back to their silver oars, but they waited. The woman made a sound like a long sigh.

"They want one of you to come with them," the fox said.

Gregory bit his lip. "My father will be home soon," he muttered, looking at the pale planks of the moon-ship. "He'll be able to cut the branches."

"The day is passing, Gregory!" bellowed the captain. "We need to move now."

I looked down at the truck, its paint still gleaming in the sunlight like an ember. There was an accident, I told myself. I willed myself to feel crushed legs, see the spidered glass and the sun beyond it. The black, tangled branches were the cracked glass. They were across my own fading vision. This had all taken perhaps a moment, which was why the sun had not moved.

I willed myself to feel it, but I did not.

"I'll go," I said.

Gregory was saying something, but I stepped onto the silver boat again. This time the figures ignored me and moved to the oars. They strained against them, and I felt the moon inch forward. The rope between the ships tightened and sang with a thousand tiny screams. Time stretched like the rope, and then there was a deep groaning behind us. I turned to see the sun floating free above the trees, the sailors aboard pumping their arms and the captain grinning down at Gregory and the fox as he passed.

"Tell your father to chop these damned trees!"

The woman was beside me, and her features were becoming clear through the veil. The rope still stretched between the ships.

"We will teach you to row," she was saying. "We will teach you the paths of the seas of the sky."

I tore the veil from her face and ran across the deck. The fabric was like ice in my hands. As I ran I twisted it around my wrist. At the ship's edge I stepped over and in one motion looped the fabric of the veil over the rope and grasped the other end. For an instant I hung there, a speck on a thread between sun and moon.

The sun was still below us but rising quickly. I kicked off from the moon and slid, gritting my teeth against the hiss of the veil on the rope. On the golden ship they caught me in a tangle of orange and yellow arms. The captain was yelling something and slapping me on the back. Below us I could see the boy waving wildly with the fox beside him.

The sailors let out the sail, and the ship continued to rise.

. . .

I wrote this all down on some sheets that I found in a trunk below decks. There were jewels as well, of course, but I found these sheets, a quill, and a diamond vial of ink. The ink kindled on the page like fire but faded to black as it dried. The next time we pass over our town beside the lake I will fold these sheets into the shape of cranes the way you showed me and let them fall from the ship's side. If you (or anyone) find them, don't look for me in the truck below the trees. Don't look for me at all.

We are sailing west.

This work © 2016 Stephen Case.

Beginning or End of the Universe
by Martin Heavisides

One key individual is crucial to saving the world from irrevocable destruction—possibly the universe (talk this over with editors and agents). Possibly, what with superstring theory and such, every available parallel universe—or most of them (what would be the effect on your writing style if you really had nine, or fifteen, or eighty-one dimensions to play with instead of a paltry three?) Let's say one of the available parallel universes, how many? nobody's really counted, survives—you'll admit the position of that one lone glimmering universe would be a perilous one. Let's not drop the ball guys, ok? But wait! by a time-paradox known only to our hero(ine) plus an intrepid team of supersmart confederates who may be killed off at will for the greater good of the story (after all they couldn't expect to outlive the universe anyway now could they? if they do nothing, or their plans fail, they'd only be advance scouts for the general catastrophe—that's good! work that into a nobly dying speech) where was I? Right, by a time-paradox known to the universe at large but generally scoffed at and disbelieved, it may be possible to pull all the lost universes back into existence through a strategically placed black hole, and then the onus isn't so much on the one universe left, illimitable though its inhabited worlds are. Of course there's a catch— ten black holes spaced about the galaxies seem likely candidates, but only one can be the right one, and the likely result of choosing wrong would be to implode, messily, the one universe we have left. There are tests that can be run, but the results they yield are only probable, with wide margins of error. One test would be irrefutably conclusive— unfortunately, in nine cases out of ten, no less than universally conclusive.

What to do? The universe is in no immediate danger that we're aware of, so perhaps best not upset the status quo ante. On the other hand, nobody expected the sudden annihilation

318

of all the other universes either—wouldn't want to be caught napping twice. Why keep all your eggs in one basket if you can fill it to the brim again? Wait a minute! by that analogy, is a universe an egg or a basket? Literally of course it's neither.

(How many other universes are there anyway? None of our committee of thirteen has been to more than three besides our own, at least consciously. With overlaps, amongst ourselves, we could vouch for twenty-nine or perhaps thirty. The Confederation President has visited six on frequent business, and had gone insane through sheer overload of mourning at the moment of near-universal catastrophe, having strong personal ties to each of them as well. I think that's the record though, and as for an exact count there's simply no counting.

How many times any of us have visited other universes unconsciously no one knows. How it's done of course is that you inhabit the parallel person (or place or thing, if it's a person-impoverished universe) whose role corresponds to yours in your universe of record. Sometimes people rapidly slip(ped) into and out of parallel universes in not too many blinks of an eye. In a universe very close to your own it might be possible to spend a day, or a week, without noticeable disorientation—though not without your place in ours being taken by the person you've displaced. Has this happened? Theoretically—up to a half year ago at least—it seemed inevitable, but there's never been any empirical proof, largely because it's hard to get any sort of a grip on what would constitute evidence of it happening. It's long been known however, that déjà vu, presque vu and jamais vu are conditions associated with unconscious universe hopping. Jamais vu, the most extreme, is a result of finding yourself in a universe different enough that you're momentarily certain you've never been there before—which of course is true, but you wouldn't necessarily notice if the contrast with what you do know weren't so extreme.

When I say it's long been known about déjà, presque and jamais vu, I mean of course that it's long been the subject of heated speculation and debate. It's only been known for certain in the last half year, since nobody's experienced any of those states since every universe but one vanished in a general catastrophe. We miss it, along with many other phenomena we hadn't realized were associated with a multiplicity (as opposed to a singularity) in the universe department.

Jamais vu of course isn't quite the most extreme reaction a universe hopper can be, especially when you consider how brief a visit jamais vu always entails. If the universe you're jumping from differs sufficiently from the one you land in, instant death or permanent madness is the result. Return seems impossible in such cases—certainly in every one we've been able to monitor.

We've had very little luck analyzing the mad state of universe hoppers, simply because those we're able to study differ from us so profoundly in their initial make-up that it's impossible to determine what their mental state would be if we could restore it. Which is a pity, since it drastically limits our options in treating them—a few starved and a few others were poisoned while we determined by trial and error simply how to feed them—but we try to do our best, knowing we have hoppers of our own dependent on the kindness of races as supra-alien to us as we are to these. By now, of course, our hoppers have hopped into the void, and we'll have no more such shattered visitors—not unless we choose a black hole to shoot our time paradox through; and choose right.)

Uh-oh. I'm part of the Committee of Thirteen—don't even know how I arrived at that number. Better make sure I am the hero(ine) or at least a secondary principal who's indispensable to the sequel—second or third part of the trilogy I guess that would have to be. Don't see writing a credible follow-up to this, but why should I save uncountable universes in a one-off—surely that'll spin to three volumes, *Lord of the Rings* fat or thereabouts? Yeah—better hope I'm indispensable to plot development and action—don't want to go before my time, in my own book yet!

So: what to do? the universe will die sooner or later if we do nothing, but considerably sooner—is our best guess—if we do something and it's incorrect. "Incorrect is a considerable understatement. At least there'd be nobody alive to indict us for crimes against humanity."

"Not to mention everything and everyone else." "That too." A couple of strong voices. Have to work on them a bit, come up with names eventually. They'd be on the side of skepticism and caution. They wouldn't be alone.

I wouldn't be with them though. I can already see myself insisting we proceed—after due deliberation (three volumes to fill) but with necessary haste (sooner or later it has to become a forced option and debate superfluous—need that for reader adrenalin)—roll the dice, finally, people: shoot that time-paradox off at whatever seems likeliest of the available holes. We have nothing to lose but everything, and a lot more everything to gain back if we succeed. Pascal would've taken the bet.

This work © *2016, Martin Heavisides – Originally published in* Sein und Werden

A Little Song, A Little Dance, A Little Apocalypse Down Your Pants
by Robert T. Jeschonek

I come back from the dead suddenly, the way I always do, with a great heaving gasp as air and light and consciousness rush into me all at once.

"Easy now, Jody Lee." Binky the Bring-Back Bot says the same thing every time he resurrects me, the same damn thing. "Slow, even breaths, dear. In through the nose, out through the mouth."

Meanwhile, I'm twisting and flopping around naked in what I call the Humpty-Dumptynator—a rectangular glass box half-full of slimy blue goo and squirming anti-maggots. (They give life instead of feeding on it.) No matter how many times I've been through this—and believe me, there've been thousands—I still wake up with the same shock and nausea, spazzing out like this is my first freaking life restoration.

While at the same time, I know I've gotta get over it but fast, as Binky reminds me.

"Snap out of it, honey." The silver-skinned bastard jabs my left bicep with a hypo needle in the tip of his index finger, shooting me full of something that takes the edge off. "Remember, you've got another show tonight." He shoots me with a pale green light from his right eye, which is also soothing. "You have to die again in three hours if you want to get paid."

\#

Once I get cleaned up, I go for a walk, trying to blow the stink off. My long black hair's tied in a ponytail, and I'm wearing a Selfie Suit, which looks like whatever I want depending on who's looking. A hot guy might see me in a little red dress, a not-so-hottie might see me in overalls...and I myself just see a casual black pantsuit.

322

I can't hold back a yawn as I walk through Tesseractus Prime 'cause it's just another pan-galactic mega-casino in just another multidimensional hotel-cathedral-singularity. It's the same old thing, the same old crowd, in the same old place.

And by that, I mean it's a looney tune wonderland to the zillionth power.

A unicorn centaur in a diaper gallops past, fleeing a flock of mocking blackbirds trying to bomb his horn with poop. A guy with an accordion-shaped body bounces by, burping filthy limericks every time his midsection crumples. A priest, a rabbi, and Hitler walk into the nearest bar, saying something about buying a dog a drink...and then they all turn into poodles.

Welcome to humanity circa 100,000 A.D., when science that might as well be magic makes all things possible. Everyone can be as wacky as they wanna be, in every imaginable way. The universe is one big joke...but nobody's laughing anymore.

And that's where I come in.

#

"I have never been more miserable in my life." Standing onstage in the massive theater at the hotel-casino-cathedral, I gaze out at the crowd arrayed before me. It's a panoply of every silly, crazy, bizarre, surreal, and just plain insane character you can imagine...and everyone's laughing their heads off (some literally, if the heads aren't attached very well). "I mean it. I wish I were dead."

For a long moment, the roar of laughter and applause drowns me out. I stand there and let it flow around me, watching as the horde of ridiculous figures howls in hilarity.

A glowing purple clown in the front row blasts a bicycle horn and stomps his huge red shoes (which are also laughing). Beside him, a gorilla in a pinstriped suit hops up and down, making with the monkey shrieks and whipping banana peels and poo at the stage.

In other words, I'm killing. Again. Because I'm the best. I know what makes 'em laugh.

When the roaring dies down, I start talking again. "Seriously, I'm at the end of my rope." That gets a few titters from the crowd. "The more you people laugh, the more I long for oblivion." Cue a slew of scattered guffaws.

Then, a thing that looks like a giant pretzel with eyes instead of grains of salt zips up to the stage and flies around me a dozen times, laughing like a maniac. The audience follows suit with a roar that sounds ten times louder than before.

"Enough of this mortal coil!" The spotlight follows me as I stomp across the stage toward a long table covered by a red velvet shroud. "It is time to end my suffering!"

Everyone cheers and claps and howls with laughter as I pull the shroud from the table, revealing a selection of swords and knives. People shout out suggestions; some even teleport up beside me to point at the weapon of their choice. I shoo them all away and pick up the samurai sword.

"This is the end for me." I kneel on the stage and hold the sword out away from me, pointing the tip at my belly. "I go now to the big comedy show in the sky."

Hands shaking, I falter, and the crowd urges me on. I continue to hesitate, building suspense; it's all part of the act.

"I have the courage to do it at last!" I nod forcefully. "Death, I fear not thy sting!"

Then, before I can slide the sword through my stomach, there's a deafening boom from somewhere off stage. A cannonball blows through my midriff from side to side, cutting a swath where the sword was supposed to cut.

The top half of my body plops down to close the gap. For a moment, as the crowd gives me a standing ovation, I kneel there, my top and bottom halves disconnected but adjacent.

Then, the top half drops over backward, and the darkness of death swirls over me. I feel my mind sliding into the abyss like leftovers sliding from a plate into a trash receptacle.

And then I'm gone, into the great and fathomless unknown. Just like I am every time I do this—two shows a day, six days a week, 52 weeks a year.

\#

Three and a half hours later, I'm staring at a bowl of thin broth in one of the 100,001 ever-changing restaurants in Tesseractus Prime. The broth keeps telling me to eat it, literally—it's conscious cuisine with a mind of its own—but I can't force it down. Binky the Bring-Back Bot put me back together just fine after the cannonball, but my stomach still remembers being blown apart just a little too well.

"Excuse me?" Just then, a horse's ass—an actual horse's ass, minus the horse—clops over to my table. "Have you seen a setup come this way? I seem to have lost mine."

Great, just what I need. Another lost punchline looking for the rest of his joke. "Can't help you, buddy." I stir my bowl of broth as if I'm actually going to eat it.

The broth gets all worked up and starts to yap. "Oh yes, oh please put me inside you, dear famous Jo Jawdropper! Eat me right up, you vixen!"

The tail on the horse's ass switches excitedly. I can see there's an eyeball staring back at me from its bunghole. "Ohmigod! I can't believe this! I'm talking to Jo Jawdropper!"

I never thought I could hate my stage name any more than I already do...but hearing it spoken in the squeaky whine of a horse's ass really does the trick. "Check, please!"

"No check yet!" screams the broth. "You've gotta slurp me up first!"

Just as I'm starting to freak out a little, someone clears his throat behind me. "Get lost, ass." His voice is as deep as the croak of a down-dirty drunk just before he turns himself sober so he can start drinking all over again. "Amscray!"

Turning, I'm surprised for two reasons: one, he's shorter than I imagined because of that voice, all of five-foot-five; and two, I recognize him, from his black leather jacket to his bald head to his bushy red mustache. I used to work with him, back in the day.

"Now git!" He stomps over and gives one of the horse's ass's butt cheeks a powerful slap. "Don't make me kick you!"

"Kiss my you-know-what," snaps the ass, and then he clops off through the restaurant.

"What an ass," says the guy. "Probably doesn't know himself from a hole in the ground."

"Well, well." I smile and hold out my hand. "If it isn't The 'Stache."

The 'Stache (that's his stage name; he never told me his real name) gives my hand a hearty shake. "Long time no smell,

JoJo m'dear."

"Thanks for the save," I tell him. "I guess that makes you my hero." Impulsively, I pull him into a big, grateful hug. It's been such a lousy day.

Meanwhile, the broth keeps yapping. "Slurp me up! Put me inside you! Lick my bowl clean!"

"Shaddup," snaps The 'Stache. "Or else!"

"Or else what?" says the broth.

"You know the one about the fly in the soup?" says The 'Stache. "Well, I'm gonna show you the one about the soup that flies. Across the room."

With that, the broth finally shuts up.

#

The 'Stache and I catch up while taking a late night stroll on Schrödinger's Catwalk—a promenade that might or might not occupy infinite locations and realities at any given moment.

Fountains of rainbow light cascade all around us, casting colorful glows on our faces. Within the light, I glimpse an ever-changing parade of images, flickering movies of people and events from all eras and alternate worlds.

For an instant, I think I catch a glimpse of The 'Stache and me in the old days, working the comedy circuit together...but then it's gone, or maybe it was never there at all.

"I was out of the biz for a while," says The 'Stache. "Didja know that?"

"You quit show biz? For real?"

He grins, flashing gold incisors through his overabundant mustache. "For ten years real, Double-J."

"What was it like?"

"Not being on the road all the time, you mean? Not struggling to squeeze laughs out of a bunch of humorless fruitcakes every day of my pathetic life?" The 'Stache looks ahead of us and chuckles. "Why don't we ask him?"

"Ask me what?" It's an alternate version of The 'Stache with zebra stripes and elephant ears, loping toward us—one of the side effects of Schrödinger's Catwalk. You never know when you're gonna cross paths with another you from a parallel universe.

"Hey! Did I miss show biz when I gave it up for ten years?" says The 'Stache I came in with.

"You gave it up for ten years?" Other 'Stache punches original 'Stache in the shoulder on his way past. "What a maroon!"

Original 'Stache laughs and jerks a thumb at his doppelgänger as he walks off and vanishes. "That guy is such a prick, isn't he?"

"You're back in the game, aren't you?" I ask him. "That's why you're here, right? You're doing standup again."

"Maybe I'm just here to see you," says The 'Stache.

"So what made you do it? What made you want to get back onstage after ten years away?"

"Because I'm gonna be the greatest comic who ever lived," says The 'Stache. "And I'm gonna make it happen in a one-night-only performance, tomorrow night." He smiles and takes my hand. "You want in, JoJo? For old times' sake?"

"Sure." I say it with a smirk, waiting for the punchline. "How can I possibly say no?"

The 'Stache stops walking and faces me. "Dead serious here, partner. This ain't a bit."

"Izzat so?" Notice I haven't stopped smirking. "So how do you propose becoming the greatest ever in just one night?"

"I've done it before, haven't I?" The 'Stache winks and squeezes my hand.

"Ten years off the circuit is like a hundred years in comedian time." I pull my hand free and shake my head. "You're gonna have to sell your soul to Maxwell's Demon just to make a comeback, let alone become the greatest."

"Kiss my brain!" The 'Stache laughs and jabs a finger between his eyes.

"Huh?"

"Kiss it!" The 'Stache keeps jabbing. "Because it knows, darlin' JoJo. It has a plan that will set the worlds on fire."

Just then, someone taps me on the shoulder. Turning, I see an alternate me made of rippling green palm fronds. It hurts to look at her flashing gold bouffant hairdo, and she's chewing some kind of squealing gum or bite-sized creature, I can't see which.

"He's right, honey mustard," says Palm Frond Me. "Big Daddy here's got the goods."

"Hear that?" The 'Stache unveils his broadest grin yet. "If you can't trust your salad-based alternate self, who can you trust?"

I could say I don't want anything to do with Delusional Dudley Doofus here…but that would be a bald-assed lie. Truth is, he's got me curious; anything to break the boredom of my daily lives and deaths.

Not to mention, he and I used to be a thing once upon a once-upon. Maybe that's in the back of my mind a little, too.

Also other places, like ten feet away, where alt versions of me and The 'Stache just appeared in flagrante delicto. In the middle of the act, in other words, and I don't mean comedy.

So what does my 'Stache do? Gives 'em a standing-O, of course. "Yeah! Wooo! Bravo!" He whistles and claps for all he's worth.

It's been sooo long since I did what they're doing, I applaud, too. My alt-self, who's on top, laughs and shoots me a big thumbs-up.

Good thing I'm not the type who might get a funny idea from seeing something like that.

#

So let's just say I get a funny idea after all, and the rest is history. And by history, I mean super-nasty sex.

So sue me. It's the first time in I don't know how long (literally) that I've done anything other than eat, sleep, kill myself, or rise from the dead. Breaking out of a rut is a good thing (or is that rutting till you break?)

Don't bother me about guilt and regret. This isn't our first time at the rodeo. Forget about illusions, too.

Not that all the mystery is gone. There's still a burning question hanging over us.

"Got any coffee?"

Not that one, though it's the first thing I ask him in the morning.

"So what's this plan of yours?" That's the one.

"You mean the plan where I ravish you?" says The 'Stache as he tickles my tummy. "Check and double-check."

Did I just giggle? I never giggle. "The other plan."

"You mean the one with the fifty porcupines, the nudist camp, and the case of bubble gum?"

Did I just giggle again? "The one about becoming the greatest comic who ever lived."

"Oh, that one." The 'Stache rolls over and kisses me. "It's a secret."

"A secret?"

"But who knows?" The 'Stache shrugs. "Maybe we can scare up an exclusive preview if you can pencil me in this morning."

"Hey, wait!" I laugh as he makes a grab for me. "What're you doing?"

"Sorry." He doesn't stop. "I thought we meant pencil me in..."

#

"I know, right?" The 'Stache gives my shoulders a squeeze. "Kinda small, isn't it?"

"Yeah." I'm standing on the field of Hypercube Center, the biggest sports stadium in all of Tesseractus Prime. It's breathtakingly vast, stretching off for miles in all directions. "A real intimate venue."

"My thoughts exactly." The 'Stache gives me a peck on the cheek and undrapes his arm from my shoulders. He walks a few steps away and lets loose a loud whoop that echoes through the stadium. "I want everyone to feel like I'm close enough to reach out and touch."

"Then mission accomplished." Part of me keeps thinking he's pulling my leg, even after I saw his name on the marquee out in front of the place. How he got booked in a venue this big after so long away from the biz beats the hell out of me.

"I'll be a hot ticket, with so few seats to fill," says The 'Stache. "What're we lookin' at? Five thousand, max?"

"If that," I say, though of course we both know it's more like five million. "Guaranteed sell-out, I'd say."

"No need to beef up this bill." The 'Stache grins. "Though I might make room for you, if you need the work."

"Lemme think about it."

"I can always use an opening act." He shrugs. "Just sayin'."

"Very generous of you. Thanks loads."

"Fair warning, though. This'll be old school all the way." The 'Stache turns and gazes across the miles-long field. "Just a spotlight, a glass of water, and a microphone." He spreads his arms wide and looks up into the distant heights. "Plus a ginormous mother-lovin' communications array beaming to the fringes of the known freakin' universe in every possible signal and frequency."

Shading my eyes against the glare of the stadium lights, I can just make it out—a spindly silver grid hovering high above, punctuated with upturned disks and spiny antennae. How I completely missed it until now, I don't know; maybe it's got one of those Inexhaustible Apathy Filters that dims external stimuli to the brain based on natural human aversions to Getting Involved.

Whatever the reason, one thing's clear. "That thing's huge."

"It's all customized." The 'Stache proudly plants his hands on his hips. "I designed it myself and personally supervised the construction."

"You did?"

"I'm a cosmological engineer, Double-J," says The 'Stache. "I didn't spend those ten years away from show biz just workin' on my memoirs and keepin' it real, y'know."

"But how'd you pay for it? How'd you get permission to install it here?" I sweep an arm around to take in the field and seats. "How'd you get booked here at all, for that matter?"

"I made boatloads of money in cosmo-engineering." The 'Stache grins and nods. "Big projects mean big bucks. I worked on everything from Starhenge to the Great Space Roller Coaster, with plenty of hyperdrive bypasses in between." He waves for me to join him. "With the cash I made from my work and investments, I just bought the damn stadium and booked myself! Then I gave myself permission to install the array."

I walk over to stand next to him, looking up at the sprawling grid in the sky. "So what's it for? Streaming a pay-per-view special to the cosmos? Beaming a feed to distant primitive cultures so they'll come to worship you as a god?"

"It's something bigger and better than you can imagine." He puts his arm around me again.

Looking down, I slide him a frown. "Seems like a lot of trouble to go to. What's the punchline?"

"Wait and see," says The 'Stache.

"C'mon, tell me."

He shakes his head. "A punchline ain't worth much without the element of surprise, is it?"

I pop an elbow in his side. "What if full disclosure is a condition of my being on the bill?"

"Then I guess you'll miss out on being a headliner at the event of the millennium." Why the bleep is he still grinning? "No skin off my chin, Gunga Din."

Is this the part where I'm supposed to sigh and give in? Because damnit, that's exactly what I do. My curiosity couldn't be more piqued; my gut instinct is kicking the crap out of all my intuitions, taking their lunch money, and spending it on magic beans.

And yes, Mom, my heart might have something to do with it, too.

"All right," I tell him. "Good thing I happen to have the day off."

#

That evening, Hypercube Center is filled to capacity and then some. Every seat in the stands is occupied, and every square inch of standing room on the field is packed. Even the sky is swimming with wall-to-wall spectators; everyone who can sprout wings or rotors or jets or antigravity nards is drifting overhead, angling for the best view in the house.

The only open space within that immensity is the stage itself. As The 'Stache promised, it's a bare bones affair, just a plain black square with a mike stand in the middle and a pitcher of ice water with two glasses on a skinny pedestal table nearby. Old school all the way.

Which begs the question: What's The 'Stache cookin' up? (And the corollary: What's he smokin'?) Without the ingredients of modern comedy—samurai swords, knives, guns, cannons, elaborate Rube Goldberg suicide machines—how the fun does he propose to get any laughs?

"Just go with it," he tells me when I ask him that very question. "Trust ol' Baba Looey here, he won't let you down."

I don't believe him for a second, but I feel better when he folds me in his arms for a pre-show hug. Even better when he stands on tiptoe to give me a long, loving kiss. Am I really that chickified that a little mush can drown out the voices of reason in my head?

Yes, apparently. The voices of reason are screaming for me to make like a banana and get the flock out of Dodge. But the next thing I know...

...I'm standing at the mike onstage, introducing The 'Stache.

Yay me, I get a standing-O all my own, just for being there. It takes a while for the applause to die down enough for me to be heard.

At which point, I put everything I have into singing The 'Stache's praises. I really pour it on, telling the crowd what a great comedian and unique talent he is—what an influence he's had on my career and those of so many others. I tell 'em how lucky they are that he's returned to the stage, what a privilege it is to be there to introduce him to the universe again. I tell 'em how great he is in bed, and how I'm probably mostly doing this because we're romantically involved, so don't blame me if he sucks, bites, and blows. (I skip that last part, but the mind readers out there might catch a whiff.)

Then I start applauding. "Ladies, gentlemen, invertebrates, intangibles, incomprehensibles, unmentionables, and all other lifeforms, artforms, and colorforms, I present to you the once and future comedy genius known far, wide, and in-between as The 'Stache!"

The crowd roars with deafening cheers and applause. I've done a great job warming them up; now it's up to him to close the deal.

The 'Stache bursts out from behind an Apathy Curtain that kept him invisible until now. Waving and grinning at the crowd like a beauty pageant contestant, he marches up and takes my place at the mike. Then he winks at me and gestures at a mark on the floor, a glowing red X ten feet behind the mike where he wants me to wait.

As I take my position and the crowd settles down, he starts talking.

"What is comedy?" That's how he starts. "It's what makes you laugh. And that changes through time as humanity changes."

The 'Stache spreads his arms wide to encompass the crowd around him—the millions of people who are listening in dumbstruck silence. He sounds more eloquent than usual, as if he's channeling his inner Einstein instead of his typical Wisenheimer. "Humans have evolved to a level where technology enables them to do so many things...things that would have been considered magic to their ancestors thousands—even hundreds—of years ago.

"And these human beings of today, so changed now from what they once were, have a very different definition of comedy. Since almost anything is possible to them, even commonplace...and every bizarre situation that might once have been the basis of a joke is now the basis of reality...they no longer laugh at what they once did."

At that moment, the crowd shifts. I can see and feel and hear it from the stage. The people in the stands and on the field and in the air have waited through what's amounted to a lecture so far, but they've passed the tipping point. It's just a matter of time until they turn ugly.

The question is, does The 'Stache know it's coming? And does he have something planned to head it off?

If he does, he gives no sign of it. "So what does it take to make humans laugh in this modern day and age?" He counts out the answers on the fingers of his right hand. "Cruelty. Shock. Atrocity.

"This is what their sense of humor has become. Laughing at someone mutilating or killing themselves." He shoots a glance in my direction.

Suddenly, a loud male heckler shouts from the audience. "What the Fermi are you talkin' about, 'they'?"

The 'Stache ignores the heckler and keeps talking. "But here's the irony...the ultimate irony, that none of them can see.

In the course of their evolution to a less funny species, humans have stumbled upon the biggest joke of all time."

Again, the heckler calls out from the crowd. "What's with the 'them' and 'they'?"

A second heckler joins in. "We're human, and we're right in front of you."

The 'Stache ignores them. "It goes like this. It took billions of years for the universe to evolve...for the planet Earth to evolve in such a way that the conditions were optimal for sentient life to develop...and for that sentient life, humanity, to evolve to its current, highly advanced state. It has taken that long for human beings to reach a level of technological advancement that makes them masters of their own bodies and minds and the physical laws of the universe itself.

"Have they used this mastery to transcend their limitations and set out in search of greater knowledge? To probe the hidden mysteries of existence itself?"

Another heckler interrupts. "Why does he keep calling us 'they'?"

"What has humanity done?" continues The 'Stache. "They've used their mastery to turn themselves into a trillion variations on the same self-referential silliness...the same images of clowns and celebrities and fictional characters they've been recycling for the past ten millennia. They've got the power to become gods, and they're still pissing around in the same damn kiddie pool, laughing at the suffering of their fellow men and women.

"In this way, humanity itself has become the greatest joke in the history of the universe! The kind of joke that my audience will appreciate!"

By now, the crowd is restless to the point of open rebellion. I smell danger in the air like smoke from a fire.

There's a murmur through the crowd, a susurration of thousands of disaffected voices...but the shout of the first heckler still manages to punch through above them all. "For the last time, why do you keep calling us 'they'? We are humanity. We are your audience."

A dark smile curls its way across The 'Stache's face. "What the eff gave you that idea?"

The murmur of the crowd drops away as all ears lock onto his next words.

"I'm not talking to you people." The 'Stache points upward. "I'm talking to them."

"The airbornes?" asks the heckler. "The flying-room-only people?"

"Not even close." The 'Stache raises his arms overhead and spreads them wide. "I should've said I'm talking to it. The universe."

Just then, I remember the communications array he installed above the stadium, the one that's "beaming to the fringes of the known freakin' universe in every possible signal and frequency." I figured it would be streaming his show to people on distant worlds and vessels...but maybe I was thinking too small.

"That's who this whole show was meant for," says The 'Stache. "You people are just here to prove my point."

"You're full'a shazbot," shouts the heckler. "The universe isn't sentient!"

"Sure it is!" says The 'Stache. "And I just told it the funniest joke it's ever heard!"

Suddenly, a deafening blast of thunder crashes through the stadium, and everyone falls silent. The airborne audience scatters like cockroaches from a kitchen light, and everyone in the stands and on the ground looks up.

"Hear that?" The 'Stache hikes a thumb toward the sky. "I'd say somebody's getting the joke!"

There's another blast of thunder, and another—each progressively louder than the one before. The stars in the sky dance and swirl like gold dust in a prospector's pan, flashing in unnatural rhythms.

Down below, the ground rumbles and shakes. That sets the earthbound crowd in motion, as everyone stampedes toward the exits. Millions of screams rise together, exploding through the miles-long/miles-wide stadium in a tsunami of cascading terror.

Not that The 'Stache looks the slightest bit worried. His face is calm as he turns and gestures for me to join him.

I wonder if I ought to be fleeing for the exits instead, but I run to his side anyway. "What's happening? What is this?"

The ground shakes harder than ever, and the thunderous blasts keep coming. Every light in the stadium blows out at the same time, showering the crowd with sizzling shards of glass.

The 'Stache wraps his arms around me. "I'm killing, that's what!" He grins up at the reeling stars in the sky. "They freakin' love me!"

The booming thunder becomes a continuous roar. The stars spin faster and faster, and the ground splits apart. Thousands of fleeing audience members tumble into the widening crevices.

The 'Stache tightens his grip on me. "Don't worry, Double-J!" He has to shout for me to hear him over the cacophony. "You and I have nothing to worry about! We'll be fine!"

A powerful wind rushes past us, a hurricane wind—only it's not trying to blow us away. It's sucking everything upward, pulling people and pieces of stadium into the sky with inexorable, furious force.

"How can you say that?" My voice is a terrified shriek.

"Because!" says The 'Stache. "I haven't done an encore yet!"

Just as he says it, the wind hauls us off our feet. We both go tumbling toward the stars, still locked in our embrace as if that will save us somehow.

#

At some point after we leave the ground, I lose consciousness—which is probably a blessing, given the circumstances.

Then, I awaken in The 'Stache's arms. His eyes are locked on mine, and his smile is gentle.

"Hey there, sleepyhead." He kisses me softly on the cheek. "Rise and shine."

As awareness returns more fully, I realize our surroundings are calm. There seems to be no trace of the apocalyptic mayhem that engulfed Tesseractus Prime.

"Wait." I push away from him and look around. It's only then that I see where we are: in a transparent bubble, floating through uninterrupted white space.

"What is this?" My voice quivers when I say it.

Robert T. Jeschonek

The 'Stache runs his hand along the surface of the bubble, which flexes and stretches under his fingertips. "Nothing...yet."

I feel panic twisting inside me, straining to burst free. "What're you talking about? What just happened?"

"Pretty sure the universe just laughed," says The 'Stache.

"What do you mean, it laughed?"

"What do you think all the noise and shaky-shaky were about?" The 'Stache's eyes glitter as he grins.

Things still aren't making sense to me. The white space, the bubble...our lives, which somehow still exist. "But where is everything?"

"Out there somewhere." He waves dismissively at the milky void. "Compressed into a super-dense, super-heated ball of energy. The seed of a new universe, in other words."

"Wait, what?" Am I losing my mind here? Did he just tell me... "The universe ended?"

He waggles his hand and squints. "More like reset. It suddenly contracted..." He jams his hands together. "Now there's a pause, like a breath. And soon..." He makes a whooshing sound as he pulls his hands apart. "It'll reboot."

"Like a big bang, you mean?"

He touches the tip of his nose. "Exactamundo. There'll be a shiny new universe in place of the old one. Happens once every 14 billion years or so."

"And what about us?" When I press my hand against the bubble, it feels like a warm rubber balloon. "Why didn't we get mashed up with the rest of the old universe?"

"Funny you should ask." The 'Stache takes my hand. "It's been talking to me..."

"The universe."

"Yup. Apparently, it likes my work so much, it wants me to help set up the next version of itself. I mean the next joke."

My head is spinning. I'd think he's lost his mind if we weren't floating in a transparent bubble through some kind of white void after witnessing a cosmic apocalypse.

"So that's it then?" A hysterical giggle escapes my lips. "Our universe—the one we knew, our home—is just gone?"

"Gone forever." The 'Stache nods.

Again, a crazy giggle escapes me. "Forever? Everything we know is gone forever?"

"Yeah, and wouldn't ya know it?" The 'Stache laughs and shakes his head. "Now I'm hungry for Chinese all of a sudden!"

I think about it, chewing a fingernail. More giggles slip out.

"What is it?" asks The 'Stache. "What's so funny?"

I laugh a little harder now. "All those times I killed myself for comedy...and now here I am, a last survivor while everyone else is dead."

The 'Stache nods. "It's ironic, all right."

I keep laughing. "And you know what really cracks me up? I can't figure out whether the joke's on them, the people who are gone...or on me."

"Then everything's as it should be, Double-J. Remember the Groucho Marx Effect from physics: A universe simple enough to be understood is too simple to produce a mind capable of understanding it.

"Or as Groucho himself put it..." The 'Stache flicks an invisible cigar and waggles his eyebrows. "'I wouldn't want to belong to any club that would have me as a member!'"

Robert T. Jeschonek is an award-winning writer whose fiction, comics, essays, articles, and podcasts have been published around the world. DC Comics, Simon & Schuster, and DAW have published his work. According to Hugo and Nebula Award winner Mike Resnick, Robert "is a towering talent." Robert was nominated for the British Fantasy Award for his story, "Fear of Rain." His young adult urban fantasy novel, My Favorite Band Does Not Exist, *was named one of Booklist's Top Ten First Novels for Youth. Visit him online at www.thefictioneer.com.*

Why Mary Margaret Road-Grader?
by Kevin Cheek

Howard Waldrop swears this is not a Lafferty story. He has written a Laffertarian story, "Willow Beeman" republished in *Feast of Laughter #2* last year, so he should know what he is talking about. He said this story came to him from the Story Place as a complete story—just hit him in the head already in the voice in which he typed it.

So what's it doing in a book/zine dedicated to Lafferty?

It has a lot of elements that complement Lafferty. Its Native-American milieu serves as a wonderful companion to the Native pastiche in what Daniel Petersen has dubbed Lafferty's Buffalopunk stories—stories like "Days of Grass, Days of Straw" and "Assault on Fat Mountain." More subtly, it presents Native-American inspired characters not as some romanticized stereotype, but as complex, and even conflicted individuals.

The post-apocalyptic setting is strongly reminiscent of some of the same things Lafferty was pointing at in stories like "And Walk Now Gently Through the Fire" and even to a degree "The World as Will and Wallpaper." Though in this case Waldrop shows an evolution in the newly static world—both a hope for change and regret for lost tradition.

Exuberance with language is something this story most definitely shares with Lafferty. It is almost gleefully drunk on words. And then there's the storytelling technique of standing archetypes in for characters. Read "Mary Margaret Road-Grader" twice. The first time, read it for sheer enjoyment. The second time through, look at the characters like Winston Mack Truck and Elmo John Deere. Haven't you known these characters all along? Try this in your own writing; it is a short-handed introduction that takes a very deft hand to pull off. But then ask yourself: for how long have you known these characters all along? This is a question Lafferty often asks in books like *Fourth Mansions*, in stories like "Where Have You Been, Sandaliotis?" Were the things that you have known all along there as recently as yesterday, or even this morning?

Were these archetypes always there, or were they subtly suggested as character types you feel you ought always to have known? This is a trick of Lafferty and very few other writers.

And of course the other reason to include "Mary Margaret Road-Grader" is that it is a truly magnificent story that any editor would love to include in any collection, and thanks to the graciousness of Howard Waldrop, we can.

Introduction © 2017 Kevin Cheek

Mary Margaret Road-Grader
by Howard Waldrop

Soon to be a major motion picture!

It was the time of the Sun Dance and the Big Tractor Pull. Freddy-in-the-Hollow and I had traveled three days to be at the river. We were almost late, what with the sandstorm and the raid on the white settlement over to Old Dallas.

We pulled in with our wrecker and string of fine cars, many of them newly-stolen. You should have seen Freddy and me that morning, the first morning of the Sun Dance.

We were dressed in new-stolen fatigues and we had bright leather holsters and pistols. Freddy had a new carbine, too. We were wearing our silver and feathers and hard goods. I noticed many women watching us as we drove in. There seemed to be many more here than the last Sun Ceremony. It looked to be a good time.

The usual crowd gathered before we could circle up our remuda. I saw Bob One-Eye and Nathan Big Gimp, the mechanics, come across from their circles. Already the cook fires were burning and women were skinning out the cattle that had been slaughtered early in the morning.

"Hoo!" I heard Nathan call as he limped to our wrecker. He was old; his left leg had been shattered in the Highway wars, he went back that far. He put his hands on his hip and looked over our line.

"I know that car, Billy-Bob Chevrolet," he said to me, pointing to an old Mercury. "Those son-a bitch Dallas people stole it from me last year. I know its plates. It is good you stole it back. Maybe I will talk to you about doing car work to get it back sometime."

"We'll have to drink about it," I said.

"Let's stake them out," said Freddy-in-the-Hollow. "I'm tired of pulling them."

341

We parked them in two parallel rows and put up the signs, the strings of pennants, and the whirlers. Then we got in the wrecker and smoked.

Many people walked by. We were near the Karankawa fuel trucks, so people would be coming by all the time. Some I know by sight, many I had known since I was a boy. They all walked by as though they did not notice the cars, but I saw them looking out of the corners of their eyes. Music was starting down the way, and most people were heading there. There would be plenty of music in the next five days. I was in no hurry. We would all be danced out before the week was up.

Some of the men kept their strings tied to their tow trucks as if they didn't care whether people saw them or not. They acted as if they were ready to move out at any time. But that was not the old way. In the old times, you had your cars parked in rows so they could be seen. It made them harder to steal, too, especially if you had a fence.

But none of the Tractor Pullers had arrived yet, and that was what everybody was waiting for.

The talk was that Simon Red Bulldozer would be here this year. He was known from the Brazos to the Sabine, though he had never been to one of our Ceremonies. He usually stayed in the Guadalupe River area.

But he had beaten everybody there, and had taken all the fun out of their Big Pulls. So he had gone to the Karankawa Ceremony last year, and now was supposed to be coming to ours. They still talk about the time Simon Red Bulldozer took on Elmo John Deere two summers ago. I would have traded many plates to have been there.

"We need more tobacco," said Freddy-in-the-Hollow.

"We should have stolen some from the whites," I said. "It will cost us plenty here."

"Don't you know anyone?" he asked.

"I know everyone, Fred," I said quietly (a matter of pride). "But nobody has any friends during the Ceremonies. You pay for what you get."

It was Freddy-in-the-Hollow's first Sun Dance as a Raider. All the times before, he had come with his family. He still wore his coup-charm, a big VW symbol pried off the first car he'd boosted, on a chain around his neck. He was only seventeen summers. Someday he would be a better thief than me. And I'm the best there is.

Simon Red Bulldozer was expected soon, and all the men were talking a little and laying a few bets.

"You know," said Nathan Big Gimp, leaning against a wrecker at his shop down by the community fires, "I saw Simon turn over three tractors two summers ago, one after the other. The way he does it will amaze you, Billy-Bob."

I allowed as how he might be the man to bet on.

"Well, you really should, though the margin is slight. There's always the chance Elmo John Deere will show."

I said maybe that was what I was waiting for.

But it wasn't true. Freddy-in-the-Hollow and I had talked in English to a man from the Red River people the week before. He made some hints but hadn't really told us anything. They had a big Puller, he said, and you shouldn't lose your money on anyone else.

We asked if this person would show at our Ceremony, and he allowed as how maybe, continuing to chew on some willow bark. So we allowed as how maybe we'd still put our hard goods on Simon Red Bulldozer.

He said that maybe he'd be down to see, and then had driven off in his jeep with the new spark plugs we'd sold him.

The Red River people don't talk too much, but when they do, they say a lot. So we were waiting on the bets.

Women had been giving me the eye all day, and now there were a few of them looking openly at me; Freddy too, by reflected glory. I was thinking of doing something about it when we got a surprise.

At noon, Elmo John Deere showed, coming in with his two wreckers and his Case 1190, his families and twelve strings of cars. He was the richest man in the Nations, and his camp took a large part of the eastern end of the circle.

Then a little while later, the Man showed. Simon Red Bulldozer came only with his two wives, a few sons, and his transport truck. And in the back of it was the Red Bulldozer, which, they say, had killed a man before Simon had stolen it.

It's an old legend, and I won't tell it now.

And it's not important anymore, anyway.

So we thought we were in for the best Pull ever, between two men we knew by deeds. Simon wanted to go smoke with Elmo, but Elmo sent a man over to tell Simon Red Bulldozer to keep his distance. There was bad blood between them, though Simon was such a good old boy that he was willing to forget it.

Not Elmo John Deere, though. His mind was bad. He was a mean man.

Freddy said it first, while we lay on the hood of the wrecker the eve of the dancing.

"You know," he said, "I'm young."

"Obvious," I said.

"But," he continued, "things are changing."

I had thought the same thing, though I hadn't said it. I pulled my bush hat up off my eyes, looked at the boy. He was part white and his mustache needed trimming, but otherwise he was all right.

"You may be right," I answered, uneasily.

"Have you noticed how many horses there are this year, for God's sake?"

I had. Horses were usually used for herding our cattle and sheep. They were pegged out over on the north side with the rest of the livestock. The younger boys who hadn't discovered women were picking up hard goods by standing watch over the animals. I mean, there were always some horses, but not this many. This year, people brought in whole remudas, twenty-thirty to a string. Some were even trading them like cars. It made my skin crawl.

"And the women," said Fred-in-the-Hollow. "Loose is loose, but they go too far, really they do. They're not even wearing halters under their clothes, most of them. Jiggle-jiggle."

"Well, they're nice to look at. Times are getting hard," I said. The raid night before last was our first in two months, the only time we'd found anything worth the taking. Nothing but rusted piles of metal all up and down the whole Trinity. Not much on the Brazos, or the Sulphur. Even the white men had begun to steal from each other.

Pickings were slim, and you really had to fight like hell to get away with anything.

We sold a car early in the evening, for more plates than it was worth, which was good. But what Freddy had been talking and thinking about had me depressed. I needed a woman. I needed some good dope. Mostly, I wanted to kill something.

The dances started early, with people toking up on rabbit tobacco, shag bark and hemp. The whole place smelled of burnt meat and grease, and there was singing going on in most of the lodges.

Oh, it was a happy group.

I was stripped down and doing some prayers. Tomorrow was the Sun Dance and the next day the contests. Freddy tried to find a woman and didn't have any luck. He came through twice while I was painting myself and smoking up. Freddy didn't hold with the prayer parts. I figure they can't hurt, and besides, there wasn't much else to do.

Two hours after dark, one of Elmo John Deere's men knifed one of Simon Red Bulldozer's sons.

The delegation came for me about thirty minutes later.

I thought at first I might get my wish about killing something. But not tonight. They wanted me to arbitrate the judgment. Someone else would have to be executioner if he were needed.

"Watch the store, Freddy," I said, picking up my carbine.

I smoked while they talked. When Red Bulldozer's cousin got through, John Deere's grandfather spoke. The Bulldozer boy wasn't hurt too much, he wouldn't lose the arm. They brought the John Deere man before me. He glared at me across the smoke, and said not a word.

They summed up.

Then they all looked at me.

I took two more puffs, cleaned my pipe. Then I broke down my carbine, worked on the selector pin for a while. I lit my other pipe and pointed to the John Deere man.

"He lives," I said. "He was drunk."

They let him leave the lodge.

"Elmo John Deere," I said.

"Uhm?" asked fat Elmo.

"I think you should pay three mounts and ten plates to do this thing right. And give one man for three weeks to do the

345

work of Simon Red Bulldozer's son."

Silence for a second, then Elmo spoke. "It is good what you say."

"Simon Red Bulldozer."

"Hmmm?"

"You should shake hands with Elmo John Deere and this should be the end of the matter."

"Good," he said.

They shook hands. Then each gave me a plate as soon as the others had left. One California and one New York. A 1993 and a '97. Not bad for twenty minutes' work.

It wasn't until I got back to the wrecker that I started shaking. That had been the first time I was arbiter. It could have made more bad trouble and turned hearts sour if I'd judged wrong.

"Hey, Fred!" I said. "Let's get real drunk and go see Wanda Hummingtires. They say she'll do it three ways all night."

She did, too.

The next dawn found us like a Karankawa coming across a new case of 30-weight oil. It was morning, quick. I ought to know. I watched that goddammed sun come up and I watched it go down, and every minute of the day in between, and I never moved from the spot. I forgot everything that went on around me, and I barely heard the women singing or the prayers of the other men.

At dusk, Freddy-in-the-Hollow led me back to the wrecker and I slept like a stone mother log for twelve hours with swirling violet dots in my head.

I had had no visions. Some people get them, some don't.

I woke with the mother of all headaches, but after I smoked awhile it went away. I wasn't a Puller, but I was in two of the races, one on foot and one in the Mercury.

I lost one and won the other.

I also won the side of beef in the morning shoot. Knocked the head off the bull with seven shots. Clean as a whistle.

At noon, everybody's life changed forever.

The first thing we saw was the cloud of dust coming over the third ridge. Then the outriders picked up the truck when it came over the second. It was coming too fast.

The truck stopped with a roar and a squeal of brakes. It had a long lumpy canvas cover on the back.

Then a woman climbed down from the cab. She was the most gorgeous woman I'd ever seen. And I'd seen Nellie Firestone two summers ago, so that was saying something.

Nellie hadn't come close to this girl. She had long straight black hair and a beautiful face from somewhere way back. She was built like nothing I'd seen before. She wore tight coveralls and had a .357 Magnum strapped to her hip.

"Who runs the Pulls?" she asked, in English, of the first man who reached her.

He didn't know what to do. Women never talk like that.

"Winston Mack Truck," said Freddy at my side, pointing.

"What do you mean?" asked one of the young men. "Why do you want to know?"

"Because I'm going to enter the Pull," she said.

Tribal language mumbles went around the circle. Very negative ones.

"Don't give me any of that shit," she said. "How many of you know of Alan Backhoe Shovel?"

He was another legend over in Ouachita River country.

"Well," she said, and held up a serial number plate from a backhoe tractor scoop, "I beat him last week."

"Hua, hua, hua!" the chanting started.

"What is your name, woman?" asked one of Mack Truck's men.

"Mary Margaret Road-Grader," she said, and glared back at him.

"Freddy," I said quietly, "put the money on her."

So we had a Council. You gotta have a council for everything, especially when honor and dignity and other manly virtues are involved.

Winston Mack Truck was pretty old, but he was still spry and had some muscles left on him. His head was a puckered lump because he had once crashed in a burner while raiding over on the Brazos. He only had one car, and it wasn't much of one.

But he did have respect, and he did have power, and he had more sons than anyone in the Nations, ten or eleven of them. They were all there in Council, with all the heads of other families.

Winston Mack Truck smoked awhile, then called us to session.

Mary Margaret Road-Grader wasn't allowed inside the lodge. It seemed sort of stupid to me. If they wouldn't let her in here, they sure weren't going to let her enter the Pull. But I kept my tongue. You can never tell.

I was right. Old man Mack Truck can see clear through to tomorrow.

"Brothers," he said. "We have a problem here."

Hua Hua Hua

"We have been asked to let a woman enter the Pulls."

Silence.

"I do not know if it's a good thing," he continued. "But our brothers to the East have seen fit to let her do so. This woman claims to have defeated Alan Backhoe Shovel in fair contest. She enters this as proof."

He placed the serial plate in the center of the lodge.

"I will listen now," he said, and sat back, folding his arms.

They went around the circle then, some speaking, some waving away the opportunity.

It was Simon Red Bulldozer himself who changed the tone of the Council.

"I have never seen a woman in a Pull," he said. "Or in any contest other than those for women."

He paused. "But I have never wrestled against Alan Backhoe Shovel, either. I know of no one who has bested him. Now this woman claims to have done so. It would be interesting to see if she were a good Puller."

"You want a woman in the contest?!" asked Elmo, out of turn.

Richard Ford Pinto, the next speaker, stared at Elmo until John Deere realized his mistake. But Ford Pinto saved face for him by asking the same question of Simon.

"I would like to see if she is a good Puller," said Simon, adamantly. He would commit himself no further.

Then it was Elmo's turn.

"My brothers!" he began, so I figured he would be at it for a long time. "We seem to spend all our time in Council, rather than having fun like we should. It is not good, it makes my heart bitter.

"The idea that a woman can get a hearing at Council revolts me. Were this a young man not yet proven, or an Elder who had been given his Service feather, I would not object. But, brothers, this is a woman!" His voice came falsetto now, and he began to chant:

"I have seen the dawn of bad days, brothers.
But never worse than this.
A woman enters our camp, brothers!
A woman! A woman!"

He sat down and said no more in the conference.

It was my turn.

"Hear me, Pullers and Stealers!" I said. "You know me. I am a man of my word and a man of my deeds. As are you all. But the time has come for deeds alone. Words must be put away. We must decide whether a woman can be as good as a man. We cannot be afraid of a woman! Or can some of us be?"

They all howled and grumbled just like I wanted them to. You can't suggest men in Council are afraid of anything.

Of course, we voted to let her in the contest, like I knew we would.

Changes in history come easy, you know?

They pulled the small tractors first, the Ford 250s and the Honda Fieldmasters and such. I wasn't much interested in watching young boys fly through the air and hurt themselves. So me and Freddy wandered over where the big tractor men were warming up. The Karankawas were selling fuel from the old Houston refineries hand over hose. A couple of the Pullers had refused, like Elmo at first, to do anything with a woman in the contest.

But even Elmo was there watching when Mary Margaret Road-Grader unveiled her machine. There were lots of oohs and ahhs when she started pulling the tarp off that monster.

Nobody had seen one in years, except maybe as piles of rust on the roadside. It was long and low, and looked much like a yellow elephant's head with wheels stuck on the end of the trunk. The cab was high and shiny glass. Even the doors still worked. The blade was new and bright; it looked as if it had never been used.

The letters on the side were sharp and black, unfaded. Even the paint job was new. That made me suspicious about the Alan Backhoe Shovel contest. I took a gander at the towball while she was atop the cab unloosening the straps. It was worn. Either she had been lucky in the contest, or she'd had sense enough to put on a worn towball.

Everybody watched her unfold the tarp (one of those heavy smelly kind that can fall on you and kill you) but she had no helpers.

So I climbed up to give her a hand.

One of the women called out something and some others took it up. Most of the men just shook their heads.

There was a lot of screaming and hoorawing from the little Pulls, so I had to touch her on the shoulder to let her know I was up there.

She turned fast and her hand went for her gun before she saw it was me.

And I saw in her eyes not killer hate, but something else; I saw she was scared and afraid she'd have to kill someone.

"Let me help you with this," I said, pointing to the tarp.

She didn't say anything, but she didn't object, either.

"For a good judge," called out fat Elmo, "you have poor taste in women."

There was nothing I could do but keep busy while they laughed.

They still talk about that first afternoon, the one that was the beginning of the end.

First, Elmo John Deere hitched onto an IH 1200 and drug it over the line in about three seconds. No contest, and no one was surprised. Then Simon Red Bulldozer cranked up; his starter engine sounded like a beehive in a rainstorm. He hooked the chain on his towbar and revved up. The guy he was pulling against was a Paluxy River man named Theodore Bush Hog. He didn't hook up right. The chain came off as soon as Simon let go his clutches. So Bush Hog was disqualified. That was bad, too; there were some darkhorse bets on him.

Then it was the turn of Mary Margaret Road-Grader and Elmo John Deere. Elmo had said at first he wasn't going to enter against her. Then they told him how much money was bet on him, and he couldn't afford to pass it up. Though the excuse he used was that somebody had to show this woman her place, and it might as well be him, first thing off.

You had to be there to see it. Mary Margaret whipped that roadgrader around like it was a Toyota, and backed it onto the field. She climbed down with motor running and hooked up. She was wearing tight blue coveralls and her hair was blowing in the river breeze. I thought she was the most beautiful woman I had ever seen. I didn't want her to get her heart broken.

But there was nothing I could do. It was all on her, now.

Elmo John Deere had one of his sons come out and hand the chain to him. He was showing he didn't want to be first to touch anything this woman had held.

He hooked up, and Mary Margaret Road-Grader signaled she was ready.

The judge dropped the pitchfork and they leaned on their gas feeds.

There was a jerk and a sharp clang, and the chain looked like a straight steel rod. Elmo gunned for all he had and the big tractor wheels began to turn slowly, and then they spun and caught and Elmo's Case tractor eased a few feet forward.

Mary Margaret never looked back (Elmo half turned in his seat; he was so good working the pedals and gears, he didn't need to look at them) and then she upshifted. The transmission on the yellow roadgrader screamed and lowered in tone.

I could hardly hear the machines for the yells and screams around me. They sounded like war yells. Some of the men were yelling in bloodlust at the woman. But I heard others cheering her, too. They seemed to want Elmo to lose.

He did.

Mary Margaret shifted again and her feet worked like pistons on the pedals. And as quickly as it had begun, it was over.

There was a groaning noise, Elmo's wheels began to spin uselessly, and in a second or two his tractor had been drug twenty feet across the line.

Elmo got down from his seat. Instead of congratulating the winner (an old custom) he turned and strode off the field. He signaled one of his sons to retrieve the vehicle.

Mary Margaret was checking the damage to her machine.

Simon Red Bulldozer was next.

They had been pulling for twelve minutes when the contest was called by Winston Mack Truck himself. There was wonder on his face as he walked out to the two contestants. Nobody had ever seen anything like it.

The two had fought each other to a standstill. When they were stopped, Mary Margaret's grader was six or seven inches from its original position, but Simon's bulldozer had moved all over its side of the line. The ground was destroyed forever three feet each side of the line. It had been that close.

For the first time, there had been a tie.

Winston Mack Truck stopped before them. We were all whistling our approval when Simon Red Bulldozer held up his hand.

"Hear me, brothers. I will accept no share in honors. They must be all mine, or none at all."

Winston looked with his puckered face at Mary Margaret. She was breathing hard from working the levers, the wheel, the pedals.

She shrugged. "Fine with me."

Maybe I was the only one who knew she was acting tough for the crowd. I looked at her, but couldn't catch her eye.

"Listen, Fossil Creek People," said old Mack Truck. "This has been a draw. But Simon Red Bulldozer is not satisfied. And Mary Margaret Road-Grader has accepted. Tomorrow as the sun crosses the tops of the eastern trees, we will begin again. I have declared a fifth night and a sixth day to the Dance and Pulls."

Shouts of joy broke from the crowd. This had happened only once in my life, for some religious reason or other, and that was when I was a child. The Dance and Pulls were the only meeting of the year when all the Fossil Creek People came together. It was to have ended this night.

Now, we would have another day.

The cattle must have sensed this. You could hear them bellowing in fear even before the first of the butchers crossed the camp toward them, axe in hand.

"Where are you going?" asked Freddy as I picked up my carbine, boots, and blanket.

"I think I will sleep with Mary Margaret Road-Grader," I said.

"Watch out," said Freddy. "I bet she makes love like she drives that machine."

First we had to talk.

She was ready to cry she was so tired. We were under the roadgrader; the tarp had been refolded over it. There was four feet of crawlspace between the trailer and the ground.

"You drive well. How did you learn?"

"From my brother, Donald Fork Lift. He once used one of these. And when I found this one . . ."

"Where? A museum? A tunnel? Or some . . ."

"An old museum, a strange one. It must have been sealed off before the Highway wars. I found it there a year ago."

"Why didn't your brother pull with this machine, here, instead of you?"

She was very quiet, and then she looked at me. "You are a man of your word? That must be true, or you would not have been called to judge, as I heard."

"That is true."

She sighed, flung her hair from her head with one hand. "He would have," she said, "except he broke his hip last month on a raid at Sand Creek. He was going to come. But since he had already taught me how to work it, I drove it instead."

"And first thing off you defeat Alan Backhoe Shovel?"

She looked at me and frowned.

"I . . . I . . ."

"You made it up, didn't you?"

"Yes." She bit her lip.

"As I thought. But I have given my word. Only you and I will know. Where did you get the serial plates?"

"One of the machines in the same place where I found my grader. Only it was in worse shape. But its plate was still shiny. I took it the night before I left with the truck. I didn't think anybody would know what Alan Backhoe Shovel's real plate was."

"You are smart," I said. "You are also very brave, for a woman, and foolish. You might have been killed. You may still be."

"Not if I win," she said, her eyes hard. "They couldn't afford to. If I lose, it would be another matter. I am sure I will be killed before I get to the Trinity. But I don't intend to lose."

They probably would like to kill her, some of them.

"No," I said. "I will escort you as near your people as I can. I have hunted the Trinity, but never as far as the Red. I can go with you past the old Fork of the Trinity."

She looked at me. "You're trying to get into my pants."

"Well, yes."

"Let's smoke first," she said. She opened a leather bag, rolled a parchment cigarette, lit it. I smelled the aroma of something I hadn't smoked in six moons.

It was the best dope I'd ever had, and that was saying something.

I don't know what we did afterwards, but it felt good.

"To the finish," said Winston Mack Truck and threw the pitchfork into the ground.

It was better than the day before — the bulldozer like a squat red monster and the roadgrader like avenging yellow death. On the first yank, Simon pulled the grader back three feet. The crowd went wild. His treads clawed at the dirt then, and the roadgrader lurched and regained three feet. Back and forth, the great clouds of black smoke whistling from the exhausts like the bellowing of bulls.

Then I saw what Simon was going to do. He wanted to wear the roadgrader down, keep a strain on it, keep gaining, lock himself, downshift. He would dog his way into the championship.

Yesterday he tried to finish the grader on might. It had not worked. Today he was taking his time.

He could afford to. The roadgrader was light in front; it had hardrubber tires instead of treads. When it lurched, the front end sometimes left the ground. If Simon timed it right, the grader wheels would rise while he downshifted and he could pull the yellow machine another few inches. And could continue to do so.

Mary Margaret was alternately working the pedals and levers, trying to get an angle on the squat red dozer. She was trying to pull across the back end of the tractor, not against it.

That would lose her the contest, I knew. She was vulnerable. When the wheels were up, Simon could inch her back. The only time he lost ground was when he downshifted while the claws dug their way into the ground. Then he lost purchase for a second. Mary Margaret could maybe use that, if she were in a better position.

They pulled, they strained, but slowly Mary Margaret Road-Grader was losing to Simon Red Bulldozer.

Then she did something unexpected. She lurched the roadgrader and dropped the blade.

The crowd went gonzo, then was silent. The shiny blade, which had been up yesterday, and so far today, dug into the ground.

The lurch gained her an inch or two. Simon, who never looked back either, knew something was wrong. He turned, and when his eyes left the panel, Mary Margaret jerked his bulldozer back another two feet.

We never thought in all those years we had heard about Simon Red Bulldozer that he would not have kept his blade in working order. He reached out to his blade lever and pulled it, and nothing happened. We saw him panic then, and the contest was going to Mary Margaret when . . .

The black plastic of the steering wheel showered up in her face. I heard the shot at the same time and dropped to the ground. I saw Mary Margaret holding her eyes with both hands.

Simon Red Bulldozer must not have heard the shot above the roaring of his engine, because he lurched the bulldozer ahead and started pulling the roadgrader back over the line.

It was Elmo John Deere doing the shooting. I had my carbine off my shoulder and was firing by the time I knew where to shoot.

Elmo was trying to kill Mary Margaret, he was still aiming and firing over my head from the hill above the pit. He must have been drunk. He had gone beyond the taboos of the People now. He was trying to kill an opponent who had bested him in a fair fight.

I shot him in the leg, just above the knee, and ended his pulling days forever. I aimed at his head, but he dropped his rifle and screamed so I didn't shoot him again. If I had, I would have killed him.

It took all the Fossil Creek People to keep his sons from killing me. There was a judgment, of course, and I was let go free.

That was the last Sun Dance they had. The Fossil Creek People separated. Elmo's people split off from them, and then went bitter crazy. The Fossil Creek People even steal from them, now, when they have anything worth stealing.

The Pulls ended, too. People said if they were going to cause so much blood, they could do without them. It was bad business. Some people stopped stealing machines and cars and plates, and started bartering for food and trading horses.

I wasn't going to get killed for anything that wouldn't go 150 kilometers per hour.

The old ways are dying. I have seen them come to an end in my time, and everything is getting worthless. People are getting lazy. There isn't anything worth doing. I sit on this hill over the Red River and smoke with Fred-in-the-Hollow and sometimes we get drunk.

Mary Margaret sometimes gets drunk with us.

She lost one of her eyes that day at the pulls. It was hit by splinters from the steering wheel. Me and Freddy took her back to her people in her truck. That was six years ago. Once, years ago, I went past the place where we held the last Sun Dance. Her roadgrader was already a rustpile of junk with everything stripped off it.

I still love Mary Margaret Road-Grader, yes. She started things. Women have come into other ceremonies now, and in the Councils.

I still love Mary Margaret, but it's not the same love I had for her that day at the last Sun Dance, watching her work the pedals and the levers, her hair flying, her feet moving like birds across the cab.

I love her. She has grown a little fat. She loves me, though.

We have each other, we have the village, we have cattle, we have this hill over the river where we smoke and get drunk.

But the rest of the world has changed.

All this, all the old ways . . . gone.

The world has turned bitter and sour in my mouth. It is no good, the taste of ashes is in the wind. The old times are gone.

This work © 1976 Howard Waldrop.

Author's note: I was born in 1946, and I've been getting published since 1969, and in all that time, I've been given three stories, ones that just came to me, from the Story Place, whole and unbidden. "Mary Margaret Road-Grader" is one of them. I was at a friend's house, sleeping on a couch. I got up to put on some coffee (they were all upstairs doing Fun Stuff) and as I passed the stereo I turned it on. The song was Simon and Garfunkel's "Bridge Over Troubled Water." Before I got the water in the pot, "Mary Margaret Road-Grader" came to me —nearly all of it, just like that. By the time everybody came down about noon, I was finishing the first draft. That was 1974. I was thankful. If writing were always that easy, anybody could do it.

"Mary Margaret Road-Grader" originally appeared in *Orbit 18*, edited by Damon Knight (Harper & Row, 1976).

Howard Waldrop is the multiple award winning author of "The Ugly Chickens" and about a hundred other stories, each one a gem. His latest collection is Horse of a Different Color, *out from Small Beer Press. Howard has been inspired by Lafferty for several decades and has kept a model streetcar on his writing desk ever since reading "Interurban Queen."*

Brief Thoughts on "The Rod and the Ring"

by Lawrence Person

"The Rod and the Ring" contains many of the standard Lafferty tropes: an Oklahoma setting, historical trivia (Harry Greb did indeed fight in the Floto Outdoor Arena, where he beat an Otis Bryant with a TKO in the third round), and the usual off-center erudition coming out of every pore. The Lafferty story it most reminds me of is "Thus We Frustrate Charlemagne," in that both feature groups of strange people carrying out arcane, obscure rituals that remake (or destroy) the world, only to be pulled back by a last-second status quo ante bellum reprieve.

Even for a Lafferty story it's odd, with a cast of 13 characters we never get to know (indeed, many seem to remain unnamed) talking about a battle that can unmake the world, but with very little of the actual battle shown.

It's also vaguely reminiscent of the "new people" segment of Argo, where tearing up the old consensus has the effect of destroying all existing "old" people (also undone by force of will of Melchisedech Duffy), as well as "Great Day in the Morning," also featuring Duffy, also featuring the destruction of the old world.

Indeed, each of these could be seen as stories of Tzadikim Nistarim, the Kabbalistic belief that there are 36 righteous men who secretly hold together the world. In Lafferty stories, frequently there pop up men who, by their stubborn belief, prevent the destruction of the world by the skin of their teeth. "The Rod and the Ring" presents yet another version of that story.

An interesting work, but not a patch on any of Lafferty's best.

This work © 2017 Lawrence Person

Lawrence Person is a science fiction writer living in Austin, Texas. His fiction has appeared in Asimov's, Analog, Postscripts, Fear, *Jim Baen's* Universe, Galaxy's Edge, *and several anthologies, including* Rayguns Over Texas *and* Cross Plains Universe. *His non-fiction has appeared in* National Review, Reason, SF Eye, *and* NYRSF. *He runs* Lame Excuse Books *(http://www.lawrenceperson.com /lame.html) and owns a celebrated library of Science Fiction first editions, including a nearly complete R. A. Lafferty collection.*

Thoughts about Lafferty's "The Rod and the Ring"
by Darrell Schweitzer

I can't say I am surprised that an unpublished R.A. Lafferty short story has turned up. Lafferty said to me in the interview I did with him that his method was to write a story "until it busts." Maybe, in the view of some editor, this one busted.

I once heard an editor say of Lafferty, "Don't be in awe of the name. The stories come in huge bundles. Some of them are good, some of them not." When, early in 1977, I came to work for the late George Scithers on Asimov's SF (called IA'sSFM in those days) I soon saw that this was true. Lafferty's agent would send the stories around in bundles, letting editors pick a few, then return the rest. This was not, in my view, a very good marketing strategy. You are competing with yourself. You are less likely to sell everything (which is the agent's job) if some stories are visibly better than others, and there are enough to make a comparison. No, the best way to do it is to pass them out one at a time, as if each is a precious, unique gem.

But that is commercial thinking. It's agentish thinking. (I have been just enough of a literary agent myself to be fluent in the idiom.) It is not, very clearly, how Lafferty thought about his own work. He was clearly someone who just wrote because a voice within him spoke. It is true that when he started out, he wrote a couple mainstream stories, a couple genre stories of other sorts (western and mystery, I think it was), and then followed the lead when his science fiction started to sell. But what other field, other than the fantastic, could possibly have accommodated him? He was certainly not the sort of writer to follow a trend because it was hot, or to try to rewrite one of John W. Campbell's editorials and sell it back to him, as certain writers used to race to do about the time Lafferty started writing. The result of this uncommercial approach was that he did pile up a substantial backlog of unpublished material. About 1980 I was visiting my friend Robert Whitaker, and I noticed, in the hall of his apartment, a long row of piled up boxes about the size of reams of paper. I asked him what they were. They were unpublished R.A. Lafferty novels. He had borrowed them to read. I don't remember if there were twenty-five or forty. I will let Robert describe them sometime if he chooses, because he is far more of a profound Laffertian than I shall ever be. My role in all this was merely to tell my editor at the Donning Company that these manuscripts existed. The result was the Donning edition of Aurelia and a planned edition of More Than Melchisedech that got as far as a color rough for the cover but never came out.

Maybe some of those novels "busted." Maybe some of them were just too odd even for the science fiction field, which was considerably looser than it is today, at least at a commercial level. As for the short stories that went around in bundles, how many were there? I don't know. How many are still unpublished? All I can say is, with "The Rod and the Ring," one less than before.

Did this story "bust"? I don't think so. One of the novels, I was told, was difficult to publish because it had too many viewpoint characters. The opening of this story, with the comment that "The set-up here is like the Greater Tulsa Telephone Book" almost seems to be a satirical riposte to a comment Lafferty must have heard often. Another character replies that thirteen isn't many. It could have been eight thousand.

We are definitely in familiar Lafferty territory here. A lot of Laffertian motifs are repeated in miniature. There is a small cabal of people whose actions decide the fate of the world. (It breaks apart.) There is the eccentric dialog and description. The nature of reality itself is called into question.

More to the point, if you read half a page of this you know you are reading Lafferty and no other writer. Isn't that what we always want from him?

This work © 2017 Darrell Schweitzer.

The Rod and the Ring
by R. A. Lafferty

"The set-up here is like the Greater Tulsa Telephone Book," Randy Andy Oglesby stated. "Too many characters, and a weak or non-existent story line. It will have to be a 'loosening' encounter. Well, I suppose I'm the loosest of us."

There were strong smells of Corrosive Sublimate, of animal musk and of combat musk, of brimstone and of sulfur dioxide, of flesh rot and of plant rot, of hot fractured stones, of fetid swamps and of slack salt-water, of adrenaline uncorked, of rancid ozone, Mexicali mushrooms, Devonian tar-pits, the smell of things coming apart, of very large things coming apart, the smell of entrenched insanity. There is nothing like rampant smells to set up a murderous mood.

"Thirteen characters aren't very many," Bertigrew Bagley said thoughtfully. "Some of the arrangements have up to eight thousand characters."

"Eight thousand pawns, maybe, not characters. Seven vivified characters can be critical mass. Nine can be dangerously critical mass. And you yourself know how very chancy as many as thirteen can be."

"I know," Bagley said. Bertigrew Bagley was Patrick of Tulsa. One of the characters, Killer Flegle, was Emperor of Tulsa (very sloppy thinking and naming, that). And Bagley could slip into that role easily. "And thirteen at table is said to be unlucky, as if there weren't already a strong enough smell of unluck about the arrangement."

"Thirteen characters and only two props," Apollonia Woods said in her soft voice that had been likened to 'whispering acid.' "Except that the characters are also props, and the two props (the Rod and the Ring) are also characters. Yes, I know that the ring is given mistakenly as a watch in the arrangement. But a ring with a dial on it (thirteen dials in the present case) is still a ring, an educated ring. This is the ultimate arrangement though. Oh absolutely! Can you not see that?"

"You fit the character of Apologia Dubois perfectly, Apollonia," Bagley said. "But then you fit a lot of characters perfectly."

There were subliminal sounds and murmurations coming from the arrangement. They were below the regular threshold of the ear, and yet they carried relentless anti-arguments and destructions.

"I don't quite fit this character," Apollonia said. "There is a place for outright insanity in putting these arrangements together, but such insanity should at least be creative. I invoke the 'minor change option' here before I step into the Apologia character. 'One blue eye, which is on the left on Mondays, Wednesday, and Fridays; and one green eye.' A lack of imagination that extreme almost cries to heaven for vengeance. I'll keep the green eye, and I'll change the blue eye to a red one. I already have my amber-colored nose, and I can flash it on and off. Maybe I can pick up a little extra money working as a traffic light somewhere. What is this crabby little place we're in, Bertigrew? And are the snakes here real? Yes, I know that the specifications call for a place 'in an extreme state of decay.' This dining room couldn't have been much even when the place was younger. With our big table sitting the thirteen of us here, there's just not much room left for anything else. And the arena part of the building isn't very big. It won't sit over five hundred. And the pit itself might be fine for a point-blank combat, but it sure hasn't room for far-ranging battles."

"This is what's left of the Floto Bowl," Bertigrew (Flegle) Bagley said. "It may have been better, but not bigger, in its palmy days which were about sixty years ago. Harry Greb fought here once."

"Who or what was Harry Greb?" Horatio McElroy asked.

"A prize fighter, in the days when they were dull but honest. He was middleweight champion of the world. Boxing was illegal in Tulsa County then, but this place is over the line in Osage County. It was quite a few things, a high-stakes gambling place (there was a lot of big money in the Osage then), a speak-easy, a good supper club (buffalo rib-racks were a specialty, and so was rattlesnake meat before it caught on elsewhere), and an arena. Yes, the arena pit is small, barely room for a boxing ring in it. It was a cock-pit."

"A cock-pit? For what sort of vehicle?" Hermione McElroy asked.

"A cock-pit for cock fights," Bagley said. "There was a lot of money bet on cock fights then. I fed the specifications into a computer; it considered all the places in an extreme state of decay and came up with the Floto Bowl. It does fill most of the requirements, including 'old blood-soaked ground to underlie it all.' Ah, the snakes here are real, Apollonia."

The supper was good. The buffalo rib-rack was excellent though the buffalo (from Crab Tree Ranch Number Four) had been costly. Those fellows hadn't been about to kill *half* a buffalo.

These 'arrangements' take on a life of their own after a bit, when a specified setting has been occupied, when the characters have been matched with the testers, when the theme begins to unfold itself, when the confrontation-and-combat comes to first blood. And there were daring (ruinous really) notions playing like lightning between the thirteen of them there. There were the exponentially-exploding dangerous thoughts feeding on each other and growing great. But in the present case there seemed to be a new recklessness.

The stimulants tonight were not unusual, Agaric and Mexicali Mushrooms, Psychic Puffballs, Oxytropis Splendens, Snow, White Rum with Bhang, Ghost, Arabian Palmer Weed. And there were other stimulants that came with the arrangement, borderline narcotics and mind-benders and 'Utter-Depravity Crystals.' These were dream-effect things and not immediately exciting. But 'loosening' was the theme that ran through it all, 'destruction by loosening.'

The spoiling of the personality and of the personality-consensus seemed to be the aim of the group that had composed the arrangement. There had been some very unsavory minds involved in creating those characters, but unsavory minds were the 'big in' with all the arrangements this year.

The rationale that came with the arrangement was mostly concerned with 'breaking the consensus' and with that even more daring thing 'breaking the world which is built entirely on consensus.' This rationale was spoken to each of them subliminally and relentlessly. It bypassed their intelligence and attacked and conquered them.

"You believe that the world is based on any other thing than the consensus?" the silent voice assaulted them. "Break the consensus and find out. You believe that the tilt towards predominant mind-madness will not shatter this planet? But the planet has already been shattered, and its shards are held together by only the most tenuous bonds and by common agreement. An insane world will fly apart every time. You doubt that you can literally smash the world? Try it. With all the rot and loosening at hand, try it. This game, this 'Lose the World Game,' can be won." So the silent voices talked.

Meanwhile two combatants were down in the cock-pit, down in the arena itself. Every arrangement has a fight to death at its core. They were down on that small area of forever blood-soaked sand. Maurice Fantome-Glaive had the role of Monsieur Jean-Marie the greatest swordsman in history. And he fought under the aegis and totem of the ring.

"I'd have thought it would be the rod," Hermione McElroy said, "since the sword is a sort of rod."

"No, no," her sibling Horatio McElroy protested. "The sword is a rod only when it is at rest or when it is broken. When in action it is everywhere, flashing like a ring, a shield, a sphere, a cogent realm. It is a globous cloud of lightning. But it should never be separated from the rod, never opposed to it. When that happens, the consensus, the concord is already broken."

Toro Manatee had the role of the Male Warrior who was the master of sorcery, archery, and horsemanship. He it was who fought under the totem of the rod. His horse (it had not been seen there before the moment when the combat was joined) was named Bellerophon. But wasn't Bellerophon the rider and Pegasus the horse? Not in this arrangement, no.

"It's cheating," Hermione complained. "The horse is really the fourteenth character, and only thirteen characters are listed in the arrangement."

"I believe that the horse is one of the thirteen," Horatio hazarded. "One of us was already the horse in disguise. Which one of us thirteen is missing? Oh, we are scattered all about the balustrade till there's no checking us off. The horse may be myself. I feel vacated here."

"Yes, I've often referred to you as 'My brother the horse,'" Hermione said. "I never knew why until now."

The rod and the ring should never have been separated. Together they were the scepter, the royal rod with the royal sphere on the end of it, the authority of the world. Whenever they were separated, the authority of the world was broken and the world came apart.

It is a psychological commonplace that if ever the majority of the inhabitants of the world become schizophrenic, then the world itself will become schizophrenic. And to be schizophrenic is to fly apart.

The ring, which is also the sphere, the world on the end of a stick as well as a dialed instrument, is also a time machine of a special sort; it is an alternate-time machine, really a possibility machine. And whenever the unity is broken and the rod and the ring are separated, then time can break all categories and run wild.

Fantome-Glaive the greatest swordsman ever, and Toro Manatee the master of sorcery, archery, and horsemanship, had joined in shining and resounding battle. The sword of the swordsman did generate a perfect and impervious sphere with its speed and deftness; and the sorcery of Toro kept that sphere at bay.

"Oh, I am to be Jessica, the elderly lady who remains as the sole inhabitant of falling-apart Earth," Jasmine Maloney cried, realizing her role for the first time. "But I am *not* an elderly lady. Why is the arrangement pushing that role onto me?"

"Oh, Jazz, you were always in a world of your own," Apollonia quipped in her 'whispering acid' voice.

The cosmic battle between Fantome-Glaive and Toro Manatee was so intense that no one even breathed while it went on. The horse added color and blood to the melee. The preternatural combatants spilled their own blood on the sand of the pit that already held in its memory and residue the blood of ten thousand game cocks and several dozen boxers and wrestlers. But other things were concurrent with this engrossing battle.

Manatee shot an arrow point-blank at Fantome-Glaive, and it sped toward him at one hundred and eighty miles an hour. For three feet it sped toward him at that high speed. Then it hung in the air motionless.

Hung in the air motionless? For how long a time?

Oh, not for any time at all. Time was elsewhen. Remember that the many-dialed ring, miscalled the watch, was an alternate-time machine. And no one of them could say whether they went from alternate time to true time or from true time to alternate time. But, in that elsewhen in which they found themselves, they were present at the destruction of the Planet Earth, which destruction was brought about by themselves.

The old planet was falling apart because the consensus ropes that bound it together were all dissolved in the 'big loosening.' The world broke up into twenty-two thousand pieces, large and small.

"Oh come off it!" Apollonia Woods acid-whispered to whatever powers were in charge. "This is preaching, sticky preaching."

"This is the Destruction of Merope," a subliminal voice was uttering. Well, it was 'good show' that destruction, though rather too large to comprehend.

"The name Merope has been given to the 'Lost Pleaid' (that exploded star)," the subliminal voice out of the arrangement was still informing them, "and also to the 'Lost Planet' between Mars and Jupiter (that supposed exploded planet). But in reality this daughter of Atlas and Ethra is the Planet Earth, the 'Lost Planet' that is between Venus and Mars (this exploded planet). You all resist us a little bit. When did this happen? you ask. It happens in the explosive present. Aspects of the happening can be seen in one of the projections of the Ring, that alternate-time machine."

"Subliminal voice, you have lost me," Jasmine Maloney protested. "It's too big to relate to. If this is our own world coming apart, where is our viewpoint? Where are we?"

"We assume that you have read the words on the cover," one of those subliminal voices came crawling up over the threshold to inform them. "These are the words that read: 'The game can never be played the same way twice. Why not?

Because it changes the world every time it is played.' You should always read what is on the cover before you go to what is inside."

"Those are only words," Bagley (the Patrick or the Emperor) protested. "They are advocacy words, they are psychological words, they are slanted words. But they aren't words to apply to a real and material world. Should a world be governed by words that appear on the cover of a box?"

"Sure," the subliminal voice pushed words up over the threshold to them. "If it's the box that the world came in, the world should be governed by the words on the cover."

"It's still too big," they all began to shout. "It's like a big mud-ball coming apart, a world-sized mud-ball. It's too big for us to relate to. Show us where we are located in it or on it. We can relate to that."

"Oh all right. Relate to this then," the voice sub-sounded. "We'll go on local focus."

The arrow that Toro Manatee had shot point-blank at Fantome-Glaive sped towards him once more at one hundred and eighty miles an hour. For three feet it sped towards him at that high speed. Then it hung in the air motionless, touching but not transfixing the throat of the gallant Fantome-Glaive.

"Whew, that was close," at least twelve of the characters called out.

"Whew, that was close," at least one of the subliminal voices spoke.

Hung in the air for how long a time? Oh, not for any time at all. Time was elsewhen. Remember that the many-dialed ring or sphere was an alternate-time machine.

In the everwhen in which they found themselves now, they were once more present at the dismembering and destruction of the Planet Earth (identified by the arrangement as Merope). But now they were on local focus. They were on the smallest of the twenty-two thousand pieces of shattered Earth.

"Dammit, this is subjective. It's not really happening," Bagley protested.

"All worlds exist by a balance of the subjective and the objective," a subliminal voice from the arrangement kit was communicating to them. "Worlds without life have the best

369

balance as their subjectivity is spread through every atom of them. Worlds with life on them have their subjectivity concentrated in that life. Worlds with intelligent or quasi-intelligent life have their subjectivity further concentrated. That's why they are so easy to unbalance and to knock off. Enjoy this. Listen now. There will be a recording of Groben's 'Music to Knock Worlds Off By.'"

The thirteen characters were on a very small and jagged asteroid not over fifty yards in diameter, an asteroid or body that was splitting up into thirteen smaller bodies.

Twelve of the characters were jubilant.

"We've done it!" they howled. "We've won the game, and it's the ultimate game. We have destroyed the world, and we were never so glad to see anything destroyed. This is a big 'first' for games, and a big 'last.' Now there is a separate world for each of us."

"But only one of them will be the Earth," Jasmine Maloney put in her claim. "I am the youthful-elderly lady who is staying as the last person on Earth when everybody else is leaving because the planet is falling apart. Ow, ow, ow, it just did, didn't it! My piece isn't the biggest, but it is the Earth because I claimed continuity first. And now there is an exclusive world for each of us. I'm going to like it that way. I never liked other people anyhow."

"Are we unanimous?" Randy Andy Oglesby (playing the role of Arnold Andrew Oglethorpe III) demanded from his own rock. "All that we need is a declaration of unanimity. Then we have won the ultimate game and destroyed the world. Right on, everybody?"

"No, no, wait, wait, I'm not sure," Bertigrew Bagley protested. "This is all grubby insanity."

"Not sure!!!" his words rolled back from destroyed local space like ironic thunder. When you're about to finalize the destruction of a world you had better be sure!

"Of course it's grubby insanity. We are grubby insane characters," Hermione McElroy gibbered. "So were we devised, so shall we be."

"But we are caught up into the squalid insanity of the characters we portray," Bagley still argued. "Isn't that dangerous?"

"The ultimate game is supposed to be dangerous," Apollonia spoke (there wasn't any air now, so their voices were coming to each other subliminally like the voices from the arrangement kit). "It's necessary if we want to win the game, necessary that we be squalidly insane; and you had better not interfere."

"It's getting awful cold and awful dark," Bagley pointed out. "Blinding dark, killing cold."

"Compared to what???" Toro Manatee roared. "We'd have it made already if you hadn't taken exception, Bagley you fink. I still think we have it made. We operate under 'small universe rules' here. It isn't cold and it isn't dark unless we have something to compare it to. Now I'll just create the brightest and warmest thing possible, and it will suffice in a small universe. Killing cold, Bagley you fink? Compared to what?"

And Toro Manatee struck a match to bring about an incomparable state of brightness and warmth.

"Compared to that little flame, I am the killing cold," a cosmic voice spoke. The match went out. It couldn't have burned without air anyhow. And all of them froze to death instantly.

But not really.

They were back at the old game-cock pit. The arrow shot by Toro Manatee, going once more at a hundred and eighty miles an hour, went clear through the throat of Maurice Fantome-Glaive the greatest swordsman in the world. Fantome-Glaive fell down dead and destroyed and with a disgusted look on his face. And eleven others of them were angry and disgusted.

"Bagley, you unspeakable fink!" they roared. "We had the game won, the ultimate game. We had the world destroyed, and you botched it. You rat, you fink, you obstructionist! You wouldn't let us dismember the world. Look to yourself then in this dismembering moment!"

****

371

REPORT OF TEST GROUP RX2 on the game 'The Rod and the Ring':

"This is the ultimate game. Other games calling themselves ultimate are not really so. This game is expensive, fifty thousand dollars for a cubic yard of gaming material. That is all right. It will keep the cheap-jacks out. Test group RX2 had two members killed in the testing of this game. One of them had an arrow shot through his throat. One of them was torn to pieces by the eleven remaining testers. But such deaths of test persons are to be expected when a really daring game is tested.

"The Rod and the Ring is billed as 'The game that can never be played the same way twice because it changes the world every time it is played.' In truth, it is the game that destroys the world every time it is played correctly, and thus it may be played correctly a maximum of one time. Make no mistake about it: this is the ultimate game, *and it can be won.*"

We urge that this game be approved and marketed. We urge all groups to play it to the hilt. This game can be won and it will be won. And, once it is won, it will be won forever and by everybody. And we'll be rid of this tedious world.

"Buy the game. Play it to win. And it can be won, if you don't have a rotten obstructionist fink in your group. Be sure that you do not.

"Highly recommended."

END

Illustration © 2016 Anthony Ryan Rhodes

The Day After the World Ended
by R. A. Lafferty

(Notes for Speech for DeepSouthCon '79, New Orleans, July 21, 1979)

I'm going to talk about the peculiar science-fictionish circumstance and condition in which we are living. It is, unfortunately, an overworked theme and situation that has been used hundreds of times and has never been well-handled even once. It is the *Day After The World Ended* situation, subtitled *Grubbing in the Rubble*. It is the business of making out, a little bit, after a total catastrophe has hit. There are possibilities for several good stories in this situation, and I puzzled for a long time as to why no good ones had ever been written. I even myself tried and failed to write some good ones based on this set-up. And only recently have I discovered why plausible fiction cannot be based on this situation.

The reason here is that fact precludes fiction. Being inside the situation, we are a little too close to it to see it clearly. Science Fiction has long been babbling about cosmic destructions and the ending of either physical or civilized worlds, but it has all been displaced babble. SF has been carrying on about near-future or far-future destructions and its mind-set will not allow it to realize that the destruction of our world has already happened in the quite recent past, that today is *The Day After The World Ended*. Science Fiction is not alone in failing to understand what has happened. There is an almost impenetrable amnesia that obstructs the examination of the actual catastrophe.

I am speaking literally about a real happening, the end of the world in which we lived till fairly recent years. The destruction or unstructuring of that world, which is still sometimes referred to as "Western Civilization" or "Modern Civilization", happened suddenly, some time in the half-century between 1912 and 1962. That world, which was "The World" for a few centuries, is gone. Though it ended quite recently, the amnesia concerning its ending is general. Several historiographers have given the opinion that these amnesias are features common to all "ends of worlds". Nobody now remembers our late world very clearly, and nobody will ever remember it clearly in the natural order of things. It can't be recollected because recollection is one of the things it took with it when it went.

Plato once said or wrote, "Man is declared to be that creature who is constantly in search of himself. He is a being in search of meaning." But Platonic Declarations don't seem to apply on *The Day After The World Ended*. Man is not now a being in search of meaning. He does not recollect and he does not reflect. All the looking-glasses were broken in the catastrophe that ended the world.

There is a vague memory that this late world had a large and intricate superstructure on it, and that this came crashing down. There is some dispute as to whether we gained by the sweeping away of the trashy construction, or whether we lost a true and valid dimension in the unstructuring of our Old World, and whether we do not now live in *Flatland*. There is no way to settle this dispute since the old structure cannot be recaptured or analyzed.

There is even some evidence that *Flatlands* are the more usual conditions, and that the worlds with heights and structures are the exceptions. Even if we could go back there, a time machine from Flatland and eyes from Flatland would not be able to see dimension not contained in Flatland.

Now we come to the phenomenon or consensus named "Science Fiction." When trying to identify an object, the first question used to be "What's it good for?" But that is a value question, and values are banned under the present condition of things. Other questions that might be asked in trying to determine the function of Science Fiction are "How does it work?" and "What does it do?" An answer to "What does it do?" might be "Sometimes it designs new worlds." This trait of SF may be timely because our previous world is destroyed and there is presently a vacuum that can only be filled by a new world.

Science Fiction is an awkward survivor in the present environment because there is no fiction possible in this present environment, and that shoots half of it. The curious thing known as prose fiction was one of the things that was completely lost in the shipwreck of the old world.

Sometimes we hear about a contractor building a house on a wrong lot. Sometimes we hear about a man plowing a wrong field. Both these things are hard to do. How do you unplow a field? But we ourselves have been trying to plow a field that isn't there any more, and hasn't been there for between two and seven decades.

Prose fiction was a narrow thing. As a valid force it was found only in Structured Western Civilization (Europe and the Levant, and the Americas and other colonies), and for only about three hundred years, from *Don Quixote* in 1605 to the various "last novels" of the twentieth century. The last British novel may have been Arnold Bennett's *Old Wives' Tale* in 1908 or Maugham's *Of Human Bondage* in 1915. Both of them have strong post-fictional elements mixed in. The last Russian novel was probably Gorki's *The Bystander* in the 1920's, and the last Irish novel may have been O'Flaherty's *The Informer* about the same time. In Germany, Remarque's *All Quiet on the Western Front*, published in 1929, was plainly a post-novel in a post-fictional form. But the structured world did not end everywhere at quite the same time. In the United States there was a brilliant "last hurrah" of novels for several decades after the fictional form had disappeared in Europe, and Cozzens' *By Love Possessed*, published in 1957, might still be considered as a valid fictional work.

That special form of fiction, the Short Story, was of even shorter duration, beginning with Hoffmann in Germany and Washington Irving in the United States, both writing real short stories from about 1819, and continuing to the *Last Tales* of Isak Dinesen in 1955.

There are apparent exceptions to all this, but they are only apparent.

The thesis is that prose fiction was a structured form and that it became impossible in a society that had become unstructured, that prose fiction was a reflection of an intricate construct and that it ceased when it no longer had anything to reflect. A shadow simply can't last long after the object that has cast it has disappeared.

Well, if a thing is clearly dead and yet it seems to walk about, what is it? Maybe it's a zombie. And we do presently have quite a bit of stuff that might be called zombie-fiction. This is personal posing and peacock posturing, this is pornography and gadgetry, this is charades and set-scene formalities. There are pretty good things in the "new journalism" and in the "non-fiction novels." There is plain truculence. But there isn't any fiction any more. There is the lingering smell of fiction in some of the branches of nostalgia. But fiction itself is gone.

—except mis-named Science Fiction, the exception that proves only the exception. And it was never a properly fashioned fiction. It didn't reflect the world it lived in. It has always been more of a pre-world or a post-world campfire story than a defined fiction. But it still walks a little, and it isn't a zombie in the regular sense.

The ghost of some other fiction might say in truth to Science Fiction: "You're not very good, are you?" But Science Fiction can answer "Maybe not, but I'm alive and you're dead."

We are now in an unstructured era of post-musical music, post-artistic art, post-fictional fiction, and post-experiential experience. We are, partly at least, in a post-conscious world. Most of the people seem to prefer to live in this world that has lost a dimension. I don't know whether the condition is permanent or transitory.

We really are marooned. The world really has been chopped off behind us. Just how the old world ended isn't clear. There is a group amnesia that blocks us out from the details. It *didn't* end in Armageddon. The two world wars were only sidelights to a powerful main catastrophe. The so-called revolutionary movements did not bring anything to an end. The world had already ended. Those things were only the grubbiest of brainless grubbings in the ruins.

There is nothing analogous or allegorical about what I'm saying. I'm talking about the real conditions that prevail in the real present. At the worst, we've lost our last world. At the best, we're between worlds. We're living in Flatland, and we're not even curious about the paradoxes to be found here.

Life here in Flatland is like life in a photographic negative. Or it is life in the cellar of a world that has blown away. It is life in a limbo that has taken the irrational form of a Collective Unconscious. And we do not even know whether there is to be found somewhere the clear picture in whose negative we are living, or whether the negative is all there is.

But for technical reasons we can't stay here. Somebody had better be remembering fragments of either a past or a future. We can't stay here because the ground we are standing on is sinking.

Well then, does Science Fiction have any place in this post-world world? It seems to be a semi-secret society so confused that it can't even remember its own passwords. And yet it does have cryptic memories and elements that extend back through several worlds. It is a club of antiquarians, and it contains a lot of old lore in buried form. It is a pleasant and non-restrictive club to belong to. It provides varied entertainment for its members. It offers real fun now and then; and fun in the post-world period seems to be more scarce than it was when we still had a world.

With the rest of the marooned persons-and-things, Science Fiction today is trapped in a dismal science-fictionish situation. It is right in the middle of the *Day After The World Ended* plot. But SF turns this into the dullest of themes, and it never applies it to the present time when it is really happening. Someday people might want to travel back to this era by some device to see just what it was like between worlds, to see what it was really like in a "dark age." We do not have detailed eye-witness accounts of life in any other of the dark ages. Doubt has even been thrown on the existence of dark ages in the past. And we ourselves today do not consider the present hiatus (or the present death, if it proves to be that) as worthy of the attention of Science Fiction.

"Science Fiction As Survivor" does carry, in a few sealed ritual jars, some sparks that may kindle fires again, but it is unaware that it is carrying any such things. There is some amnesia or taboo that prevents SF (and the rest of the post-world also) from looking at the present state of things generally.

And the present state of things generally is that we are in the condition of creatures who have just made a traumatic passage out of an old life form, out of a tadpole state, out of a chrysalis stage. Such creatures are dopey. They are half-asleep and less than half-conscious.

Well, what does happen after the death of a world or a civilization? The historian Toynbee in grubbing into the depths of twenty-four separate civilizations or worlds that he studied, kept running into the *Phoenix Syndrome*, into the *Fire in the Ashes Phenomenon*. So far, the Phoenix, the fire-bird that is born out of its own ashes, has been a bigger bird after each rebirth, but maybe not a better one. It may have been as big as it could get during its latest manifestation, and there's the dim memory that it crashed at the end of that life because it had become so large and unwieldy that it could only flop and could no longer fly.

If the world is reborn Phoenix-like (and it isn't certain or automatic that it will be reborn at all), what form will it take next? No dead form is ever revived. But something entirely unexpected has, so far, been born on each site of an old world after a decent interval of time. Some of these intervals have been several centuries. But others have been only a few decades, and they have been getting shorter. There are no long-lived vacuums in this arena of happenings, but there has never been as wide and deep a vacuum as there is right now.

Of one thing there is plenty: there is almost total freedom for anyone to do whatever he wishes. There is almost complete liberty of both action and thought. We live in a wide-open "people's-republic" to end all "people's-republics," and it probably will. But at the same time we are living in rubble and remnant. We are living in a series of cluttered non-governments, but the clutter isn't attached to anything. It is easily moved out of the way.

By every definition, this *is* Utopia. Of course some of us have always regarded Utopia as a calamity, but most of you have not. In its flexibility and in its wide-open opportunities, this is the total Utopia. Anything that you can conceive of, you can do in this non-world. Nothing can stop you except a total bankruptcy of creativity. The seedbed is waiting. All the circumstances stand ready. The fructifying minerals are literally jumping out of the ground.

And nothing grows. And nothing grows. And nothing grows. Well, why doesn't it?

Back to Science Fiction. The "If only" premise is at the beginning of every Science Fiction flight of fancy. But in actuality we are at the "If only" nexus right now. All the conditions have come together. All the "If onlies" are more than possible now: they are wide open. They are fulfilled. There are no manacles on anybody or anything; or else they are as easily broken as pieces of thread. But people still hobble about as if they were fettered in hand and foot and mind.

There has never been a place swept as clear of accumulation and superstructure as ours. There's an opportunity here that doesn't come every century, for not every century has the room to be creative. There is the room and the opportunity, but nothing is moving in that way.

I'm not proposing right choices or wrong choices. I'm not even pushing transcendence over gosh-awful secularism. I'm saying that we do have choices and opportunities to the extent that nobody has ever had them before. There are fine building stones all around us, whatever ruins they are from. But nobody is building.

There's an old and much-quoted Housman verse:

"I, a stranger and afraid
In a world I never made—"

—and there are stylized and self-serving ways of quoting this verse as though to justify oneself and disclaim any responsibility for the world. But this has become a crocodile verse now, for the world referred to isn't here any more. And the question to be asked of everyone is "If you are not right now making a world, why aren't you?" Group ingenuity, on an unconscious level at first perhaps, and then on a conscious level, *can* bring it about. It can be done by a small elite of only a few million geniuses. Declare yourself one of them! You can now set up your own rules for being a genius, and then you can be one. You can set up your own rules for being anything at all.

There *will* be, happily, a new world, a new civilization-culture to follow on the recent termination of the Structured Western World. All it's waiting for is ideas to germinate and a few sparks to kindle. Several of the survivor-groups of the old world-shipwreck have sparking machines, but they may not realize what they are.

"But if we can't somehow bring about the sparking, the reanimation trick, then we're really dead.

"Forget that reanimation," some of you say. "What's the matter with the way it is now?"

"Nobody's driving the contraption. That's one thing that's the matter with it."

"That's all right too," some say. "It isn't going anywhere. It isn't running. We've even taken the wheels off it. We like it that way."

But even the ruins we are grubbing in are sinking into a slough. We'll be drowned in foul muck if we don't start to move. It's up to our mouths now, and that is why we are babbling and bubbling. Soon it will be over our noses, and we can only hold our breaths for so long.

"That's all right," some still say. "We like the way it tickles our noses. Leave it the way it is."

Well, that's our choice, but it isn't the only one.

Possibly, if we don't drown in the present muck, there will be a new world. As a condition to its coming into being, it will have its new arts, new ideas, new categories of thought, new happinesses. It may even have successors to the old musics and fictions and peak experiences and immediacies. It isn't easy to predict what it may be, but it may be no more difficult to build it than to predict it.

When was the last time that we had a world? What, judging by its bones and stones lying around, was it like? No, we can't reconstruct it the way it was. All we have is a wide-open opportunity to make something new. A couple of hundred people here, a couple of billion there, working with uneasy brilliance, may come up with a stunning and unpredicted creation. The best way to be in on a new movement or a new world is to be one of the inventors of it.

Here is the condition that prevails in our non-world right now. We are all of us characters in a Science Fiction

Story named 'The Day The After The World Ended'. Well, more likely it is an animated story or comic strip in which we find ourselves to be the characters. The continuity has now arrived at 'crux point', the make-or-break point where brilliant strokes are called for. Somehow the characters have been given the opportunity of determining what happens next, an opportunity that is absolutely unprecedented.

Meanwhile the calendar is stuck. It comes up 'The Day After The World Ended' day after day, year after year. These should be the Green Years. But unless you use an inflated way of appraising things, these last few decades have not been at all creative. And if nothing grows in the Green Years, what will grow in the dry?

People much less gifted than ourselves have invented worlds in the past and have set them to run for their five to fifteen centuries. But we do not make a move yet. There is a large silence occupying the present time. Is it the silence just before a great stirring and banging? Or is it a terminal silence?

Well, what does happen now?

Can't any of the characters in this 'do-it-yourself' Science Fiction story come up with any sort of next episode? Would it help to change the name of the story from 'The Day After The World Ended' to 'First on a New Planet'?

Any character may take any liberty he wishes with this post-world story. It is a game without rules. But apparently he will not be able to climb clear out of the story.

I refrain from writing "*The End*" here. It must not end.

He was decked out in Navajo beadwork and a Sioux war-bonnet when he spoke at the supermarket in Indianapolis. Indianapolis really meant Indian City, didn't it?

R. A. Lafferty, "Royal Licorice"

Illustration © 2016 Anthony Ryan Rhodes

383

List of Contributors

Jon Braschler
Russell M. Burden
Stephen R. Case
Kevin Cheek
Andrew Childress
Gardner Dozois
John Ellison
Andrew Ferguson
Logan Giannini
Andrew M. Greeley
Joseph L. Green
Martin Heavisides
Robert T. Jeschonek
Dan Knight
R. A. Lafferty
David Langford
Gregorio Montejo
John Owen
Rich Persaud
Lawrence Person
Daniel Otto Jack Petersen
Alan Reid
Anthony Ryan Rhodes
Bill Rogers
Darrell Schweitzer
R. Ward Shipman
Robert Silverberg
J Simon
Robert Whitaker Sirignano
Sheryl Smith
Michael Swanwick
Yakov Varganov
Howard Waldrop
Gene Wolfe

The Ktistec Press

Kevin Cheek
Gregorio Montejo
John Owen
Rich Persaud
Daniel Otto Jack Petersen
Anthony Ryan Rhodes

Made in the USA
San Bernardino, CA
04 May 2017